Ghaith Abdul Ahad

About the Author

WENDELL STEAVENSON is the author of the acclaimed
memoir *Stories I Stole*. She has lived in and reported from post-
Soviet Georgia, Ethiopia, Iran, Iraq, and Lebanon. Her work
has appeared in the *London Observer*, the *Telegraph*, *Prospect*
magazine, the *Financial Times*, *Slate*, *Granta*, *The New Yorker*,
and *Time*. She lives in Paris.

The Weight of a Mustard Seed

Also by Wendell Steavenson

Stories I Stole

✖ ✖ ✖

The WEIGHT *of a*
MUSTARD SEED

✖ ✖ ✖

THE INTIMATE STORY OF AN IRAQI GENERAL AND HIS
FAMILY DURING THIRTY YEARS OF TYRANNY

Wendell Steavenson

HARPER

NEW YORK · LONDON · TORONTO · SYDNEY

HARPER

A hardcover edition of this book was published in 2009 by Collins, an imprint of HarperCollins Publishers.

First UK edition published by Atlantic Books 2009.
FIRST HARPER PAPERBACK PUBLISHED 2010.

Designed by Emily Cavett Taff

The Library of Congress has catalogued the hardcover edition as follows:

Steavenson, Wendell, 1970–
    The Weight of a Mustard Seed : the intimate story of an Iraqi
    general and his family during thirty years of tyranny / Wendell
    Steavenson.
    —1st ed.
        p. cm.
ISBN 978-0-06-172178-6
1. Janabi, Kamel Sachet Aziz. 2. Generals—Iraq—Biography.
3. Iraq—Politics and government—1979–1991. 4. Iraq—Politics
and government—1991–2003. 5. Iraq—Social life and customs.
I. Title.

  DS79.66.J385S74 2009
  956.7044092-dc22

                                                        2008024402

ISBN 978-0-06-172188-5 (pbk.)

10 11 12 13 14   OV/RRD   10 9 8 7 6 5 4 3 2 1

For Dominique Fell-Clarke
Sanity, when there was none

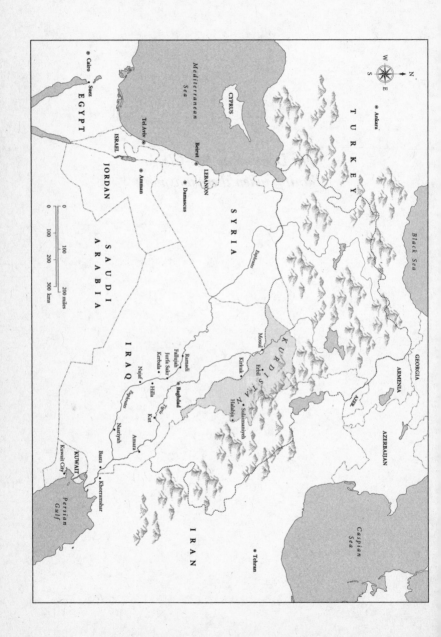

*We shall set up scales of justice for the Day of Judgment,
so that not a soul will be dealt with unjustly in the least,
and if there be (no more than) the weight of a mustard
seed, We will bring it (to account): and enough are We to
take account.*

—THE KORAN. *Chapter 21, The Prophets, verse 47*
(Translated by Abdullah Yusuf Ali)

Contents

Author's Note

I WENT TO BAGHDAD IN THE SUMMER OF 2003 AS A freelance journalist with a commission from London's *Observer* newspaper. I had spent the war in Kurdistan in the north and I wanted to see its aftermath and learn more about the locked-in years of Saddam's regime. I was in Baghdad all through that August and returned the following November for a further seven months. I lived first at the Hamra Hotel with the journalist pack, then moved to the cheaper Dulaimi next door, then into the UK *Guardian* house with a couple of armed guards in the garden. I wrote dispatches for Slate.com and articles for the *Financial Times Magazine* and *Granta* and worked on the story for this book by interviewing, with a translator, the Sachet family and friends of colleagues of General Kamel Sachet. I was interested in the story of an Iraqi general as a way of telling the story of what had happened in Iraq, not just from the point of view of the victims of the regime, but those who had participated in it. I wrote down my interviews in a notebook, and, usually the same day, transposed these notes into cleaned-up transcripts, observations and paragraphs on my laptop.

I left Baghdad in June 2004, exhausted by the stress of the violence which had ratcheted unrelenting, intending to return after a good break. Over the summer two of my friends were kidnapped—both were released after a few days—but from conversations with colleagues in Iraq it was clear that my way of working, driving about Baghdad in a regular car with a headscarf obscuring my blonde hair, but without guards or guns, was increasingly foolhardy. I did return for five weeks in January and February 2005, to cover the first elections and see what other stories I could find and to check in with the Sachets, but by that time there had been more kidnaps and it was clear foreigners were targets for bandits as well as insurgents. Seventy percent of Baghdad was controlled by gunmen and pretty much no-go, gun battles and hold-ups were happenstance every day and, although I covered myself in a big black enveloping abaya in the back of an anonymous car, was careful to visit people unannounced and stayed not more than an hour or two, it was clear than any pretense at risk-management, for an independent like me, was a sham. Later, in the spring of that year, Marla Ruzicka, who had founded an NGO working to compensate Iraqis for American collateral damage, was killed with her Iraqi colleague by a car bomb aimed at a Humvee. The following year Jill Carroll, who was freelancing for the *Christian Science Monitor*, was kidnapped for three months and her translator, Alan Enwia, who I had first met in 2003 and who was a wonderful, warm, intelligent guy, was killed during the ambush. In earlier times, Marla and Jill and I had walked over to the Babylon Hotel together to go swimming in their indoor pool.

From the summer of 2004 to the time of writing, the relative relief of the surge in 2007 notwithstanding, I don't think any Western journalists walked down any Iraqi street (except in Kurdistan) for a coffee, to go to a restaurant or to go shopping in any casual way. When I talked to newspaper colleagues in between their rotations, it was clear they were confined to their guarded compounds and embeds and that any eyes-and-ears reporting was being done by Iraqis. By 2006, even Iraqi reporter friends of mine (the ones still alive) said they could barely go out, let alone carry a camera or a notebook, in public spaces.

So after 2005 I conducted my research among the increasingly large Iraqi refugee and exile populations in London, Beirut, Damascus, Amman and Dubai. It wasn't a perfect solution, but once a story is under your skin, time and distance become just more hurdles, along with sense and sensibility, that have to be reckoned with.

In the writing of this book I have keenly felt an outsider's temerity in attempting to depict Iraqis. I have tried to get things right, of course, but I have also worried at exposing the private lives and thoughts of Iraqis in such dangerous and uncertain times. Accordingly, some names have been changed. The Iraqis who appear within these pages talked to me because they hoped that, through their stories and the story of Kamel Sachet, somehow a broader truth of Iraqi sufferance would be told and that American and British readers would understand a little better the nation they had invaded.

There are very few books written from the interior of the Baath Party state and those that have appeared in English tend to be ghost-written memoirs, fallible and full of holes. In the Great Loot of 2003, swaths of state files and dossiers were collected by various vested-interest parties—Shia, American, historian, blackmailer—but they are often handwritten in Arabic and almost all still in the piles of disorder with which they were swept from the shelves of government offices. Without written sources, I have been dependent on people's memories and these can be self-serving and elusive. Every story (except one or two smaller incidents) about the life of Kamel Sachet has been told to me by more than one person and the general trajectory of his life has been confirmed by many. The stories that people have told me about themselves, however, are uncheckable. I know that omission can be as great a lie as selective recall and I tried to push people into as much honesty as they could bear. It is the nature of the subject that this sometimes did not amount to very much. Ultimately the veracity of these stories relies on my own judgment, and nobody's judgment, just like nobody's memory, is right 100 percent of the time.

I worried too about sensitivity, how much or how little of it I should allow to the officers of tyranny I was interviewing. I explain my panderings to the sympathies of Baathies by reminding myself that these are people after all, and what person does not deserve to be listened to? None, I maintain. If we strive to understand ourselves in the other, which is the only and original reason to tell stories in the first place: None.

Paris, March 2008

Prologue

AUGUST 2003. EARLY DAYS. I HAD A NAME, DR. HASSAN al-Qadhani, and an address on a piece of paper; the telephone number written beside them, like most of the lines in Baghdad, did not work.

There was a pink rose bush overhanging the garden wall. I pushed the buzzer by the metal gate, but the electricity was off and it did not sound. My translator called up the path, several minutes went by, we called again, a woman nervously poked her head out and said the doctor would be back shortly. I did not want to intrude or frighten her so I said we would wait in the car.

When Dr. Hassan arrived, I introduced myself and he brought us in and sat with me in the formal reception room of the house. He was in his early fifties, handsome in a square way, brushed dark hair, mustache, trim physique, polite, pleasant, weary; there were dark circles under his eyes. Dr. Hassan was a psychiatrist; he told me that he had studied in Munich and London and that he had been in the army medical corps. He spoke clearly in perfect English, steadily, with a certain grimness that a couple of times flashed into a warm smile. There was a lot of ground to cover.

"Yes, post traumatic stress, soldiers who have committed suicide, self mutilation," he listed. "I have seen these effect through four," and he stopped himself to count, "yes, the war in the North against the Kurds in '74, the war with Iran, the First Gulf War and this one, yes, four wars."

His wife, blonde and well dressed, came in with two cups of coffee. Dr. Hassan started to apologize because I had waited outside in the street. I waved him down, no, no, of course.

"But my wife was afraid, you understand. Five days ago we were robbed."

Three men had broken in at dawn. Dr. Hassan had woken up with a gun pointed at his head. The robbers had pushed him and his wife and eight-year-old son into the kitchen and tied them up while they ransacked the house. They found $15,000 in cash, a gold bar and the keys to the Mercedes parked outside. This haul did not quite satisfy them. They said they knew the doctor had $100,000: Where was it? They wanted to take his eight-year-old son as hostage against this amount, but Dr. Hassan swore he did not have this money, that they had the wrong information, he asked them to leave the boy, to take the car, and go, now that it was light and morning. He pulled up his shirt to show me a large red oval bruise on his stomach where he had been punched with the butt of a Kalashnikov.

"My son," he told me, "has bad dreams and cries. He sleeps with us now. We have to walk him even to the bathroom. I told him everything was alright, that none of us were hurt and that everything would be OK. He doesn't believe me. He is always searching for my gun, to keep beside him."

But in Iraq, there was never one story, there were always many stories, layers of episodes, each one a wound. We began to talk about his recent cases, but our conversation halted with an explosion; the glass in the windows banged, a car alarm went off.

Dr. Hassan then looked down at his hands and told me that

he understood his patients, he understood the phobia, anxiety, panic, depression, restlessness, insomnia:

"I myself was once arrested under the old regime." He paused and looked out of the gap in the iron bars on the windows, which the robbers had pulled out to get inside. "These things are very sensitive," he said without looking at me. "Solitary confinement for three months . . . I have often seen torture victims, they are apathetic, withdrawn, severely depressed, often emaciated. It is difficult enough for a doctor to treat another doctor, a psychiatrist treating another psychiatrist . . ."

THE NEXT TIME I went to see Dr. Hassan, it took him several minutes to unlock the new heavy padlock he had bought and let us in through the gate. He looked better since the robbery, he smiled a little more, the dark circles under his eyes were gone and his bruise was healing.

We met several times that summer. Dr. Hassan seemed to regain a genial sense of humor, but too often his eyes shadowed, clouded with memories, and he maintained a certain strain of diffident frankness. He had kept everything shut in a box for a long time. As we talked, he cautiously unburdened. He told me he had a brother in England, that he had once fallen in love in Munich and had to give her up, that he was a Shia from the South and "they" had never trusted him. In the course of his duties he had been responsible for certifying soldiers mentally fit for duty, he had witnessed men shot for desertion and treated their traumatized executioners, healed psychosomatic paralysis and investigated spies. We talked about the Americans: what did they want in Iraq? How was a former Baath Party member to comport himself with the occupation? Cold shoulder or collaborate? He was worried for his family's safety; he talked about leaving the country. Throughout the former elite there were rumors of revenge assassinations, extortion, detentions. One of his friends had been an adviser to Tariq Aziz, the former Deputy Prime Minister, and was sitting at home, unable to sleep much or eat, losing weight, too frightened to travel on his diplomatic passport, waiting for the Americans to come and arrest him. "It is only a different kind of fear; before we had paranoia about Saddam. Now I am seeing it transferred to Bremer and the Americans!"

Invariably, though, we returned to the era before, the time of Saddam Hussein. Saddam, abusive father, super-sheikh, paranoiac—Dr. Hassan tried to explain the totality of it, even from the inside, even from his position, even with his connections and military rank.

"You had to lie against your principles. You had to say things that you did not believe. It was mental conflict. This kind of tension and suppression destroys the superego—I mean that you cannot decide anything, you are directed by the regime, your education, your military service, your job. You could see cases where people were socially withdrawn, they were afraid to go to work, they were often absent. It was somewhere between social phobia and agoraphobia. And you would see normal people too displaying signs of paranoia, not wanting to talk on the telephone, for example, afraid of the door-bell ringing at an odd time. The more extreme cases lost their jobs, suspected their families and friends. They said they were sure the police were following them, that they were being watched from satellites."

The fear was incubated, inculcated.

"To live thirty-five years like this. It becomes conditioned as a personality trait."

It had been a long sufferance. Dr. Hassan had opened the

door, not into the black and white world of oppressor and victim that I had expected, but into a grayer corridor. He had been a member of the Baath Party. He had, I discovered, attained the rank of general in the medical corps. He had participated in the regime. And yet. . .

And yet, an intelligent rational man, a man with pain and morality, regret and hubris, a wife and a son, pride and fear of humiliation.

It was just an inkling of a story then, a question hanging in my head in the blue shadow hour of a leavening dawn: Why hadn't men like Dr. Hassan just left? Why had they served such a regime? How had they accommodated their own morality? How had they lived? How had they lived with themselves?

One day, musing on some of these ideas, Dr. Hassan had told me, "You should go and see the Sachets. I don't know how much they will tell you. But they are an interesting family. Kamel Sachet was a general. A very famous general."

Chapter 1

HIS WIFE

THE SACHET FAMILY LIVED IN SAIDIYA. SAIDIYA was a district settled mostly by army officers on plots gifted from the government. It was a typical Baghdad neighborhood of cubist concrete houses stretched along highways built in the money-slick boom of the seventies, now sunk under the parched weeds and rubbish drifts and rubble of a flyblown sanctions decade liberated with an invasion.

In August the 133 degree sun switched off at dusk and the baked concrete of the city radiated into the evening. Not a cooling darkness, no puff of wind, but respite enough to venture outside, stretch your legs, sit in a café, sticky-necked in the furnace heat wreathed in kebab smoke, with a fuzzy warm Pepsi and listen to the traffic cacophony of a million second-hand cars flooding over the suddenly open border—no customs duties! No exit visas! No immigration officials! Nothing! Honking jammed in front of the traffic policeman at the intersection, stuck in a forty car line at the petrol station, brandishing a pistol at a line jumper, buying "jellycans" of fuel from the lithe and scabby black-market street boys. The shops cascaded pent-up imports onto the sidewalks: satellite dishes, electric fans (although the electricity was variably on-off—three hours on, three hours off), mobile phones (it was rumored a network would be set up soon), tinsel, gold painted chandeliers, strings of multicolored fairy lights, cherry glitter lipstick, leopard print lingerie (for a woman must look enticing for her husband), pink dolls for daughters and plastic Kalashnikovs for sons. Men sat about, in sandals with cracked heels and loose tracksuit trousers, chain-smoked and complained about the electricity, the water, the Americans, no jobs, no rights; women walked past in long gowns and headscarves carrying kilos of tomatoes; small boys crammed the new internet shops, noses pressed against dusty second-hand monitors, gleefully, heedlessly playing Gulf War One, playing Americans hunting down Iraqis because the game was designed with only one protagonist.

We drove through the shopping throng, ignored the gunshot that might have been a car backfiring except that it really was a gunshot, past the tract of waste ground, right at the half-built mosque, raw and gray under redundant construction cranes, past a small abandoned police post; wove between a palm trunk chicane, a ball of tumbleweed razor wire and a pool of emerald sewage into an unassuming street of small villas with walled front gardens.

Kamel Sachet Aziz al Janabi had been a commander of the special forces, the general in charge of the army in Kuwait City during the Gulf War and a governor of the Province of Maysan, but the family's house was a modest, pleasant, middle class affair and there was nothing of the grandiloquent marble columns and bronze glass of the elite Baathie facades. The formal reception room for guests, where I was received, was large, bright and comfortable; I sat on a sofa in front of a glass coffee table laid with crocheted table mats and a vase of plastic roses, my translator sat next to me. The Sachets were very proud of their father and were happy to talk about him. We met in that first summer, each of us full of curiosity, optimism and excitement. They had a lot of questions for me: Why had the Americans invaded? Was it for the oil? What kind of government would they install? But by the following winter, the Abu Ghraib rumors and detentions and hard knock raids had depressed all of us and I was reduced to apologizing—shaking my head, as abject and angry as they were—for the occupation.

Once or twice the daughters brought me into the private interior of the house, leaving my male translator behind, to show me something: how Ali, the second son, had decorated his room in pink satin and tulle for the arrival of his new wife, a new baby; or how to stuff eggplants. But usually when I visited, once or twice a week, I sat in the reception room and various members of the family would come in to say hello, bring me tea and then coffee, and sit for a talk.

KAMEL SACHET'S WIFE was Um Omar, Mother of Omar (her eldest son), mother of his nine children. In rough order: Shadwan, Omar, Ali, Sheima, Amani, Ahmed, Zeinab, Mustafa, Zaid—and a burgeoning number of toddling grandchildren. She was a warm matriarch. Kissing her hello was like putting your arms around a feathered divan; when she moved it sounded like a swishing quilted curtain. She was firm and yielding; soft and bulky and upholstered in voluminous black velvet. She had aged into house-mother doyenne, indulgent of her family brood and prone to twinges of nerves. From time to time she suffered acute but nonspecific complaints: sleeplessness, problems with her stomach—not exactly a cramp but not exactly an ache. Once she went to three doctors in a week and came back with a bag of medicine, sleeping pills, antidepressants, antibiotics and, bizarrely, typhoid tablets. I brought a doctor friend of mine to give her some proper advice. She felt dizzy, she felt sick, but she had not been sick, yes, it happened once before like this, and it was very bad, that time she had fainted, maybe it was stress—yes, she nodded as my doctor friend explained the intersection of psychosomatic and physical. He told her to relax and not to worry and then some bomb banged distantly as if in ironic response.

Her headscarf framed her face in a severe black oval, but Um Omar's features were plump and powdery and, when she wasn't upset, her mouth smiled benevolently in repose. The big garrulous Ali, then in his early twenties, who seemed to get fatter and fatter every time I saw him, told me that when they were young she was strict and hurled slippers or wooden spoons at them if they ran around the house breaking things or neglected their homework. But it was hard to imagine this sternness—although not impossible; she wore large gold rimmed glasses and I could glimpse the school-teacher she had once been. Sometimes she seemed almost the naughty one of the family: her children had been brought up proscribed by the strictures of Saddam's regime and under the firm authority of their father, but Um Omar had grown up in a more indulgent time. She often giggled, almost girlish; she would swirl her wrists in gesticulation and roll her eyes as if to say it is not as serious as all that! And then she would look over her shoulder in comic concern that Ahmed, her devout and censorious son, had caught her being frivolous.

One afternoon at the end of 2003, when I went to visit, her hands were orange.

"Oh, I know! I was putting henna in Shadwan's hair and look at me!" She upturned her fluorescent palms.

"You have been shelling fava beans also." I had noticed two large bags of discarded pods by the kitchen door.

"Oh, they are very delicious, now is the season for them," said Um Omar, smoothing her lap, "but it takes a very long time to get the little beans out of their skins." She shuddered comically at the work involved and clapped her hands on her knees, a movement that was like patting a cushion.

Presently Shadwan, her eldest daughter, thirty and unmarried, came in carrying a vast circular platter piled with rice and green fava beans. Um Omar beamed. Shadwan smiled triumphantly. Another daughter, Amani, thin and wan like a swaying reed, with a pale oval face, followed with bowls of yogurt. She looked up in docile polite greeting, but did not say a word. She carefully and noiselessly set the bowls down on the glass-topped table and then retreated, with a slight limp, back into the private interior of the house. Um Omar flapped her hands like semaphores:

"Eat! Eat!" The mountain of rice and fava beans looked like it was enough to feed the entire Janabi tribe. We bent to the task. Um Omar threw her arms up, the sleeves of her black gown fell back a few inches towards her dimpled elbows, and asked, "Is it good? I always worry if it will come out right. You know, when you are not paying attention everything works fine. When you want to do something well, it never works out."

Um Omar had just come back from Mecca. It was the first time she had ever left Iraq, and she had applied for the lottery—each Muslim country is allotted a quota of pilgrims—and was accepted for *Haj*, the pilgrimage. She had remembered me in her prayers and brought me back a handbag as a present and I was exhorted to sip from a small glass of holy zamzam water. I protested about drinking their precious supply, but Um Omar shook her head and said she had brought back several liters.

So, I asked, how was it?

"Oh yes, it was very good, very interesting, but very tiring!"

Five days it took them to get to Mecca! They went by bus to Safwan and had to wait there, at a camp where there were permanent tents for pilgrims. The toilets were very bad; Um Omar shuddered. "We were like sheep; but the group before us was worse: they had to wait in Safwan for five days!" She threw her hands up to heaven in supplication. From Safwan they traveled to Kuwait on a yellow school bus. At first Um Omar did not know anyone, but the unaccompanied ladies on the journey soon became friends. She befriended a woman who was from the elite Mansour district of Baghdad.

"She was a *Wahhabi*, but she was very kind." said Um Omar, referring to the fundamentalist Islamic strain to which the woman adhered. The Wahhabi woman had given Um Omar pamphlets and religious tracts to read, but Um Omar confessed she never bothered to read them and when she got home . . . ! Ah, an uproar of hands, Ahmed had made a big complaint and confiscated them as heretical.

The Kuwaitis had a very nice place for pilgrims to stay in; it was like a village and the bathrooms were clean and the food was fine. Then it was time to go on the airplane. Um Omar had never been on an airplane and she had been a little nervous but she thought it was a very nice experience: the stewardesses were very beautiful, "they are from Turkey, you know—and the food! It was my best meal ever!" They flew to Jeddah and from Jeddah made their way to Mecca.

In Mecca the Iraqi contingent stayed in a good hotel with an elevator which alarmed Um Omar. At breakfast there were baskets filled with foil packets of honey, milk, orange juice and cheese. Um Omar had been rather taken with the sachets, so neat!

"But many people in Mecca! And from everywhere." The crowds were thick and dense and if you got into the middle of one it was hard to get out of it. There were so many people pressing forward that on the way to Mount Arafat people would trip over the men who stopped to kneel down and pray. One old man was being continuously tripped over until other pilgrims dragged him up by his neck and told him to wait to pray later, for Allah's sake. Um Omar had wanted to stone the devil in the pillar but this was the most dangerous place for stampedes so she had given two stones to two different people to beat the devil on her behalf. "I asked two because you know, one might forget!"

The men all wore their special white robes, which left a shoulder bare. Women, Um Omar explained, can wear anything, of course, as long as it is *hijab*.

"Some of the women from Indonesia wore cosmetics and blue eye shadow!" Um Omar was shocked. And some of the Shia had brought pictures and likenesses of Hussein and this was wrong. And some of the pilgrims from England tried to give her some books and literature, but she refused them, no no! She waved her hands, waving away the foreign. Mostly, however, she was not impressed with the behavior of the other Iraqis in her group. Apparently they had quarreled and argued and caused too many problems about every little thing. Um Omar said that when she had been accepted for *Haj* she asked the man who was in charge of her tour what the most important thing to bring was and he'd replied that the most important thing on *Haj* was patience. So she was very patient through the long periods of waiting and organizing. The other Iraqis, she complained, had not been patient. She had wanted, for example, to spend more time in the second holy city of Medina on the way home, two days was not enough time at the grave of the Prophet, but there had been so much arguing that they had left early.

"It was interesting, you know, that most Saudis are Wahhabis, and they do not agree with offering prayers to Mohammed or to Ali, they say these are only men, there is only one Allah. They are right, I was convinced by their arguments. But they would not let us throw our letters from relatives and friends into the grave of the Prophet Mohammed. I had a letter from Shadwan, and I threw it away." Shadwan looked downcast and shrugged her shoulders. "And I wanted to buy a mobile phone that plays music as a gift—but they told me this was not allowed because music is *haram*! Why? It was a gift for a child!" Um Omar opened her palms in bewilderment. There was something foreign about it all, but what could you expect? "Ah. Of course, the *Haj*, like a feeling you cannot describe, like a feeling nowhere else." Um Omar looked away and then back at me. "But inconvenient!" She said she was very happy to have gone but she did not want to go again. Once was enough. "It is what God has imposed upon us, it is a duty."

Ahmed came in. He was seventeen and studied at the religious university in Baghdad. He was wearing a fawn colored *dishdasha*, extremely clean and well pressed, bowed to me hello and touched his hand to his breast in greeting, blinking his disconcertingly long eyelashes. He said he hoped one day to perform the *Haj* himself.

"A prayer in Mecca is worth 100,000 ordinary prayers. Yes, it is clear. And a prayer in Medina is worth 10,000, the same in the Dome of the Rock in Jerusalem. A prayer in a mosque is worth twenty-seven prayers compared to a single prayer at home."

PHOTOGRAPH: *A black and white snap from the sixties with a white border: Um Omar, then a university student called Shamh, young and curvy, squeezed into a dark pencil skirt and a cropped jacket with a cinched waist, is standing on the street. Her dark hair is swept up into a big beehive, her eyes are drawn with kohl like a movie star and her lashes are thick with spiky mascara. She is smiling at the camera as if she is pretending to be annoyed with it for catching her.*

"I didn't wear *hijab* then." Um Omar and I were sitting together, talking alone. I had told her I wanted to hear everything from the beginning, how she had grown up, how she had met her husband, and I had asked her if she had any old photograph albums.

"Not many," said Um Omar, and then she had gone inside and come back with a box of loose snaps. Fingering this one, she regarded her younger Shamh self fondly and then said, with jokey self-admonishment, "If my husband had been a religious man back then, he would never have married me!"

Um Omar sat closer to me and laughed at another era and her memories.

"I am glad Ahmed isn't here . . . ," she suppressed a smile. Ahmed would certainly have frowned.

Shamh had gone to Baghdad University to train as a teacher; none of her sisters had gone to university—education was her abiding ambition. When she was in her second year she began to notice a young man from the neighborhood following her. She would see him at the bus stop wearing his police uniform. She was flattered by his attention, but she did not speak to him until he sat next to her on the bus one day, told her his name was Kamel and recounted his virtues and his circumstances and said he would like to marry her. Shamh was pleased, his speech showed that his intentions were honorable, the Sachets were a known family. Shamh confided in her sister-in-law his attentions, and after a short time, he formally brought his parents to meet her parents. Shamh agreed to marry him on one condition: that he bought her a house so that they could live independently, but Kamel could not afford a house on his policeman's salary and so the plans for engagement were stalled.

Um Omar covered her mouth with her hand in a conspiratorial whisper, and explained, in mock-rueful horror at her own disrespect, the difference between her family, urban and established, and his family, recent immigrants from the village with Bedu manners. "You know I did not want to live with his family; his parents were a bit *Araby*!"

KAMEL SACHET HAD been born in 1947 in the village of Hor Rajab, the third son of an illiterate farmer's family. Life was as plain and poor as it had been for generations. Hor Rajab was only twenty kilometers from Baghdad, but there was no road or electricity or radio or even a mosque. On Fridays the village sheikh would climb a small hill and make the call to prayer without a megaphone and prayer would be held in one of the rooms of the low mud-built schoolhouse.

Kamel was tall for his age and quiet, even as a child, to the point of taciturn. His life was barefoot and *dishdasha*, blackboard and chalk, elder brothers and father, cold in the winter and burning in the summer. The government provided lunch for schoolboys: eggs, oranges, bread and milk and a daily spoon of cod liver oil that they called caviar and hated the smell of. Lessons taught by the sheikh, reading and writing and the Koran, chores at home and play. The boys in the village made their own footballs out of bundled bits of rag and scraps of shoe leather tied up with heavy string. One time a camel caravan came to the village and they scooped up tufts of camel hair and mashed it with camel milk and packed it hard to dry and make a rubbery ball that bounced, but the ground they played on was limned with salt and the salt would stick to the camel milk football and scratch up their toes as they kicked it.

Whenever I talked to Kamel Sachet's friends or military colleagues they always used two words to describe him. They said, "he was brave" and that "he was a simple man." In translation, this "simple" meant uncomplicated, straightforward, straight talking and clear-cut. But I always imagined Kamel Sachet's simplicity in another way, as a purity of mind carved out of hard-edged shadows in a single color: yellow of the sun that beat through a yellow sky onto the yellow earth. Kamel grew up in poverty that did not know it was poor—spartan, austere, *simple*. It was not the way of the village for boys to fight and scrap but to let anyone hurt you was *haram,* forbidden, and shame.

Kamel was part of the clever group of boys at school and his teacher praised him to his parents and encouraged them to send him to middle school. Whether it was for this reason or economics, when Kamel was twelve his father Aziz moved the family to the outskirts of Baghdad, to the district of Dora, a pre-suburb area that was still then fields and unpaved roads and to which electricity (and television and radio and music and news) was not to come until 1964.

Here was the teenager, testing limits and boundaries, leading his little gang into the adjacent Christian neighborhood, fighting other little gangs, studying under trees when it was too hot at home and then jumping into the Tigris to cool down, falling in love with a girl from a good Jobouri family who refused his humble proposal, becoming momentarily inflamed with Unity! Liberation! *Ishtiraqiya* [Socialism]! during the short lived Baathie coup of 1963, even temporarily manning the checkpoint near the Dora refinery with a green uniform and an Egyptian rifle ("so bad that if you dropped it, it would discharge and explode") and encouraging his father to go to the new literacy classes sponsored by the socialist revolution.

His ambition, as that of his friends and childhood gang from the neighborhood, those that had seen their fathers struggle with the land, was to work as an employee in a government position that would bring a salary and a position. Many of them, after the humiliation of "The Aggression" of the 1967 war when the Arab states were defeated by Israel, felt compelled to join the military. After passing his baccalaureate, Kamel Sachet applied for the airforce, but he was turned down and joined the police instead.

A YEAR AFTER Kamel's proposal, Shamh was chatting at the bus stop with a boy from the university, who was praising her high marks. "I can still remember his name," said Um Omar wistfully, "it was Mahmoud." Kamel saw this, and walked over with high red indignation and his fists raised. Shamh told Mahmoud to leave to avoid a confrontation, but then she reminded her suitor that he had no rights over her.

The next year he agreed to buy a house of his own and she accepted his marriage proposal. Her sisters had married people introduced through matchmakers and relatives; Um Omar chuckled that she had found a husband by herself. Her brother asked around about the reputation of a young policeman called Kamel Sachet. In general people praised him: he had a reputation for being brave, but also he had a quick temper. He got into fights. If someone cut him off at a traffic light, for example, he was liable to beat them up.

Kamel Sachet and Shamh were married in 1972.

PHOTOGRAPH: *Polaroid of Shamh-Um Omar as a young mother in the seventies. She is wearing a knee length sundress with a bright geometric pattern and a pair of towering tottering white platform sandals with bows on her toes. She's laughing and holding a baby, her first son, Omar.*

Was Kamel Sachet always religious? Didn't he impose the *hijab* on you when you were married?

"No, no! It came much later that he began to pray regularly and to study the Koran and then he regretted he had not started much earlier."

Um Omar had wanted to continue her studies with a master's degree but her husband thought it was unnecessary and in any case she quickly fell pregnant. Instead she became a teacher at a primary school called *Etedahl* (Being Straight), which later changed its name to *Emtethal* (Setting an Example). She taught general studies, geography, history and *wataniya*, national studies.

Wataniya was a kind of civics class. The syllabus explained citizens' duties, the structure of the government, the constitution, the authority of the police and the administrative divisions of the country. It also taught the duties of students: arriving on time, showing respect to teachers, taking care of the furniture and in particular, cleaning the portrait of the President which was hung in every classroom. In 1979 the face of President Bakr was taken down and replaced with the face of his usurping cousin, the self-promoted Saddam Hussein.

Saddam Hussein was the Baathie strongman and Vice President with an increasing portfolio of key controlling positions in the army, the Party, and the Security Services. With his tribal connections to the President and his inner circle, he effectively controlled the four pillars of the Iraqi state. He made sure he was the most visible politician in the country, always on TV, smiling, handsome, charismatic, well-tailored suits, polished shoes, mirror sunglasses. He would sweep into provincial towns in a black Mercedes cavalcade and emerge to cheering crowds of blushing young female university students and proud-backed Baathie Youth cadres, dispensing charm, gold watches, oil nationalization, agrarian reform. In the fat years of the seventies teachers salaries were increased, schools were repaired and built and stocked with expensive foreign equipment. In Um Omar's school, the pipes were fixed so that sewage didn't overflow in a corner of the playground, new desks and chairs arrived every year, there were modern exercise books and special dustless chalk. Saddam Hussein seemed as young and vigorous as his upwelling country and he promised a future that was as shining and rich and strong.

Through the seventies he took control of the mechanisms of state. Party members who crossed him were arrested, demoted, scared off with ringing telephone threats. Much as Stalin took advantage of Lenin's illness, Saddam overtook the aging Bakr, forcing him into the passive position of figurehead, until he was ready to take over publicly and Bakr "resigned for health reasons" in 1979. Saddam's first move as president was to invite prominent party members to a meeting. This meeting was videotaped. Saddam sits on a dais, smoking a cigar as his lieutenants announce that a conspiracy has been discovered. Saddam says, with regret and tears in his eyes, that he can remain merciful no longer. Name after name is read out. Those called stand up, shuffling, shocked, and are escorted out of the room by Amn security officers. No one dares to remonstrate, the tension builds electric, the tape goes on and on. Name after name. At the end, with the relief of expiated fear, the remaining assembled burst into applause and laud their new leader with promises of fealty. Some of them are rewarded for this display by being invited to join the execution squads of the purged. Right from the beginning there was never any doubt that the penalty for being on the wrong side of Saddam was death.

The appointed class monitor dusted the face of Saddam every morning, it was the teacher's responsibility to make sure that the frame was not broken or damaged. At the beginning of every term the pupils wrote out a selection of the President's sayings and pasted them on the wall.

Saddam liked to make surprise visits to schools to see how much progress was being made and spot-quiz the pupils in front of the television cameras. Teachers were always careful to maintain everything very neatly and in order, just in case the President dropped by unexpectedly. When the schools' inspectors came they made sure that the portraits of the President were displayed well and emphasized that ideals and ideas of *wataniya* should be integrated into every part of the curriculum. There were rallies and meetings on national holidays but Um Omar never paid attention to the rhetoric.

"No one cared about the speeches. You just had to be present. I'd rest my head in my hands; if it was a long speech everyone would be asleep. We'd be thinking about what food we had at home, about our kids, what we should cook for dinner."

Kamel Sachet left the police in 1975 and joined the army and subsequently the Special Forces as an officer. He strove to improve himself. He volunteered for every possible course of extra training. He spent three weeks in Germany in 1978 doing a course in mountain warfare. He learned Farsi and went on joint exercises with Iranian special forces under the Shah. He rose through the ranks to Major, distinguished by his leadership and ability.

He was a good husband and father. When he came back from Germany his suitcase was full of presents. For his wife, a coat with a fur collar, two blouses, a hairdryer, perfume, socks and long house dresses. He brought coats of equal value for his own mother and for Shamh's mother and blouses for her sisters and toys for the kids. On Friday afternoons he would drive Shamh around and take her to see her sisters. They would go on family picnics and the kids would throw up in the car and he would look grim about the smell. He liked to pick a picturesque isolated spot and point out a tree, a stream. Um Omar could never understand why he wanted to stop in the middle of nowhere. She would throw up her hands and say, "What are we doing in a place where there are no other humans?"

Kamel Sachet expected his family to adhere to his high standards. He did not like his wife, for example, to go out unaccompanied.

"My husband set the pace for me. He didn't let me out much. But he never imposed anything big on me. Going out is not a big thing. I could buy furniture, I could change things in the home. I could spend money or not spend money. He gave me his whole salary and he never questioned me. I was his accountant." She laughed at it, "he had his allowance from me."

And he was often away, training, and later, during the war against Iran, at the front. When he was away the house would relax, the children would be noisy, Um Omar would call up her friends and spend hours on the telephone and then, when Kamel called from the trenches and couldn't get through, she would tell him that the children must have left the phone off the hook. He bought her a car and taught her how to drive and she would go for drives with the children. She would visit her sisters and treat her nieces and her children to the ice cream parlor, admonishing them always that this was a big secret from their father. They never told. All the Sachet children grew up with the authority of their father at home, and the authority of their president outside it. They knew not to tell their father about the ice cream and they knew never to mention things he said about the government at school.

Um Omar's discrepancies were not defiance, they were the liveliness of a young woman. She knew very well her place as a wife, and her role of confidante, supporter and homemaker. It was very clear and socially ingrained and she never had a moment's rebellion. "The man tells you what to do. A woman who knows Islam obeys her husband because obeying her husband and obeying Islam are connected."

PHOTOGRAPH: *Family snap from the eighties. Shamh has filled out to a motherly bulk. She is sitting on a sofa surrounded by her children. It is a family occasion and everyone is wearing their best. Shamh had her hair dyed blonde and wedge-cut short at the back with quiffed up waves at the front. She's wearing a colorful dress with wide shoulder pads, dangly earrings and pink frosted lipstick.*

It was only in the mid-eighties that Kamel Sachet insisted on Islamic covering for his wife and daughters. Um Omar resisted and refused for three years. It took her a long time to get used to it, she did not feel comfortable and she would take her headscarf off and then put it back on and complain and submit. Her daughters wriggled and pulled but their father's will was clear. Um Omar said that children adapt to anything; for her it was more difficult. "I was in my thirties." Gradually she adjusted, relented, agreed. She began to see the truth of the religious tenet and even came to regret that she had not donned the *hijab* earlier.

The war against Iran wore on through the decade, debilitating, grindingly attritive. The longer the war went on the more religious Kamel Sachet became. He was in his thirties when he began to pray at the correct times, five times a day. He read the Koran and thought what he might have achieved if he had memorized it in his youth. His family became a strict reflection of his rectitude, his faith and his control.

One day, Kamel Sachet found an old box of family photographs. Many were of Shamh in her younger years, dressed up and made-up in high heels and lipstick. He didn't want to be reminded. He took each picture out of the box and looked at it and said, "This is not a good picture," and then cut it into strips with scissors. Shadwan—his eldest and favorite daughter, perhaps the only one who dared, spinster guardian of her family, its secrets and pride—gathered the photos that he had dropped and kept them. Only the few that we held in our hands had survived the massacre.

Chapter 2

HIS FIRST VICTORY

Z AID WAS THE SACHETS' YOUNGEST SON, THIRTEEN or fourteen when I first met him, a cool kid, played soccer, liked video games, knew all the Manchester United players. His mother wanted him to apply himself to studying English at school, she tried to help him with his homework, but Zaid was not enthusiastic. She complained, "I end up learning more than he does!"

The family had an archive of videocassettes, forty or more, that covered the years of Kamel Sachet's career. Zaid, adept at video recorders, resetting, reconfiguring and hooking them up to the TV, kneeled in front of them one afternoon.

"What do you want to watch, we are not sure what many of these are . . ."

He read out the handwritten labels. "1986, 1988; this one is of a shooting competition my father won." It was a whole life stacked up in stilted video segments, a life that was, from the labels Zaid was reading, mostly battles. "Kurdistan, Moham-ara, Fao, Kuwait, when Saddam visited . . ."

I said I thought we should begin with Mohamara because that was the first battle.

Cᴍᴍᴐ

THE VIDEO WAS dull and shaky, striated with age. It had
been shot, presumably by an Iraqi combat photographer, in
September 1980, during the first offensive of the Iran-Iraq
war. For months Ayatollah Khomeini, the leader of the new
Islamic Republic of Iran, had taunted Saddam with the rhetoric of religious revolution; Saddam in turn had reinvigorated
old border arguments. The two sides traded insults and rocket
attacks, incidents blew firestorms, propaganda machines
printed lists of enemies and denunciations. Finally, hoping to
take advantage of the revolutionary chaos inside Iran, Saddam
ordered an invasion of Khuzestan, a border province with an
ethnically Arab majority. He threw a division at the main
provincial city, a city the Iranians called Khorramshahr and
the Iraqis Mohamara. The division took half the city but was
stopped at the river; the Iranians held the bridges. Then he
sent in the Special Forces.

Their assault on Mohamara came from the desert. For much
of the footage there was no commentary and the sound was
muted. The dark green of the Iraqi army uniforms moved
against scenery which was the same dust olive dun, as if war
rendered everything khaki in tone. Beige sand, gray desert,
yellow shadows of ruts and scars stamped by tank tracks and infantry boots. The sky was filled with black plumes rising from
the red volcano fires of punctured oil pipelines. In the first
scene a tank crew poked their heads out of the hatches as their
tank rolled along a stretch of fresh poured black tarmac road.
The camera panned and clunkily refocused on an Iranian tank
on fire and beyond it, the flat desert bisected with the verticals
of skeletal metal pylons.

The bombardment of the city began. It seemed heavy: the

only sounds on the tape were the boom thuds of the artillery. An Iranian fighter jet flew across the sky, banked and fired three pairs of rockets that flashed with white flame and blew into explosions. The plane tried to climb to safety after its run but was hit by an Iraqi missile and burned in a screaming fireball, in split seconds, to nothing.

The outskirts of the city came into view. Dry concrete block houses stood isolated from each other. The tanks moved slowly, dead tread infantry spread out between them. The tape recorded the heavy gravel throb of the engines, like a mechanized heartbeat. There was also the blurred sound of distant machine gun bursts. White smoke from farther inside the city indicated Iraqi shelling.

"That's him!" Zaid pointed excitedly. His father, Major Kamel Sachet of the Special Forces was marching into Mohamara, striding forth across the battlefield, his unit following him. He wore a clean uniform and he was holding a pistol in his right hand. He wore no helmet and had a heavy black beard that obscured his face.

Zaid sat up from lolling in front of the fast-forward button, pulled his T-shirt straight respectfully, and watched his father be a hero.

The battle moved into the city. Almost the entire civilian population had left; only a few families in the ethnic Arab quarter remained. Houses, streets, angles, lines of fire, fields of fire, range and cornered obstructions; walls were parapets. The cameraman stood behind an Iraqi soldier with a long elegant Soviet Dragonov sniper rifle, propped in the empty window casement, scoping the street. Cut to a platoon of Iraqi soldiers strung out under a colonnade of dark dusty trees, advancing amid the random *ping ping* of rifle bullets. There was an explosion, they fell back a few meters and then ran forward, running across the road, with hip-laden weight, rifles shuggling at their side, heads down, in a running crouch. One stopped, kneeled, and fired a bazooka from his shoulder.

Um Omar shuffled into the room in her black velvet robe carrying a plate of jammy biscuits. "They were very brave, these young men," she commented, settling down in an arm-chair and making herself comfortable. She had just had the sofas re-covered in a brighter fabric, blue and yellow, and wanted to know if I liked them.

"Yes, very much," I told her. Zaid rolled his eyes and his mother, catching this, gave him a stern indulgent look as if to say, as I had heard her remind him teasingly on several occa-sions, "Go and do your English homework again!"

We heard gunfire outside, loud, but not close by. It was the middle of the afternoon, spring of 2004, and gunfire was common enough not to comment on but, as the gunfire inten-sified on the video, a re-echo, bursts, volleys, and single shots, it felt like watching a war in stereo.

For several minutes the action on the tape stopped around the approach to a bridge. The Iraqi soldiers at the bridge fired across the river. In the foreground, next to a splintered tree branch, lay a splayed Iranian corpse, glass-eyed and open-mouthed. The Iraqi soldiers stood a few paces from the body, firing firing, rifles recoiling and juddering with expelled car-tridges. One of the soldiers stepped back, flinching, as an Ira-nian bullet slid past his face. There was the sound of zinging pissing bullets from among a grove of decapitated date palms. Two Iraqi soldiers hauled a martyr from the house opposite. The body was slung in a white sheet and the soldiers carried it one handed, right hands gripping their rifles.

Edit. End of the battle and silence. Nothing but the streets of Mohamara and on the tape, no noise at all, a silent pan of raw history. The cheering of the Iraqi soldiers had been deleted. The camera showed only a grimy grinning line of soldiers raising their arms in the air with the two fingered victory salute standing underneath an Iraqi flag. Farther along the road, soldiers marched tired and heavy and light shouldering belts of ammunition with victory. One soldier was filmed ripping a poster of Khomeini off the wall with his bayonet. Tanks and jeeps and armored cars drove past Iranian graffiti: *"Sons of Sadr."*

After this footage came a propaganda package overlaid with a hail of bombastic martial music with a strong righteous baritone singing, "I won't stop. I won't stop."

And a voice of dooming booming wartime patriotic exhortation:

"This is Mohamara. These are the soldiers of Saddam Hussein. Do we need more evidence? They are so powerful: each Iraqi soldier equals 1,000 of the enemy. We are victorious and now move to new battles for the sake of Iraq and for the sake of all Arabs."

The camera chronicled the empty captured streets:

"Where are the sons of Sadr soldiers? Or the bodyguard of Khomeini?"

There was a scene of Iranian prisoners. They looked thin and thinly dressed and only half in uniform. Their captured ammunition belts, their rifles and their RPGs, rocket propelled grenades, were laid out on display. They were what they were standing up in, some clothes, a tired body, fear of the unknown and nothing more. They were marched off roughly and told to keep their hands on the back of their necks.

The brass voice of victory returned to the soundtrack:

"These are our heroes of the Special Forces. Their father is
Iraq, their mother is Iraq, how could these sons fail to be
heroes?"

Major Kamel Sachet appeared again. This time he was shown
conducting a brief meeting with his lieutenants in a room with
blown out windows. He was pointing at a map and the over-
voice informed the viewers:

"These soldiers are fighting for our honor and our principles."

KAMEL SACHET'S SECOND son was born on 10 October
1980, in the middle of the battle for Mohamara. Um Omar got
word to his battalion headquarters in Baghdad and they passed
him the news on a radio relay that he had a son. Kamel Sachet
wanted to call him Nasser, which means victory, but his driver,
called Ali, said that Ali would be better. Kamel Sachet agreed.

Chapter 3

HIS ELDEST AND FAVORITE DAUGHTER

SHADWAN REMEMBERED BEING SMALL AND THE Iranian planes screaming in the night. Her father was away at the front. "We all woke up, we were very afraid."

At the beginning the war went well for Iraq. Their anti-aircraft crews shot down the Iranian jets and monuments were made from the wreckage. Shadwan watched the news on television. Saddam was everywhere. "I liked his face. He was handsome and young. He wore good clothes. He was the President." At school the teachers extolled his virtues as a strong dynamic leader.

After his great victory at Mohamara, her father came home on leave. One morning she took a book down from the shelf and asked him to help her read what was written inside. He rebuffed her. "I don't want you to love me. You should give all your love to your mother." Only much later she understood that he had said this to protect her.

Shadwan looked like her father, she had his tall grace, his quietude, his seriousness. She was born nine months after her parents were married. Kamel Sachet named all nine of his children himself, and to his first, he gave the name of an island battle between the Egyptians and the Israelis in the Red Sea.

"It is a very unusual name," Shadwan told me proudly, "it was also the name he gave his Kalashnikov."

She had a soft pretty face and her father's firm jaw gave her countenance a weight, a frame, a shape of determination. Her expression was kept carefully demure. In mixed company she always wore a long housecoat, usually blue or olive green, conservative rather than drab, and a matching head-scarf. Without *hijab*, in female company, her hair was dark and wavy to her shoulders; she seemed to smile a little more and the strain of propriety was dispelled. She said little, but she was not shy to speak; in this she was also like her father. She noticed that she analyzed things in the same way as he did, carefully, judging by value, not appearance. When she was a child she was always well behaved and he would hold her up in front of her siblings as the model exemplar. She remembers him laughing at Omar and Ali's antics and getting down on the floor and playing with them like a lion with his cubs. Later, as the war went on, he stopped laughing with his children, his manner became grim and stiff, and he never played with the younger ones.

Shadwan was diligent at school, respectful at home and modest in her demeanor. All the Sachet children agreed she was always her father's favorite; Shadwan would drop her eyelashes and look down into her lap so as not to appear proud, but she would say, "Yes it's true, I was his favorite, everyone knew this," and give a small laugh, it was a point of family amusement.

All through her childhood Shadwan submitted to her father's pride with obedience. She studied hard and was at the top of her class. She was sent to an elite girls school—Saddam's daughters were in the years above and below her—but she did not go on picnics or outings or to the ice cream parlor with school friends. If she needed to go shopping she went with her mother. When she was seventeen she asked her father if she might be allowed to go to a small party her friend Sohor was giving at her home. Her father agreed and drove her to the house and picked her up afterward. When she was eighteen she asked again to be allowed to go to the birthday of her friend Amineh. Again he agreed and drove her there and picked her up afterward. At the end of the school year Amineh had a gathering to celebrate their graduation and Shadwan was also allowed to go to that. Apart from family occasions, she had only been to these three parties in her whole life. She had never felt the excitement or the rebellion of being a teenager.

Shadwan was not naturally gregarious like her mother, she had inherited a gravity, a certain contained self-solitude, from her father. In contrast to her mother's chortle, Shadwan had a shy smile that spread slowly and rarely. Generally, she preferred to stay inside at home. She told me that it wasn't so bad: if she was bored she would go to bed and sleep and in sleep there was the respite of oblivion.

One day Shadwan showed me her room. It was small and austere and lined in wood; against one wall was a narrow single bed neatly made with a green blanket. There was a wooden bedside table, a small lamp and a few shelves. The books were mostly on her two favorite subjects: religion and psychology. The room was dark and functional, no pretty thing adorned it. Shadwan smiled as I looked it over and tried to think of something to say. I could not tell if her smile was one of pride in the room's modesty or of a more intimate rue, a look between one single thirty-year-old woman to another: do I not deserve something more?

Sometimes Shadwan would show me a pair of new shoes or a headscarf or a handbag or I would glimpse a flash of diamanté at her wrist or across her toes. She had her dreams and hopes, but her life, through various circumstances—her father's position, war, lack of security—had been circumscribed, she managed a kind of diffident righteous acceptance of this, but she lamented her shut-in sufferance: "I never had any good times after secondary school." She bowed to her religion and her father's expectations. When she came of age, many suitors came to ask for her hand. Her father refused all of them.

TWO YEARS AFTER Kamel Sachet and the Special Forces had captured Mohamara, the Iranians counterattacked and retook the city. The Iraqi army was pushed back across the desert, fighting in patches, often overwhelmed and tens of thousands were taken prisoner. Saddam shot the general in charge of the retreat and announced that the army would redeploy along the Iraqi border. There was a sense on the television news and in radio reports that this would mean the end of the war; most people were quietly relieved. Perhaps Saddam hoped Khomeini would be satisfied. Khomeini, maddened and bloodied, was not. The Iraqis dug themselves into the desert and settled for a fractious stalemate. The rest of the war, six more years to come, would be mostly fought on Iraqi soil.

As the war ground on, Kamel Sachet became tougher, more formal and prone to excoriating, tight-lipped anger. The children came to fear his moods and kept a careful orbit around his preoccupation. When he was home the house was quiet, the plumb-line tension in his frown set the atmosphere. His sons looked up at him from a distance, fretted for his approval and dreaded bringing home a set of bad school marks. Shadwan remained his confidante. Sometimes he would tell her about his experiences. Once a trench wall collapsed on him during shelling and he was buried in the sand. He told her how he had waited listening to the voices of the rescue party coming closer and closer until he could hear them inches away beginning to dig him out. She had teased him, "Yes! And then you had to clean your clothes all over again!" And he had told her, "Yes, I got out of the trench brushing the dust from my tunic!"—he was always fastidious about his uniform being clean and well pressed.

One afternoon, when Shadwan was eleven, a relative who served under her father's command came to the house and talked to her mother in low tones. Um Omar was five months pregnant and when she came back into the kitchen, there were tears in her eyes and her face was stern and full of worry. She told the children that their father had been wounded and he was in hospital and that, *inshallah*, he would recover. Shadwan kept a picture of her father under her pillow, and at night, when she took it out to look at it, she would cry a little through her prayers. She heard her mother crying at night also, when the little ones were asleep.

Kamel Sachet's eldest brother, Abdullah, came to the house and brought a portrait of Saddam to hang on the wall. He told Um Omar to get rid of the religious books and to stock her bookcases with Baath Party literature. Um Omar wouldn't let him put the portrait of Saddam up, but she gave away some of the religious books and put some Baathie pamphlets in the small bookcase in the reception room where guests would see them. Various relatives came with advice. Kamel Sachet's salary had stopped, Um Omar continued working and refused all offers of money; she dared not become indebted or take charity, she would not make her family beholden. She was trying to find a way—phone calls and blind alleys—but everyone she went to for help was afraid to tell her anything. The director

at her school called her to his office and told her that if she did
not participate in the Baath Party she would not be able to
keep her position. She paid up her membership and attended
the weekly meeting as required, but Shadwan could see this
was something bitter for her. Shadwan could feel a sense of
shame in her mother and a sense too of trying to hold her head
up in the midst of it. She did not smile any more and shouted
at her children when they were boisterous. As the weeks of uncertainty lengthened, so did the space between the words and
their meaning that Shadwan overheard in adult conversation.
Shadwan began to understand that her father was not in the
hospital after all.

After three months an official came to the house and presented her mother with written permission to visit Kamel Sachet
at al Rashid No. 1 Prison. Shadwan went with her mother and
her Uncle Abdullah the following Friday. She remembered that
the guards were polite but searched everything, even the plates
of food her mother had brought. Um Omar submitted to the
inspection and said nothing as they stirred a knife through her
saffron rice and thumbed through the extra clothes she had
brought for him. They were shown into a waiting room with a
table and a sofa. It was a military place and somehow cold.

When her father came in he looked tired and thin and his
face was pale and yellow colored. His uniform was clean and
pressed although his badge of Major had been removed. He
hugged everyone and he pulled Shadwan onto his lap. He
laughed and pretended to be at ease. "Your clothes!" he scolded
them first, "they are not beautiful enough!" Um Omar looked
down at her hands. "No!" he said, "You must buy new clothes
and the next time you come I will see them and you are not to
cry!"

He told his brother not to hire a lawyer if the case went to court and not to find a solution by asking for favors.

"I am here until I am here," he said. He told his wife to call the baby Ahmed if it was a boy and Esma if it was a girl. He told them everything would be alright.

Chapter 4

INSIDE

WITH HINDSIGHT, IT SEEMED TO DR. HASSAN that the long and miserable national descent began in 1983. Three years into the war, the oil money began to run out, blood into sand. The dinar fell from its stronghold of one to three dollars and would carry on falling for the next twenty years. For the first time Iraqis needed to have official permission to leave the country, and those with strategic skills—army officers, doctors, engineers—often found permission denied. Something changed: a sense of weariness and wariness, of claustrophobia; casualties mounted; war sacrifice ate hope with increasing ravening. Life became separated into before and after; good times and times that had to be endured.

Long decades later, in the spring of 2006, Dr. Hassan and I sat in his office in safe exile in Abu Dhabi, reflecting. Dr. Hassan had been watching the coverage of Saddam's trial. In court Saddam had jabbed and lectured, cogent and defiant. In Dr. Hassan's professional opinion, Saddam was "paranoiac aggressive"; in his own world he was still President. He threw his prosecution back in the face of those kangaroos who dared to make up their own justice and declared, "I am responsible for everything!"

The formal charge against Saddam was the killing of over a

hundred male inhabitants of the town of Dujeil, reprisal for an assassination attempt in 1982.

"Did you see they read the name of the doctor who was attending the execution in Dujeil?" Dr. Hassan leaned back in his chair and rubbed one side of his face with his palm, a gesture of strain, an effort of self-reassurance. "The doctor's signature was on the death certificates." Dr. Hassan was caught by the idea that the signature could have been his own. "Dr. Huda," he recalled, distractedly, to himself, "yes something like this, it was a Christian name . . . one day if *my* name . . . and at the trial of Saddam Hussein, was read out . . ."

"When did you realize it was bad? 1983? Or earlier?"

We went back to the very beginning.

IN THE SUMMER of 1968 Hassan graduated from high school with the highest mark in all of Kerbala province. His father was in prison, wrongfully convicted of embezzlement, and he and his mother and siblings were reduced to a small rented house in Kerbala with no electricity or running water. For such a lowly family, his was an extraordinary achievement. Hassan was awarded the fortune of twenty dinars for his scholarly success and his picture was taken for the local paper. He went to Baghdad to enroll in the university.

At six in the morning on 17 July Hassan woke up to the sound of gunfire cracking. He was staying in a hostel off Rashid Street and went out into the ocher summer dawn and asked the pavement sellers setting up for the day what had happened. The defense ministry was a few streets away, they pointed.

"Another coup," said one, shrugging his shoulders.

"A coup? Do you think they will block the roads?" Hassan was mindful of the scant three banknotes in his pocket. He had

planned to return to Kerbala that day; he did not have enough
money for a longer stay.

He went back to his hostel and drank a glass of tea and listened to the radio. General Aref was finished, that much was
obvious, but it was not clear who was now in control. At sev-
en-thirty the radio issued Proclamation Number One. Various
promises were made to deal with the Kurdish problem, Palestinian guerrillas, the righting of the military catastrophe against
the Jews the previous year, the rule of law, equal opportunities
and "a democratic life." More flowery rhetoric was reserved for
the denunciation of the regime which had just been deposed:
"a clique of ignoramuses, illiterates, profit-seekers, thieves,
spies, Zionists, suspects and agents." On the streets, Dr. Hassan
recalled, no one paid much attention; there had been so many
coups and generals and presidents since the murder of the King
in 1958. Political fervor boiled with Arab pride, the injustice of
Palestine and the indignity of British imperialism. A swirl of
ideologies, the Communist current and the nationalist current
and the Baath Party current each flowed faster and faster as if it
were a race. The Baathie revolution of 1968 was expected and
came, calmly, like a break in the weather, as if in answer to the
turmoil. The lanes under the crumbling balconies of the old
Ottoman quarter were noisy with hawkers and sellers going
about their business as usual. Hassan noticed a girl walking past
with her head uncovered and wearing a skirt that showed her
legs. All the barrow-men and the porters, the tea hawkers, the
traffic policeman with the whistle in his mouth, an old man on
a mule, watched her progress, but the girl, carrying a satchel of
university textbooks, seemed to regard their lusty interest con-
temptuously. These were modern times and what did she care
for the backwardness of the dirty lower strata? Another revolution! Progress! What did this all mean for the common man?

Not much, a shoulder shrug of indifference. That day Hassan felt no ominous portent, there were no roadblocks or curfews after all, he traveled back to Kerbala in the afternoon without incident.

HASSAN JOINED THE Medical Faculty at Baghdad University but after two terms it was clear he could not afford to continue without joining the army for sponsorship, and in order to take up his commission, Hassan was told he had to join the Baath Party.

Politics were still in turmoil. On campus there were many parties: Nasserites, Leftists, Muslim Brotherhood, Progressive Socialist Workers, Islamic factions; it was a dangerous mix of popular struggle and force, strikes, arson and rallies, counterplot and propaganda, denunciations, arrests, gunfire and assassination. Students were taken out of exam rooms and never seen again; Dr. Hassan remembered a young Baathie student leader called Ayad Allawi who liked to brandish his pistol—it was a revolution after all—at communists when fights broke out in the Student Club. From time to time, government cars were bombed.

His father warned him against getting mixed up in politics, but Hassan filled in the application form without much misgiving, signed his name to a dictated paragraph declaring the socialist and Arab nationalist principles of Baathism and went to the weekly meetings as required.

Dredging this history in Abu Dhabi, one question echoed in my head: Didn't you know? Didn't you know? I was hoping to elicit the very first pricks of misgiving, things he had seen which bothered him, a disquiet, at least concern—the telephone rang. Dr. Hassan turned away from me and took the call.

Dr. Hassan put the telephone down and smiled. He resumed his chronology. In January 1969 he and the other Baathie students were ordered to Tahrir Square ("Come and enjoy the feast!" exhorted the radio), where fourteen prisoners, nine of them Jews, were to be publicly hanged as Zionist traitors. The Baath Party, insecure in their tenure, young, nascent, then just another regime in a series of overthrowing coups, was showing its boots and its bite. The chants swelled in the throats of a hundred thousand people crowded under the swinging cadavers. "Death to traitors!" "Death to Israel!"

"What did you think, standing there?"

Dr. Hassan did not excuse himself, but neither did he berate himself. Those executed were spies, they had been convicted of working against the revolution; these were the consequences.

"There was no concept of democracy, freedom of opinion, freedom of speech, the rights of an individual. We didn't feel these things, we didn't think these things, we didn't have any practice of them. I came from a religious town where you could never give your frank opinion. No one had ever been able to speak freely, contradict or question the prevailing order, or especially any kind of religious institution. There was no discussion of these things, life simply *was*, and was organized already. We did not feel mercy or pity for those Jewish spies who were hanged. We didn't know the reality, that they were innocent, that they had been tortured. People were shouting, 'Death to the spies!' OK, we shouted, 'Death to the spies!'"

In 1974 there was another coup attempt in Baghdad. Hassan and his Baathie cadre at the University were issued with rifles and sent to defend the Ministry of Defense. He waited, with his hands sweating around the wooden stock of the gun, for an attack. He thought, *What, for the sake of Allah, am I doing here?* (In the retelling his knees began to vibrate gently—a minor tremor, some latent nerve?) He admitted that he thought to himself, squatting next to a sandbag with the grit and rubble under his newly issued, heel-cracking black army boots, *This is trouble, this is trouble that we might get hurt or killed in and we cannot get out of this trouble.*

BY 1983 DR. Hassan was a major in the army medical corps with a successful private practice. He dressed well and liked Italian shoes, he bought a new car every year and rented a house where he and his friends could gather for parties, a place to bring their girlfriends and drink and relax. He was comfortable, confident, proud of himself, he had rank and respect and money.

Three days a week he saw patients at the Rashid Military Hospital. After the retreat from Mohamara, he noticed an influx of psychological casualties, shell shock, shaking, hysterical paralysis on the right, gun-holding side of the body. He began to notice waves of malingerers that coincided with each heavy assault. Gunshot wounds to the hands or feet, self-inflicted broken arms; soldiers would inject petrol into the backs of their hands and their flesh would swell and erupt like a volcano, seeping, horrendous, accompanied by a fever. The Military Amn ordered the doctors to send these deserters to prison after they were treated. The usual sentence was five to seven years, but psychiatrists like Dr. Hassan would often write "under tension" on their files and send them back to their units. Often he helped his friends out; he would write sick notes for officers, especially if there was a big attack coming up, or he would make a false medical report, "mentally depressed, unfit for service," so that eighteen-year-olds could avoid conscription. He felt sorry for them, Sunni and Shia alike, young men faced with the meat grinder of the war; he did what he could to help them avoid the front line.

Then one day, a friend of his disappeared. Dr. Hassan asked around discreetly, confidentially; no one knew—then another friend disappeared. Both were, like him, Shia from the shrine city of Kerbala, like him, they had done well in their studies and joined the Baath Party and progressed into good jobs in Baghdad. Dr. Hassan felt a cold chill and self-diagnosed anxiety. A colleague of his, Dr. Laith, confirmed in a corridor whisper, yes, his friends had been arrested. Dr. Hassan took sleeping pills and he dreamed about leaving the country but dared not apply for an exit visa. He regretted returning to Iraq after his training in Munich, but he had had no choice, now it was too late. He thought: *I should hide, but everywhere they will find me.*

One January morning he received a letter requesting him to report for an interview at the Military Amn. He put on his olive green combat dress and a fur-lined fatigue jacket to guard against the cold. He sewed 200 tablets of temazepan and Valium into the collar of his shirt and the waistband of his trousers and put only a little money and his military ID card in his pocket. He took a taxi to the Amn office instead of driving his own car; he knew he would not be returning.

Dr. Hassan presented himself for arrest. They pulled off the badge of rank from his shoulder and took his watch, blindfolded and handcuffed him and transferred him, by black windowed minivan, to the Military Amn headquarters. His head was forced forward so that he had to walk bent over with his torso parallel to the ground and he was led along an underground corridor and down seven concrete steps and pushed into a cell. The cell had a cement floor, a solid metal door with a window slot and a dirty mattress; but it had been newly painted. A single light bulb burned brightly and continuously and the buzzing blades of a ventilator fan, irregular white noise, drove him half mad with tinnitus. Twice a day, at 6 a.m. and 6 p.m., there was a toilet break, the cell doors were opened and the prisoners had to run through the corridor, herded and slapped by guards wielding cables. For three days he remained alone, lying drugged and slothful, abandoned to his own mind. He remembered twenty years before, visiting his father in prison, he remembered that injustice—now repeated! He remembered how proud his father had been when he had achieved the highest high school marks in the whole Province of Kerbala, he had waved the telegram at everyone in prison and they had all given thanks to Allah, that he, an unlucky man, had such a son. Such a son! Dr. Hassan opened his eyes but the white walls bounced cruel electric light and he closed them again into a red interior. In prison, in this country of prisons! His memories came in waves of regret. He recalled the shape of the woman he had loved in Munich under his hands and the bright green spring trees along the boulevards—why had he ever returned to Iraq? He rued and kicked at his decisions—he should have known—and his mind rewound to his duties as a junior doctor attending to prisoners during the war against the Kurds in 1974: lacerations, lesions, swellings, bruises, black eyes, septicemia, infections, toxemia, renal complications, nails extracted, one or more, sometimes all ten, third degree burns on the fingertips due to applied electricity. At night he could hear screaming and sobbing, he ate his Valium and drove himself crazy calculating what his friends might have said under interrogation, what he should say, what he would be compelled to say.

After three days they woke him at 3 a.m., handcuffed and dragged him, bent over, down the corridor. Up the seven steps, outside, a five minute walk, it was dank and cold, then inside again. They sat him on a stool. They kept him blindfolded but he had the impression that it was an old stone vault with blank walls. He could hear two guards at the door while two other officers paced back and forth and questioned him.

"Look, we know everything about you. You are a member of the Dawa Party. You and your Shia friends have been gathering for political purposes. Your friends have confessed everything and you have been arrested. You must tell us the truth. There is no point in lying so that we have to behave harshly with you." The words Dawa Party terrified Dr. Hassan, as their shadow terrified all Shia at that time. Dr. Hassan protested that he had nothing to do with the Dawa, that he was not even a religious man, that he drank alcohol and did not go to the mosque.

A voice nearby screamed in agonized pain, crying, "No! No! Stop! Don't—"

Something about the quality of the sound made Dr. Hassan think it was a recording played to frighten him. He repeated his innocence but it was irrelevant and the beating began. They used thick electrical cables and hit him on his legs and his back. At first the pain was excruciating but after the first blows the stabs of pain slackened, the anxiety of waiting was over, it was already the worst, and his assaulted body pumped blood and adrenaline which mixed with the tranquilizers he had taken; he became dizzy and disoriented, almost drowsy. He felt his body slipping and he did not stop himself falling off the chair. He collapsed on the floor, trussed and aching, his mind black, feigning black-out. The guards rushed over, worried that they had killed him. He knew if he died it meant a problem for them, forms to fill, an investigation—"Help him, help him!" He could hear real concern in their voices. A doctor's assistant came and took his blood pressure and he was taken back to the cell. He was interrogated twice more, again in the middle of the night, eventually he signed a statement admitting his relationship to his arrested friends, but he was not beaten again.

In Abu Dhabi he paused and he leaned back in his chair and put his hands together and pressed his supplication to memory against the bridge of his nose. "I was like my patients, I was like those soldiers who exaggerate their wounds so that they do not have to return to the front."

His case was transferred to the National Security Council, the authority that judged crimes concerning the security of the regime. His parents, meanwhile, had paid $20,000 to engage a lawyer because his brother was the Chief of Military Intelligence. His friend Dr. Laith gave a statement on his behalf, asserting that Dr. Hassan was a good man and had never had anything to do with the Dawa Party. In the end he was charged with drinking alcohol in uniform, having improper relations with the nurses at the Rashid hospital and helping Shia soldiers avoid their duty at the front by signing sick leave for them. After three months he was transferred to al Rashid No. 1 Prison, officers' section. His cell mate was Lieutenant Colonel Kamel Sachet.

PHOTOGRAPH: *A portrait taken of Kamel Sachet in prison. He has a full beard and his eyes are hooded and recessed into charcoal shadows, his expression slow burning in anger, defiance and fatigue.*

Kamel Sachet used to fall asleep instantly, like a switch being flipped. "You could not count to five before he would be asleep." Dr. Hassan suffered insomnia, and would ask him, incredulous, "How can you sleep so easily? Are we in the Hilton or something?" Kamel Sachet said he always slept like a stone, even on battlefields under bombardment.

Dr. Hassan knew of his reputation. He had seen the television pictures of Saddam awarding his Special Forces commander with medals, he had read the story of Kamel Sachet, brazen with courage, wearing the full uniform of an Iraqi Special Forces lieutenant colonel, walking tall through the front gate of an Iranian garrison, raising his arm as if to return the stupefied salute of the guards before shooting them: a Trojan horse for his men to run in behind.

Conditions in the officers' section of the al-Rashid military prison were reasonable. Dr. Hassan and Kamel Sachet shared a room with a window, the door was not locked at night and they had free access to a bathroom. Outside there was a stretch of open ground, a volleyball court, a patch of scrub and a few plants. Some of the officers laid out small gardens and grew vegetables to pass the time. They were allowed to read the Koran and other books were also sometimes permitted, they had a radio but no newspapers. There were fifty prisoners in the senior officers' section (after Mohamara, Saddam would brook no dissent), among them three divisional commanders, the chief of food procurement for the army who was accused of fraud and the military attaché from the Iraqi Embassy in India who had created a diplomatic incident by hunting holy birds.

In the mornings Kamel Sachet tried to involve his new friend in volleyball to keep his strength up, in the afternoons they would walk together, pace the dirt between the barbed wire fences, as Kamel Sachet practiced pronouncing the foreign English words he had asked Dr. Hassan to teach him. They talked together, they confided their recovering trauma to each other. Kamel Sachet told Dr. Hassan that he had been kept for three months in a cell too small for him to stand up or lie down in. His interrogators had not beaten him, perhaps his natural authority abated their usual brutality, but he was not allowed to wash. He said his uniform became like "dirty sand," his beard grew long and matted. "I should not have said that thing on the telephone," he once admitted.

During interrogation he was asked why he was not a member of the Baath Party.

He replied, "I am an officer in the army; the army has no relations with the Baath Party, it is not necessary to be a member." They asked him why he had criticized the order to withdraw from Mohamara. Kamel Sachet was not penitent. "That territory cost us too much blood that we should let it go so easily."

He asked Dr. Hassan to help him write a letter of petition to Saddam asking that his case be brought before a court. The letter was conveyed through some sympathetic connections. Kamel Sachet had not yet been charged and chafed at the pace of the investigation; but he maintained his trust in God and the President. He was, as ever, servant to his duty.

All the senior officers had been transferred to al-Rashid No. 1 Prison after weeks of interrogation, being beaten, chained, kept locked up, solitary in their own filth, but they never spoke of these humiliations. If Dr. Hassan asked one of them what had happened, he would shrug and say he had done nothing and walk away. Their pride bit their tongues, they recoiled from their shame. "Suspicion was the dominant behavior"; informers were ostracized. The uncertainty of their investigations lingered over the camp; Dr. Hassan noted depression and paranoia. Some obsessively pulled whiskers from their cheeks one by one.

Most of the officers prayed, it was an old consoling rhythm and observance that broke the day into manageable pieces of time. They prayed and rubbed their prayer beads through their fingers: solace, false piety, hope. "It's a defense mechanism," Dr. Hassan told me. "The stress of the situation draws you back to the unconscious point of religion and its secrets."

Kamel Sachet's observance was diligent. He prayed five times a day and spent the evenings reciting passages from the Koran. It was his dearest ambition to commit the entire knowledge of the Koran to memory; he often told Dr. Hassan he wished he had learned the Koran when he was young and his mind more impressionable for the imprint of the verses. He asked him to pray with him, but Dr. Hassan demurred. He had his Valium instead. "It is because you are a Shia," lamented Kamel Sachet. He wished Dr. Hassan was not Shia. He told him sadly, almost with regret, "You are my best friend but it is wrong that you visit these shrines and pray to those imams."

Kamel Sachet submitted to Islamic fatalism: "What is written on my forehead is written by God for me." In battle he always held his head up, eschewing a helmet, wearing only a beret, and led his men from the front. Many times, he recounted, he had heard the bullets whistle close to him, sometimes so close they burned his tunic, but he never wavered. "If I die at that moment then it means that is the time for me to die."

Dr. Hassan found his certainty unnerving, almost supernatural. Kamel Sachet's self-belief was rock. He was the champion marksman of the whole army. "I never miss a bullet."

"If you become afraid, you have lost the battle." he explained. "You have to think what your enemy is thinking. What would your enemy expect? They would not expect an Iraqi officer to walk alone with his head held up straight through their gates!"

War is psychology, Dr. Hassan agreed. He told Kamel Sachet how he had once managed to persuade a captured Iranian fighter pilot to broadcast a short statement on Iraqi television. "I befriended him." He told him how he had devised propaganda leaflets to drop over the Iranian trenches. Kamel Sachet was impressed and surprised by Dr. Hassan's world of psychiatry. He said, "I know the other commanders don't understand you, but we need more of you." He concurred that men were better rewarded than punished. He himself commanded loyalty with good treatment. He always made sure his men had enough rations, that their boots were the best available—there were some commanders who stole their units' meat and front line soldiers were left to subsist on rice and soup. Dr. Hassan nodded at these things, he had visited the front and reported on morale. He said he had seen a platoon with only a single chicken between them every two weeks because the thieves in the commissary sold what was requisitioned.

"In Mohamara," Kamel Sachet pronounced with pride, "I treated wounded Iranian prisoners as if they were my own sons and I punished those of my own men who were looters and rapists."

They talked over many long weeks. They discussed command and psychological warfare, authority and its exercise, they talked about their families and their lives before. Dr. Hassan told Kamel Sachet about his time in Munich and the easy interaction between European men and women, without shame! "Shamelessness!" Kamel Sachet told Dr. Hassan that he had been attached to the vice squad when he was in the police, and had witnessed the corruption of alcohol, the self-degradation of women, the effects of sexual assault, such stains that could never be erased—he shook his head. Dr. Hassan told him that he had tried to counsel victims of rape. Kamel Sachet narrowed his eyes and shook his head again, for him, death was the only sanction.

They did not talk about the regime. They did not talk about Saddam. Kamel Sachet remained steadfast in his loyalty, commanded by President, father, sheikh or God, the requirement of his duty was the same. A general's great glory, enshrined in the Koran and Islamic conquest folklore, was obedience to his ruler. "Who by God obeys God and his Prophet and those in command of your affairs," quoted Kamel Sachet. His country was at war, the Iranians were the same Persian enemy that the great Kaakaa had destroyed, morphed into the Shia revolution of aggression and apostasy. His world was sharply divided into black and white, he was not a political man; he never navigated; he stood clearly upright, called in no favors, reasoned with his interrogators, spoke with confidence, without guilt, and tried to benefit from his imprisonment by learning English, studying the Koran and understanding the new world of psychology that Dr. Hassan had explained to him.

In contrast, Dr. Hassan lost twenty kilos in his three months of isolation. He imploded, his soul gnawed at itself, pride collapsed. He was caught in a paradox: his rank and party membership had not insured him against arrest and yet his position had mitigated his charges and allotted him a decent prison. Sometimes he saw it all as an overturned game, it didn't matter to them what your credentials were or your position or merit. There were no rights, no right. It was a game of control but he saw that it had no rules. He had tried to follow the rules but he had been punished anyway. In prison his friendship with Kamel Sachet kept his spirits up and rebuilt some of his confidence but when he was eventually released after several months, this thin defense crumbled again. He went back to work at the Rashid Military Hospital, but he felt alienated. His colleagues distanced themselves and, like magnets repelling, he withdrew. For several months he was repeatedly called back to court as various aspects of his case came up for processing. He wanted to explain to his colleagues that in the end he had only faced the minor formal charge of drinking in uniform; but he worried that they would not believe him. He was marked Shia, they were Sunni, they took care not to be included in his circle of suspicion. Before his arrest Dr. Hassan had been a confident extrovert, afterward he became quiet, lone and pensive. His Shia friends, who had also been arrested, came to see him once or twice at his clinic, but they did not dare to renew their friendships. The shadow of his dislocation was cold, but it was a place to hide. Over time this chill internal discomfort permeated his bones. Dr. Hassan said he never really recovered his old self. The moments of a smile, a small laugh that I saw, belied geniality, but he carried a weight of a life unlived, a handicap of circumscription. Abu Dhabi exile was no respite; it was a reduction, not an escape.

Kamel Sachet was released without charge a few weeks after Dr. Hassan. He had been at home with his family only a day or two when he was summoned to Saddam's presence. Saddam gave him money and another decoration and promoted him to full Colonel in charge of his own division. This was the recalibration of loyalty. Good patriotism could not be trusted, Saddam knew very well—he preferred rod and reward, the example of stripped and banished, followed by the prodigal relief of re-admittance. He created slaves and henchmen in one mind.

A MONTH AFTER his release Dr. Hassan was sent to attend an execution at a military training compound in the desert south of Baghdad. It was unusual for a psychiatrist to be assigned to such duty, but he could not refuse the order. Six young men, fit and healthy, were tied to stakes. Their sentence of death for desertion was read out to them. Six soldiers lined up opposite, each was given thirty bullets for his task. Their platoon commander stood to one side flanked by Dr. Hassan and a religious sheikh who had also been summoned.

The men never stopped screaming and writhing in protest: "I am innocent . . . We are Muslims . . . Please believe us . . . We have children and wives who depend on us, we fought for our country, we defended Iraq, God help us, please."

Dr. Hassan bowed his head in the retelling.

"Thirty bullets," he explained, "made an independent medical determination of death redundant. Their brains were spilled everywhere, their skulls were completely smashed." For many years their blood-grimaced faces loomed destroyed in his dreams.

Chapter 5

YES, BUT

D R. HASSAN HAD REPEATED THE MANTRA THAT reassured many of his generation: "What could I do?" Certain questions or memories might induce a gut twinge, but the gall of participation was generally well insulated from accountability, wrapped in layers of "What could I do?" "But I helped people, many people!" and "I suffered also, you know"; and the ultimate trumping: "You cannot understand what it is like to live under such a regime!"

It was impossible to argue with these justifications. In Saddam's Iraq the inculcation of fear and the (threat of) violence was very real. A misstep could kill you, imprison your wife, take your son's university place and your daughter's marriage prospects away.

I met many, many Iraqis: army officers, doctors, university professors, translators, businessmen. I studied each face, listened to each story, weighed the balance of their pauses and sighs. I was mindful that my most important question, the question I had wanted to put to Dr. Hassan in Abu Dhabi, "Didn't you know? WHY?" was never answered. Each had their own permutation of indignation, explanation, rationalization. It seemed easy enough to blame Saddam, mad monster, instead of admitting that it took thousands of individuals to enforce his will;

but I knew their remonstrations were valid. It was true what they said: I could not understand what it was like to live under such a regime. I could not judge them.

I met General Raad Hamdani in Amman in the summer of 2007. He had commanded the Second Republican Guard Corps until the fall of Baghdad in 2003. Hamdani was well read and intelligent and in conversations that ranged long over ten days of interviews, I discovered a variation on the default position of blame-shift: that of equivocation.

Hamdani was short and bullet shaped, with sloping shoulders and grappling arms that curved around a tough compact body. His big domed head was shaved, he wore a trim dark beard and his eyes stared out under a smooth ominous eyebrowless brow and bored intensely dark. He had been a tankist and looked like a ball bearing—until he put on a delicate pair of rimless spectacles and his arms uncurled and his mouth smiled and his eyes twinkled and he began to talk and quote Churchill and Sun Tzu and Montgomery. His mind was nimble and thoughtful; he analyzed. He would think through one of my probes into morality or psychology and answer, "Yes, . . . but." He employed this "Yes, . . . but" so frequently that when he used it, I would raise my eyebrows and smile at the old chestnut and he would smile back; it had become his catchphrase.

Hamdani owed his bookshelf and independence of thought to the example of his father. ("An Eastern state of mind has a limited knowledge," he told me, explaining, by contrast, the background and intellect of many of his generation of officers: "The status of learning was low, the level of thought was not high, we were an educated generation, but half our fathers were illiterate.") Hamdani's father had been a headmaster in Baghdad, but, in the turmoil and dizzy years of the sixties, was demoted by the Communists and then the Nationalists and then the Baathies until he was just an ordinary teacher. In 1969 he retired and recused himself from the politicization of the classroom. It was the same year Hamdani found it necessary to join the Baath Party in order to continue his studies and commission at the Military Academy. His father counseled him on the choice that wasn't much of a choice. He told him he understood that his membership was important for his career—although he had wanted him to become an engineer like his older brother—but that he should reflect carefully on the ideology put before him and think for himself about the content of party pamphlets and meetings. Hamdani compared and contrasted and came to the conclusion that Baathism was like an Arab version of communism. It was socialist with an emphasis on Pan-Arabism, a kind of internationalist dream. "People like my father," Hamdani observed with respectful hindsight, "knew this was impossible, a fantasy."

Yes, of course there were good things about the Baath Party. They focused on the eradication of illiteracy and built schools and spent money sending graduates to America and Europe to study. They tried to diversify the economy away from a dependence on oil and agriculture into state owned manufacturing. And they encouraged the advancement of women in a secular way. . .

But they did not allow other ideas to surface. One ideology and one party; narrowed after Saddam's takeover in 1979 to one man. Hamdani, as many educated Arabs often are, was contemptuous of the Arab mindset. "Arabs are not stupid, no, but our Eastern society is a society in which ideas are imposed, either on a tribal or a religious level. The Sheikh imposes or the Imam imposes. It is a society formed by a shepherd into a flock of sheep. Our first thought is not like in the West, to judge for ourselves or to assess something, our first thought should be, as we are brought up to defer, 'What would the religious leader think?' or 'What will the tribal leader think?' I owe my father for teaching me a different way: I think by myself. But that's what the Baath Party did. Instead of a tribal leader you were given a Baathie superior. The politicians came and took the role of the tribal elder and the religious leader. Saddam Hussein was very smart. But he didn't give others around him any chance to think. He believed he should think for everyone."

PERHAPS SADDAM WANTED to end the war in 1982, but Khomeini would not let go. Over the next years of campaign he harried the Iraqis, tried to cut the Baghdad-Basra road, invaded the Fao peninsula and supported the Kurdish *Peshmerga* fighters skirmishing in the mountains in the North. The Iraqis had air superiority and better weapons, the Iranians had greater numbers and green-headband fervor. The Iranians attacked, the Iraqis counterattacked—increasingly using poison gas as a force multiplier. Battles waxed and waned from the desert to the mountains along a 1,600 kilometer front, battles piled on top of each other, campaigns rolled over themselves, repeating, year after year, ground taken, ground lost, count the dead, count the wounded, withdraw, push forward or, more usually, stand in a trench and be shelled.

This continued, hundreds of thousands dead, hundreds of thousands prisoners, hundreds of thousands wounded (no one knows the real numbers) for eight years. Hamdani would sit in his tank at night and read by map light. His heroes were the German Second World War tankists: Guderian, von Manstein and Rommel.

"There is no evidence of a country benefiting from a long war." Hamdani quoted from Sun Tzu's *The Art of War*. "The

Iran-Iraq war was like the First World War in Europe: trenches, continuous clashes, more clashes than actual maneuvers, we repeated the Somme, and because there were many clashes there were many victories mixed in with failures and defeats." Hamdani quoted Churchill ("a genius when it came to wisdom!"): "War is many battles and many maneuvers, but the successful general is the one who has more maneuvers than battles."

THE FIRST TIME Hamdani came across Kamel Sachet was in 1981 at the battle of Seif Said.

Seif Said is a mountain on the border where Iraq's waist narrows to Iran. It was a strategic height: from its summit plateau, 2000 meters up, it was possible to see, through a telescope, the outskirts of Baghdad 100 kilometers away. In January the Iranians attacked the Iraqi garrison entrenched on the top. It was raining and cold and the mountain was a fissured mass of bare brown crumbling rock. It was a desert, no animals, not even birds. On the lower slopes shepherds had led their flocks along the narrow sheep-worn contour tracks to graze the meager spring grass and camp in a cave called the Cave of Death. "It was grim and everyone hated it," said Hamdani, "we lost so many soldiers there."

At the opening of the battle Hamdani, then a major, led an armored scout unit to discern the enemy's position and line of communications. He found an old track to an abandoned Ottoman fort and observed the Iranians reinforcing their vanguard across a narrow pass. Then he drove to the nearest village, al-Maalla, the Iraqi staging point twenty kilometers away, to deliver his report.

It was a wet dim gray January day. It would rain hard and then stop, rain hard again. Hamdani pulled the neck of his military sweater over his head, the rain soaked through his combat jacket. The Iranian shelling was heavy on the slopes, lighter on the outskirts of al-Maalla. In the village there was the mash of military confusion, a triage center had been set up in a surgical tent under red crescent flags; a thousand dead those first three days, maybe three thousand wounded. It was the first Iranian offensive of the war, the shelling was heavy, the mud was heavy, there was shock that the Iraqi garrison had been repulsed and there were so many wounded, shaken down the gravel roads over swollen rivulets in bloody muddy ambulances and overloaded groaning jeepfuls.

The general in charge of the counterattacking 2nd Corps was General Latif, who Hamdani (and others) described as a courageous but bone-headed brutal man who thought that every battle should be fought as a head-on collision. Hamdani knew him from the 1974 war against the Kurds as a heavy drinker who would distribute beer to his men. ("It was permitted to drink then, but of course not on duty.") Hamdani found his headquarters in a police station, from where two infantry brigades had been ordered up the mountain to assault the Iranians directly. Hamdani had seen the Iranian reinforcements go over the pass beneath the Ottoman fort at Joboura and he wanted to explain in his oral report that operations should be directed at choking this pass. But the atmosphere inside the headquarters was curled and mean. "Very bad." Hamdani shook his head. A colonel and a captain and six soldiers had been accused of an unauthorized retreat and Latif had ordered their execution. The prisoners, handcuffed and blindfolded, were led outside into the yard, and a squad of soldiers were lined up in front of them. These soldiers were hesitant, cradling their guns in their hands, miserable and tense. Latif had a rifle in his hand and he screamed at the execution squad, "If you will not shoot them I will shoot you and then I will shoot them myself."

Hamdani could not bear to watch. He went to Sharkashi's deputy, a wise and sympathetic officer called Barhawi, and explained his plan for cutting off the pass. Barhawi was despondent. He said to him, "Yes, you are right, but what can I do with this man? All he will do is hit them with straight-on attacks."

Hamdani left the scene and drove farther back behind the lines to the town of Mendali where the Iraqi staff had set up headquarters and gave his oral report about the Joboura pass to his commanding officer. A little while later he was requested to deliver his report directly to more senior commanders and directed into an underground bunker.

He walked down a few concrete steps and inside, smelling cigar smoke in the damp concrete room. Sitting around a table was Saddam Hussein, smoking a cigar, Adnan Khairallah, Saddam's cousin and popular Minister of Defense, the head of the Istikhbarat, the military intelligence, and a bodyguard-aide. As Hamdani came in, Saddam was scolding the head of the Istikhbarat: "This is all happening because of your failures! We did not have the correct information." The Istikhbarat chief's face was lifeless, it was impossible to tell if he was angry or ashamed. Adnan Khairallah was calming the situation down, saying "you win some, you lose some," that war was not all victories—Saddam responded slowly and with sarcastic venom and continued to stare at the Istikhbarat chief.

Hamdani proudly pulled himself to attention and gave his first report to his president. He explained his unit's position, pointing at the map tacked up on the wall of the bunker, the enemy's line of supply and how the Joboura pass could be cut. Saddam nodded. Adnan Khairallah nodded. Then, just as he finished, General Latif came in, wearing a military motorcycle helmet and a uniform (Hamdani noticed, slightly shocked) that was old with a frayed hem. Hamdani took the opportunity to salute and leave. He went out into another trench where an operations room had been dug out and lined with sandbags. Staff officers sat around its edges with radios, telephones, maps and radar equipment and gave him a cup of tea and pointed out topographies until he was called ten minutes later to come and have official photographs taken. Saddam, Adnan Khairallah, the lambasted Istikhbarat chief and Saddam's bodyguard gathered together to commemorate the moment. Saddam was trying to be a little nicer to the Istikhbarat chief, perhaps regretting his earlier harshness, and called him an "old comrade," but the Istikhbarat chief remained shocked and silent. Saddam continued talking, and ordered that the attack should be halted for a few days to allow more reinforcements to be brought up. "Let's wait, prepare ourselves and then regain this lost ground." General Latif, Hamdani was alarmed to notice, was unaccountably waving his Kalashnikov around, trying out different poses, and for a moment managed to point its barrel at Saddam. The bodyguard abruptly intervened, gripped the barrel of the gun and pointed it down to the ground. After the shutter click and formalities, Saddam and his entourage left by helicopter.

So the fighting stopped for a few days and reinforcements were called. In those early months of war the Iraqi army was small and thinly stretched and the Iranians had American Cobra attack helicopters left over from the arms shipments to the Shah which devastated Iraqi armor with their rockets. The Iranians were emboldened and used the time to pull heavy guns up to the top of Seif Said and commence a distracting attack in the Kurdish mountains in the North.

When the fighting resumed, Major Kamel Sachet's Special Forces brigade, the heroes of Mohamara, were part of the 10,000-man assault General Latif sent, again in blunt fashion against Iranian machine guns, up the slopes. The battle continued for a month, with various offensives and skirmishes, but the Iraqi forces were unable to break through. When it was clear that the assault had failed Latif sent Kamel Sachet and a number of other commanders, under charge of dereliction, to a military tribunal in Baghdad. Hamdani's version was that Saddam himself personally intervened in Kamel Sachet's case, remembering his bravery at Mohamara and, impressed at how he defended his actions at Seif Said with an honest assessment, released him and a number of other officers.

Whether this is what happened, or some approximation, is not perhaps as important as the idea of this episode as a template for the war, and for Kamel Sachet's place in it, that followed. Seif Said was the first Iranian attack of the war, the first Iraqi defeat (the Iranians maintained a force at Seif Said until the end of the war in 1988 and when they left, they withdrew unilaterally), and the first battle in which commanders were shot for failure. Thereafter, battles were often pointlessly bloody, directed by orders that could never be questioned and the death bullet could come from in front or from behind. For Kamel Sachet and officers like him, the threat of execution was a deep imprint of fear twinned with the mercy and reprieve of Saddam. After Seif Said, Kamel Sachet would trust in his president and for a while this trust would serve his career well.

HAMDANI AND I talked over several days in his office in Amman, where he was doing some kind of consultancy work for a rich Iraqi exile. He drew maps for me in blue ballpoint, arrows, attacks, lines of trenches, and answered his phone to take calls from various Iraqis and Iraq players who were revolving around the Baghdad-Amman-Damascus-Beirut-Washington circuit: Ayad Allawi, former Iraqi president appointed by the Americans, canvassing support for a rerun, the commander of the American marines in Anbar province who wanted advice, a cousin of the Iraqi foreign minister who wanted to talk about a new Kurdish political party—such was the exile's coffee-tea dance of meetings. Hamdani was always very solicitous and apologized for these interruptions and would resume drawing the troop formations at the third battle of Shalamche or a diagram of the Iranian fortifications of Fish Lake and explain how the tank battles in Fao opened up the front or why Penjawin was strategic. . . .

The Iran-Iraq war was a long term meat grinder. It was also, for the Iraqis, a total war, much more so than for the Iranians, who fielded an army out of triple the population. All of Iraqi society was militarized in the national effort.

Pupils and teachers dressed in scout uniforms every Thursday and saluted an Iraqi flag in the playground, there were veteran battalions and schoolboy battalions, even women's battalions, and policemen were sent to the front once a year so that they might be exposed to the fight as the infantry were. An officer was respected as a brave patriot, and went to the head of the queue, Republican Guards were well paid and when they were deployed in convoy the streets were lined with children throwing water and sweets and saluting them. Even babies were dressed in the camouflage fatigues and rank of their fathers and Saddam proclaimed them "sons of our soldiers." A former general once told me, with the boom of proud nostalgia, "We were 27 million Iraqis and 27 million soldiers."

And with the long war came the undertow of prolonged and hopeless fighting. Some soldiers cut their wrists or shot their feet, many relaxed in a Valium fug (the Iranians had opium to forget the pain and numb sense into courage), officers would go into battle drunk to stop themselves from shaking or "turning yellow" and some took refuge in their religion, the superstition and calming rituals of Islam warded off the horror, gave it a mysterious purpose and promised paradise.

Hamdani did not fall in with such palliatives. He seems to have retained his own independent self. He watched the summary executions on the front lines and adjudged: *yes*, on the positive side it meant that a soldier would prefer to be killed by the enemy than be labeled a coward and his family receive no pension, so positions were more ruthlessly defended, *but* the negative aspect was that there were always more losses than was necessary—"Of course to shoot a solider was a disgusting thing, a horrendous thing, any officer trained in the right way would refuse such a thing."

I asked him about his own experience, as commander and commanded. He replied, "It's a very touchy subject," and then he repeated that he had taught himself from books the British model of officer behavior and that this had always brought him trouble. "This was the pressure I felt, but I couldn't unlearn the British way. So I went in the middle. *Yes, . . . but.*" He attempted a smile to accompany his catchphrase and drew his analysis upright again. Command at gunpoint: it meant, he explained, that the new generation of commanders would always wait for a written order before they carried out any maneuver. This hesitancy became a feature of Iraqi command, officers were afraid to take responsibility, they waited for orders, insisted on clarifying positions, telephoned the high command—"This killed the spirit of the Iraqi army," rued Hamdani. Many, he said, chose to die a hero's death rather than retreat tactically and be castigated as a coward. Kamel Sachet, according to Hamdani, suffered the same hesitancy. He was undoubtedly a courageous and excellent soldier, but not very well read, and not much given to debate or thoughtfulness. Hamdani believed, watching his career progress, listening to the staff officers gossip, that for Kamel Sachet, the risks of responsibility weighed as treacherously heavy as the fear of defeat.

KAMEL SACHET PUT his trust in God, his president and his own prowess. On his release from prison in 1983 he was sent to Penjawin in the Kurdish mountains, where the Iraqis held positions on the high jagged-tooth promontories. Anxious to prove himself, he would challenge his fellow officers when they went on foot to inspect high forward positions. Although he was still weak from his incarceration he always arrived first.

The following year at the battle of Fish Lake (more of a filthy canal) in the desert outside Basra, Colonel Kamel Sachet drove his jeep to the front line where the Iranians were dug in 100 meters away and the bullets fell like rain and calmly sat and asked for tea to be brewed. The battle lasted a week over Saddam's birthday, came to be called the "Birthday Battle," and was a happy victory. After two divisions had been thrown at the Iranian positions a tank division was deployed and the Iranians were finally pushed back across the canal, thousands drowning under fire.

Kamel Sachet was promoted in double time. He leapfrogged the staff jobs and held command positions throughout the war. Major to colonel to general. In 1987 he was promoted to the Command of the Baghdad Division of the Republican Guard and his troops stopped an Iranian attack at Shalamche which threatened Basra.

After the battle there was a medal ceremony at the Republican Palace. The ceremony was held in a great state room lined with marble and hung with giant crystal chandeliers and Saddam sat, wearing his habitual wartime green uniform, on a gilt throne at one end. TV cameras bustled at one end of the hall, party officials mingled; here there were always medal ceremonies after a battle, victory or not. By the end of his career Hamdani had fifteen medals. Kamel Sachet, as his son Ali once showed me, had 18 medals of bravery, including the Sash of Rafidain, the Sash for the Mother of All Battles and the decoration "Commander of the Two Rivers." Medals were accompanied by cars, land and cash; model, quality, and amount dependent on rank and favor. Over the course of his career Kamel Sachet was given cash, many cars and a farm near Hilla, already planted with fruit trees. He loved to spend time among his orchards, but the cars he sold and he used the proceeds for charitable works and for building mosques.

Hamdani did not talk to Kamel Sachet on this medal occasion—they were barely acquaintances, he knew him by reputation only, but he remembers Saddam's extravagant praise of him. "Look at General Sachet!" Saddam pronounced as he shook Kamel's hand in congratulation. "The Iraqi soldier should be in every way like this! Look at him! Look at how fit he is! Look at his courage! Look at his good manners! Kamel Sachet is a commander I treasure."

KAMEL SACHET'S COURAGE was hard and straight and upright. He was not a political man and had no taste for the ambitious margins of war. He did not profit from it or turn his position into currency. He was not in the artillery or ever in a staff position: he must have witnessed the poison gas attacks on Iranian positions, seen the summary execution of POWs and heard the stories of the Anfal campaign against Kurdish villages in the North, but I never heard evidence (despite due diligence and a trip to Kurdistan to talk to former *Peshmerga* commanders there) that he was directly involved in these atrocities.

There was a story, however, which Hamdani told, that seemed to suggest Kamel Sachet had not managed to go through the Iran-Iraq war without absorbing the military shift in morality. When the penalty of death becomes a commonplace, perhaps it becomes unremarkable to order it.

Six years after the battle of Seif Said, after which he found himself on the capital charge of dereliction, in the latter months of 1987, Kamel Sachet was Commander of the Second Division headquartered in Kirkuk. There was a battle at the mountain of Shemiran. Republican Guard reinforcements could not be spared from the fighting in Fao in the South and for two weeks Kamel Sachet ordered his men to attack uphill to dislodge the Iranians. The Iraqi attacks were repulsed, there were no reinforcements to be had, losses were heavy, artillery pummeled over the peaks from inside Iran. The Iraqi line pulled back defensively, but Kamel Sachet ordered them to continue and to break through. According to Hamdani (although I have never managed to verify this), when it was clear the assault had failed, Kamel Sachet and his senior commander Nizar Khazraji ordered the commander of a Special Forces brigade, a Colonel Jafar Sidiq, and several other officers to be executed. Colonel Jafar Sidiq got word of his arrest, fled to Baghdad and managed to get an audience with Saddam Hussein. The colonel explained the difficulties of the battle and their heroic efforts, he said that most of his men had been martyred or wounded and that it was not right to execute the heroes of the Iraqi army. Saddam ordered Kamel Sachet and Khazraji to stop the executions, but his order came too late, seven had already been shot.

Saddam had managed to draw a very neat psycho-circle for his generals, a circle, abused to abuser, like a noose.

A FEW MONTHS later, March 1988, not far from Shemiran, was the massacre of Halabja. Halabja is a Kurdish town backed up against the mountains. The Iranians and the Kurds coordinated an assault; the Kurds retook Halabja and the Iranians pushed toward the dam at Darbandikhan which, if destroyed, could flood Baghdad. On 15 March *Peshmerga* units captured Halabja; the next day the Iraqi high command, in retribution, frustration and genocidal anger, ordered the town bombed with poisoned gas. Families huddled in their basements from the bombardment, loaded into farm trucks to escape or ran to each other's houses. They collapsed in the street with frothing mouths, their burning lungs drowned, lay sprawled in doorways, cradling dead children, retched in blind lines of refugees up mountain paths. No one knows how many dead, some say five thousand, lay in clumps of limp, tangled bodies with milk crusted eyes.

For many years the gassing of Halabja was confused by the Iranian offensive at the same time: the Iraqi propaganda machine blamed the Iranians for the gas attack, or claimed that there were Iranian troops in the town (there were only a few Iranian intelligence officers). Hamdani called Halabja "a political mistake," and denied it had happened in the way the Kurds said it had. "This thing about Halabja was a lie. That everyone there was obliterated was a lie. There were some civilians left in the town, but the Iranians had occupied Halabja." He was upset by the sentence of death that had just been passed on Sultan Hashem, the well liked and well respected (even by a former Kurdish *Peshmerga* commander I talked to in

Sulaimaniya who had been under his command as an intelligence officer in the early eighties) head of the army at the time
of Halabja. He blamed it on Kurdish revenge justice and said
clearly, "An army is not responsible for political mistakes."

Hamdani's rebuttal of Halabja reminded me of the slippery
prevarications of the Nazi defendants at the Nuremberg trials
. . . excesses, mistakes: *yes, . . . but*. I read Albert Speer's *Inside
the Third Reich*. Speer was Hitler's favorite architect, a civilian
who rose to become Minister for Armaments in the latter years
of the war. Speer was held up for many years as the Nazi who
admitted collective responsibility for Nazi atrocities, who put
his hands up and refused to excuse his own participation. But he
categorically and continually, throughout his trial, his twenty-
year imprisonment and until his death in 1981, denied that he
knew about the extermination of the Jews or the extent of the
slavery of the legions of forced labor that his ministry relied
on for war production. In fact, in the whole of his 600-page
long, extraordinary, compelling, best-selling rendition of his
relationship with and attraction to Hitler I found that only two
pages addressed the issue of slave labor in the armaments indus-
try he was responsible for.

After I read Speer I read Gitta Sereny's meticulous biography, *Albert Speer: His Battle with Truth,* in which she tried to
probe the shadows behind his erudite dissembling. She wrote,
"The truth, of course, is that lies are not necessarily simple,"
and came to the conclusion that despite his protestations, Speer
must have, in fact, known about the Final Solution. But it was
something that Speer's daughter remarked that caught my attention: "How can he admit more," she asked Sereny, "and go
on living?" After all, I thought, what person does not sustain
themselves with self-myth? How would it be possible to look
in the mirror without it?

Denial is a psychosomatic anesthetic. The truth, the truth about oneself, sheer and plain, is too blinding, too painful to fully realize. Locked inside our own skulls, none of us can claim perspective enough to judge ourselves clearly. But maybe, somehow, the truth does exist, like a kernel, deeper than thought and thinking, beyond the reach of rationalization, society, memory, conditioning, experience . . . Perhaps this kernel is sometimes called the conscience. . .

In the early months of 1944 Speer was hospitalized for several months. His illness, an attack of some kind of neurological exhaustion, was never satisfactorily diagnosed but Sereny, and Speer himself, although characteristically less explicitly, hypothesize that it was some kind of subconscious reaction to the stress of realizing the real horror of what the Third Reich had become.

Sometime in 1987, when he was commander of the Second Division in Kirkuk, after the battle of Shemiran and at the time of the Anfal campaigns, Kamel Sachet came to Dr. Hassan's clinic in Baghdad complaining of chest pains. He was admitted to hospital but the medical investigation found nothing wrong with his heart. Dr. Hassan suggested that his pains might be psychological, a result of anxiety. Kamel Sachet nodded and said simply, "There are too many troubles in the North." Dr. Hassan knew he had a complicated relationship with Nizar Khazraji, the then Chief of Staff, and that the military situation in the North was critical, but he could see that his friend did not want to talk about it further and so he did not press him.

HAMDANI SHOOK HIS head at the bullshit trial in Baghdad and all the injustice of the new Iraq (dis)order and I sat back a little. I liked him and his intelligence but Hamdani was a man who had risen unscathed through the Iran-Iraq war, who had continued his ascent through the corruption and suspicion of the nineties and who had managed to convince the Americans (in much the same way he was convincing me, with his candor and his admiration of Western mores) of his good nature and co-operation, so that although he spent several months being interrogated by army historians and CIA debriefers after the fall of Baghdad, he was never faced with Sultan Hashem's fate.

I asked him how he had managed to steer his career through Saddam's regime. He said that it was his forthrightness, his espousal to the "British way" that was always getting him into trouble, that he had almost been a martyr to his principle. At the end of 1990 he spoke out during a meeting of senior commanders: he said there was no point in discussing the defense of Kuwait when the only thing to be discussed was the withdrawal from Kuwait. For this heresy, he was called an American agent and a traitor, confined to barracks for two weeks and threatened with a military tribunal. His release was secured by Qusay, Saddam's second son. He had been Qusay's commanding officer during the Iran-Iraq war, Qusay liked him and after the retreat from Kuwait he found himself promoted rapidly under his sponsorship and protection. The nineties were the decade of sanctions and corruption and Qusay's star, eclipsing that of his psychotic murderous brother Uday, was in the ascendant. Certainly if Hamdani had managed to hitch his fortunes to that of the favored son, it made sense that he would have done well out of it and stayed safe.

Maybe Hamdani was as good a man as he said he was. I believed Hamdani, mostly. But at the back of my mind, in every interview I ever conducted with Iraqis, was the knowledge that duplicity was as much a part of being Iraqi as excessive pride, excessive hospitality and love of the kebab. In order to thread their way through the economic detritus, the agents and the sharp-edged apparatus of the Baathie state, Iraqis developed the trick of multiple personalities. They could be belligerent or obsequious, efficient or lazy, in charge or needy, drunk or pious, according to the requirements of the official whose caprice they had to navigate. Flattering and dissembling, Iraqis had learned first to present themselves in whatever shape was convenient to the situation and second to figure out how to get their due benefit from the arrangement. Their dealings with the Americans was no different. One story for the American sergeant of the foot patrol that handed out sweets to the neighborhood kids, another for the Shia official with a bristly beard and no tie who might employ you to build part of a new ministry, another for your red-check-scarfed neighbor who wanted to blow it up. I began to understand that lying was how Iraqis had survived—those that managed to—through the vicissitudes of revolution, war and occupation, mosque and army unit, classroom and government report, promotion and arrest.

Hamdani was talking to me, a Westerner, and he knew that he must praise Western traits. Perhaps he really believed in them, perhaps not. But several times he highlighted his belief in straightforwardness and lamented that it was so disparaged in Arab cultures.

"It often got me into trouble with Saddam Hussein, this frankness! . . . The truth is, in our culture, frankness is disrespect." In 1995 Hamdani had presented a paper, "Criticism on the Strategy of the Second Gulf War," at a military forum chaired by Saddam and including 180 senior officers. As he spoke, his words echoed louder into the stunned silence that received them. The moderator tried to move the microphone away from him. "There was a silence in the room like the silence that precedes the hurricane. Saddam of course was very angry." Saddam had stood up and brought his fist down on the table.

"Look at General Hamdani! This man is a casualty of Western ideology caused by continual reading and listening to Western media! If he was correct about his thesis, there would be no one in this room left alive today! I do not allow—" and at this he pointed his finger directly and emphatically at Hamdani.

Hamdani looked at the faces around him and saw they were all looking down into their laps, as if they didn't want to look at a dead man.

"This decision to discuss only the bright points of anything consumed the truth," and the truth was layered with the lies that the authority demanded. This was Hamdani's second reproach. A year earlier Saddam had mooted a reinvasion of Kuwait; Hamdani had challenged this and Saddam had been furious.

Saddam. Saddam was the concentration of everything.

"Sometimes you would feel so close to him that you could spill your heart to him and other times you felt you were in a cage with a hungry lion." Hamdani had thought long and hard about Saddam, his character, the contradictions and hubris, intelligence and stupidity. For Hamdani, even the mad monster deserved some *yes, . . . but.* "Saddam had strong charisma. Face to face you felt that he looked right through you to your mind and your feelings, that he knew everything about you. He was a good reader and often a good listener and other times the exact opposite and would brook no other opinion. And other times he would ramble on some trivial subject: the worst thing was his speeches! They were long with no point, they were the opposite of a tidy and analytical mind. For example, everyone knew that he would receive letters, from Bush Senior, from John Major and Arab leaders and these letters would be five sentences long and he would reply with ten pages! He had aspects of greatness and he built the country. But then he destroyed it. He destroyed his own ambition, when he crossed a red line that he himself had drawn. In February 1980 he gave a famous speech and said that an Arab should not fight another Arab and then he became the leader of the first [sic] Arab nation to invade another Arab nation. He talked of democracy but he was a dictator. Once he heard that one of his ministers had slapped a common civilian and he called the minister and the civilian who he had slapped and ordered the civilian to slap the minister back. But then he executed many, many. . .

"Saddam had more than one personality. If you had Sigmund Freud and Adler and others and set them to analyze this personality I don't think they would come to any one single theory. He was a thinker, he had a great humanitarian aspect, he was very generous and softhearted. But there was a murderous personality, very hard—the kind of hardness that would not even be taken by a beast. And he was a simple farmer, uncivilized and shackled by village ways. The difficulties of his early life and his ambitions—that went way beyond anything. At fourteen he used to dream of leading the Arab world, to be a second Saladin, that history would remember him always. He made history, yes, but there will always be a debate—"

Hamdani had tried to keep his own sense of self intact and to balance his opinions with his duty. He tried to command as fairly as he could, and to question when he could. When he could no longer question, "I tried to continue indirectly so that I wouldn't lose the thing I had built in myself, because to lose this would mean the loss of my life."

Hamdani shook his head, perhaps at his own failures, perhaps at the echo of these failures, perhaps at his country's descent, which seemed to last longer and plumb deeper than a patriot could bear. We returned to a discussion of the Iran-Iraq war, to the ironies of proud medal ceremonies and the battles that scraped Iraq raw. "Although the war was victorious in terms of the military," said Hamdani, equivocating, as was his wont, and then delivering the final and devastating assessment: "it destroyed the Iraqi economy and Iraq. The psychological problems that rose through the Iraqi social life and the criminal age we have today came out of that war."

IN 2003 HAMDANI was commander of the 2nd Corps of the Republican Guard in charge of the southern theater and the defense of Baghdad, the city the Americans promised to shock and awe. "Of course," said Hamdani, "I knew from the beginning we would lose." When the phone rang in his house he would pick it up and find a recorded message talking to him: "There is no way to oppose the United States!" "Stay in your home where you will be safe!" He hung up. The Mukhabarat, the intelligence service, were certainly listening, and in any case it was an obvious piece of psyops.

He planned to fight for as long as possible. He thought the Iraqi army might be able to hold out for two or three months at best.

The American F16s bombed his division to smithereens. After only a few days his troops were smashed and he found himself without a single vehicle—not a jeep, not even a commandeered taxi; everything had been destroyed—in a band of thirty-odd survivors. He split the men into groups and told them to disperse, traveling by foot on the dirt back-roads through the farmlands south of Baghdad. He made his way to the house of a cousin in Youssifiya. He liked this cousin, who had given up his government post as an engineer and taken a second wife and gone to live in the countryside. It was an odd sort of life for an educated man, but Hamdani respected his desire for independence. The cousin welcomed him and gave him the use of a shepherd's hut on the edge of his land; it was safer than in the main house where he might be seen.

Hamdani felt himself grateful, empty and exhausted. His face and arms were scratched from the blasting bombs, he had a pebble of shrapnel in one calf, his limbs ached from walking. He took off his uniform and folded it carefully and hid it with his Kalashnikov in a duffel bag and put on a borrowed pair of trousers and a flannel shirt. One of the wives brought him food, one of the small sons brought him a pen and writing paper and he began to rewrite the diary that had been burned when his jeep had been hit. The small sons watched him write and shook their heads: "Is he studying for his exams or something?"

Baghdad fell on 9 April and the Americans toppled Saddam's statue. Hamdani was sitting in his cousin's guest room with a few of his cousin's friends when he heard the news. There was no electricity and the kerosene lamps made small pools of yellow light. Hamdani described his mood as almost "dying from grief." He could not eat. He thought about his cousin's life, how he had teased him about his big family and the two wives—unusual for an educated man, and living so far out on a farm in some kind of oblivion; his cousin had laughed at his jibes and said he was happier: "I can start my own tribe!" Hamdani had chided him for favoring one of his sons above the other: "Be careful or they will end up like the story of Jacob!" Now he remembered his own sons, both of whom had been deployed with the Republican Guard and who were now, like most of the army, and himself, missing.

One of his cousin's relatives was very happy Saddam was finished. "Thank God we got rid of Saddam and the Americans are here! Soon they will rebuild everything."

Hamdani told him he thought this was a very naïve view. "We won't have the power and authority that has ruled this country and there will be a vacuum and this will be very dangerous."

"So if you know all this and you are so clever why didn't you organize a coup against Saddam? You are a high commander!"

"This is another naïve view," Hamdani replied quietly. "You don't understand the complexities. If there is no power to equal the power that has just been removed then there is no one to take control and this could end in civil war."

The happy optimistic man said, "Well, I am betting on the Americans, we'll meet again in the future and you will see that I was right!"

The following day Hamdani hid near a brush fence and watched two American armored Bradlee vehicles position themselves at the village crossroads. He had fought the Americans in two wars, but this was the first time he had been able to observe their soldiers up close. He saw how young they were and this surprised him for some reason. He also noticed the standard of their professionalism, their discipline, the way they always held their guns in the ready position with their index finger horizontal, flat above the trigger guard. He saw that not one of them took off their armor or their helmets, despite the heat. During the day he crept around in irrigation ditches to see more. At another intersection he found tanks. He saw that on each tank the razor wire was looped neatly and hung on a hook, that the jerrycans were stored in their own brackets, and that everything was kept neatly in its proper place. Two months earlier he had stopped two officers of the Republican

Guard driving toward him on the barracks road, both had been bare-headed and he had berated them for leaving their berets off. "We have talked about this before and I gave you a photograph of an American soldier and an Iraqi soldier, the American was clean and tidy and the Iraqi was disheveled and holding his gun awry and I know you were both there when I showed these pictures and I asked you all then, which looks the more impressive soldier and most of you replied, the American."

After a few days a warrant officer brought him news that his family was safe at a relative's house in Diala and that his son Osama was with them, but that his other son, Ahmed, was missing and there were rumors that he had been killed or wounded in the battle for the airport road. Hamdani put on a *dishdasha* and borrowed the ID card of a man who looked roughly like him and went to look in Baghdad.

He hardly knew where to begin, everything was broken and in chaos. He searched in different areas. "Where can you look? But you are a father so you must look." He walked the airport highway through the burnt tanks and Humvees and he wondered why the Americans had not imposed more control, why there was not even a curfew? The roads from the South were lined with makeshift graves, heaped earth or white sheets, each marked with a stake. The weather was hot and dusty and there were streams of poor people walking home. An American private, wilting and exhausted from the sun beating, held up a stretcher he had made into a sign painted with the word "Dead" so that the people walking would not step on the fresh graves. Hamdani saw every pathetic mound as his dead son, the American private holding up the sign in the heat and the dust, asking the herding people to go around, struck him as some surreal polite detail in all the mess.

Finally after several days and relayed messages from the

family in Diala, Hamdani got word that one of his relatives had found a note in the admissions book of a hospital in the Adhamiya district of Baghdad: *"Ahmed: 2nd Lt. Rep. Gd."*

Ahmed had taken three bullets on the airport road, two through his upper thigh and one through his bicep. He lay bleeding, unable to walk, next to a corporal who was slowly dying, when an American medic came up the road and crouched down to examine them. The dying corporal reached up a little and whispered for help, "I am a Christian like you!" and he fingered the gold cross around his neck. The American medic told him his name was David and said a few prayers as the corporal died. The medic said he would try to stay with Ahmed too, "Because you wear glasses and I wear glasses just like yours," but soon his unit was moved forward and he went away. Then a Republican Guard officer came out of a hiding place and dragged Ahmed, hitching car to car, until they reached the hospital in Adhamiya. There a doctor cleaned his wounds but they had no bed for him, so the Republican Guard officer took Ahmed to his own house, which was nearby. A relative tracked him down and by the time Hamdani got back to his family in Diala, Ahmed was already there, splayed and pale, tended by a local nurse (they did not dare entrust him to a hospital) being fed with antibiotics and broth.

After another week or so passed, Hamdani went to Baghdad to see if there was any remnant of the high command to which he should report. He found his former colleagues and friends too scared to sleep in their own houses. There were Americans looking for the deck of playing cards, Chalabi's militia in their American uniforms, Kurdish *Peshmerga* in baggy pantaloons requisitioning ministerial houses, the Badr Brigade guarding bridges. Thousands of Shia were on the roads walking to the shrine of Kerbala for the anniversary of the death of the martyr Hussein, performing a pilgrimage so long forbidden. They walked past burned government buildings still picked over by looters and the wreckage of his tank units on the south highway and Hamdani could see very clearly that everything was going to be different now.

Hamdani stayed for a few days at his mother's house and found an army medic he knew to go to Diala and take care of Ahmed because they were worried about gangrene. He was afraid at first to return to his own house and kept moving every few nights in case he was recognized, but after a few weeks Hamdani was tired of hiding and so with the help of some neighbors he managed to evict a family of squatters who had taken over his house and moved back in.

On the street he saw the faces of thieves and murderers and so he shut himself indoors and lapsed into depression. By the beginning of June, the American net was closing, his name was on the blacklist of the 200 most wanted. Helicopters seemed to hover exactly over his house, Humvee patrols seemed more frequent. His wife begged him to turn himself in, but he was reluctant. Eventually he was put in touch with a Mukhabarat officer exile, who said he had been under his command in 1983 together with Qusay and Uday (Hamdani couldn't remember him) and that he was now working with the Americans and could arrange for him to turn himself in safely.

So he surrendered himself to the Americans and agreed to co-operate. He was treated well and allowed to go home every night and sleep in his own bed. Once his house was stormed by American troops at night, he and his wife and daughters were bundled into the garden illuminated by the bright helicopter light above and handcuffed before he could explain that there had obviously been a mix-up and that he had already turned himself in. For several months, he went every day to be debriefed. He told them he would answer every question and that he would answer them truthfully. In his interrogations he was interviewed by different officers, historians, analysts and intelligence. Some focused on WMD and their whereabouts, others wanted him to explain the structure of the Iraqi army, others had more strategic questions about the relationship between Saddam Hussein and the Republican Guard and how decisions were made. The Americans, he acknowledged, treated him well and with courtesy. Hamdani could not resist a self-serving comment on the increasingly cordial atmosphere of these discussions. "Even in custody I told the Americans that they would lose. They hated me at first for saying this but now the new staff is coming to Amman to talk to me."

IN MANY WAYS Hamdani conformed to the way most generals and senior commanders reflected on the past twenty-five years of their combat careers. Iran was an enemy that deserved to be attacked. Gas was (regrettably) used for reasons of expediency, the Anfal campaigns were more of the order of counter-insurgency measures than genocide, the invasion of Kuwait was a monumental blunder of Saddam's hubris, the uprising that followed was Iranian backed, the nineties were years of corruption and stagnation and they had come to hate Saddam and his destruction of the army and the country in its wake. Yes, but.

Culpability. Moral Responsibility.

After several days of conversation, after the whole history had been laid out on his desk and illustrated with lines of blue ballpoint and flashes of gesticulation, I asked Hamdani directly about his own sense of guilt and morality and how he justified to himself having served a terror regime.

At first he reiterated how terrible Saddam had been. "Yes," I concurred, "but you were his general."

Then he understood what I was asking and he leaned across his desk to look at me directly, intensely, eye to eye. I met his gaze and we stared at each other for a minute or so. I looked as carefully as I could into his eyes but could discern no tremulous depth. Perhaps there was something sealed, farther back, behind—but I began to be uncomfortable and I looked away so that he had won the staring match and was able to ramble his final, concluding thoughts. I wrote them down just as he spoke them; I cannot vouch for their sincerity or veracity.

"You feel very sad, the high command was gone, it was the stupidity of our own decisions combined with the stupidity of American decisions. You feel very sad about what Iran will gain, the destruction of the country and a civil war I told my debriefers I hoped I would not live to see—

". . . The idea of participating—it's much bigger than what you are capable of understanding. I graduated from military college, a new regime came . . . It's not easy. The mistakes were not only Saddam Hussein's mistakes. It was the mistake of a whole society, it was a mountain that grew, stacked up. How much could you change it? At the time it was a very bad system, a bad regime, but there were red lines, if you didn't cross the red lines you were OK. But now? Now it's nothing: why am I out of Iraq now? I never would have left Iraq, but it has become worse, I had to . . . It kept piling up, there were more and more restraints. As a good commander, as a good person, what can you do? I tried to lessen the evil in the regime. I worked to correctly bring up good honorable soldiers to perform for their country, not for the regime. You carry out an order, but in a good way to obliterate the evil in it. I was never a tool in killing. I never killed another Iraqi, I never killed an Iranian prisoner of war, I never attacked a Kurdish village when I was part of the forces in the North. This was as much as I could do. A human being is held accountable according to the amount of freedom he gets. Who would dare to object to his plans? Or say he would lose this war? I set ninety percent of the deserters in my units free. I did not even have a jail at my division headquarters. I did not have bodyguards, it was just me and my driver. Qusay and Saddam Hussein were always criticizing me for this. And I would always answer them by asking if there was any problem in the fighting capability of my division, or their training or preparations. I had no jail but I had the best battalions in fighting skills and power." Here his pride expanded and he quoted von Manstein's *Soldiers' Memoir*, "The greatest status you reach in the military and its highest rank is to be an excellent soldier. I wished to end my career being an excellent soldier."

"You chose to be a part of it," I told him. "You could have resigned, you could have gone to live in the country like your cousin."

"One of my American debriefers asked me the same question. He asked me why I continued to fight against the Americans. I told him it had nothing to do with Saddam Hussein. It's hard for you to understand, but it was a matter of military honor, being part of a country and within that comes your loyalty to your high command. I asked the American debriefer, 'Why are you in my country asking me this question?' He replied, 'I am under orders.' I told him, 'I was also under orders.' I asked him,

'Do you like President Bush?' He admitted he did not. 'So,' I asked him, 'Why did you carry out his orders?'"

AFTER EIGHT YEARS, the war against Iran finally came to an end in 1988. Zaid, Kamel Sachet's youngest son, put another video in the machine for me to watch.

General Kamel Sachet, wearing his neatly pressed olive green uniform and the dark maroon beret of the Special Forces, is standing in front of a military map and points with a pointing stick at various circles, ovals and arrows of deployment. He is presenting a televised lecture, as a special broadcast, describing the last battle of the war, Tawakalna Ala Allah IV (We Put Our Faith Upon God IV; also translatable as "God Help Us IV"), in which he was overall commander of operations.

The lighting is dark and brown, the camera watches like a bored student, Kamel Sachet's dignity and charisma and his upright carriage look stiff and uncommunicative on television. The map behind him is flat and devoid of any geography, no town or river or mountain contour, as if the troops moved about in blank spaces. Every few minutes his briefing is intercut with a scene of battlefield footage. Infantry advance in strung lines through scrub desert toward a rocky outcrop. The quality of the picture is bad and shaking, the landscape dun and it is hard to make the soldiers out, small figures, lost against the landscape, flecks of moving camouflage.

Kamel Sachet's voice is calm and dull, as if he were reading under duress.

"Due to the orders of our President Saddam Hussein to liberate our national lands from the enemy and to destroy as many of the enemy as possible in the battle of Tawakalna Ala Allah, Saad is safe and we have taken Sanoba from the enemy. In the area between the Shoshren Valley in the south and Chihaman in the north . . ."

Chapter 6

HIS THIRD AND MOST RELIGIOUS SON

AHMED, KAMEL SACHET AND UM OMAR'S MIDDLE son, had delicate bones and a beautiful face. His dark eyes were limpid like unfathomable pools of poetry, his long glossy lashes blinked like Bambi, but he held himself carefully; he wore clean well-pressed *dishdashas* buttoned at his throat or a neat pair of jeans and a black sweater. No gesture was superfluous or excited, his hands kept still. His rosebud mouth delineated calm certitude.

An explosion boomed the window glass.

Ahmed smiled a pretty line of perfect white teeth: "Like music to us."

Ahmed had been five when the war against Iran ended; it was one of his earliest memories. His father had put him in the car and they had driven up Abu Nawas Street, along the banks of the river, by the strip of park and open air fish restaurants. He remembered fireworks, great red and green starbursts like sparkling magical chrysanthemums. Shopkeepers were distributing sweets to passers-by, rich men hired musicians to play in front gardens; there were parties and all over town kids would douse those who walked past with buckets of water, hauling honking motorists out of their cars to drench them in the great

Baghdad water fight. Gunfire cracked in celebration for days— Saddam had to go on television and ask people to calm their exuberance because too many people were getting injured by stray bullets. Ahmed remembered his father, touched by the excitement, firing his pistol in the air out of the car window. Ahmed never saw him do anything as spontaneous or as delighted as that again. Eight years! And the war was over.

"LADIES AND GENTLEMEN: We got him."

In December 2003 the Americans found Saddam in a hole. Wild-haired, grimy, bearded, defeated, his sons killed, his country occupied. Iraqis watched an American army doctor probe his mouth, look inside his ears and check his hair as if for fleas. These were the only images released. They provoked a strange mixture of fascination and umbrage. In some way Saddam's humiliation seemed to resonate in many Iraqi hearts. I heard, even from the mouths of his tortured victims, "This is not the way to treat him, after all, he was our president."

Gunfire erupted, inevitably, *ratttatattatata* all over the city; mixed outrage and celebration. The Sachets were all very happy and their house hummed with satisfaction. Um Omar smiled broadly and told me that Ali, always the impetuous one, had wanted to get the gun and fire it in the air but she and his sisters had restrained him.

"No no! Don't fire your gun or the Americans will arrest you!"

Ali pretended to look sheepish, but we all laughed about it. I teased them that gunfire expressed all Iraqi emotion: celebration for weddings and beating the Kuwaitis in soccer, frustration in traffic jams, anger, warning, joy for the birth of a son. . .

They politely pretended to laugh with me as Ahmed came into the room and touched his hand to his breast in greeting. It was Ramadan and they were fasting. Ahmed looked a little drawn from his religious exertion. Yes, it was a matter of celebration that Saddam had been captured, but he could not thank the Americans for it. The occupation was a national humiliation.

"When I see an American I want to kill them myself," said Um Omar, without losing the kindliness in her voice.

"Perhaps if we kill them they will go away," Shadwan hoped.

For Ahmed the Iraqi police were the same as the Americans. The police were collaborators with the occupiers and betrayed the names of the *mujahideen*.

"They deserve to die more than the Americans," said Ahmed; treachery was worse than occupation. "They are helping the oppressor."

Ahmed was studying at a religious college and he rose every morning for dawn prayer and to read the Koran. He told me he could not choose a favorite *surah* because all its verses were perfect. The Koran was all knowledge, law and prophecy, the sum of history and future, God's incarnate word, entire and complete. Ahmed's big brown eyes shone with its beauty. He memorized a little more of the great book every day. At night he dreamed of his father, and in his dreams his father was wearing his uniform and exhorting him, paternal and firm, to learn the Koran as he himself had always wanted to, because in the Koran there was peace. "The point is to show the Koran is right," Ahmed told me. "It is ahead of us. Everything is already written in the Koran, and then we discover it."

AHMED HAD NOT been a good student when he was a boy, mathematics was complicated for him. He remembered his father testing him from his Arabic textbook and becoming furious with his wrong answer. Ahmed, in retelling, shuddered at his father's authority. Another time, Ahmed told his father he was going to do something "tomorrow." Kamel Sachet told him no, he should always say *inshallah*, God willing, when he spoke about the future. This stricture seemed to Ahmed as integral as the authority that had delivered it.

"When he told you to do something, there was no now or later, you did it immediately. It was like a military order. If you hadn't done anything wrong, it was fine, but if you had done something wrong—well, I didn't want to sit next to him if I had done something wrong."

When he was ten or eleven Ahmed went to summer school at the mosque and began learning the Koran. For Ahmed the mosque was a clean slate. He found he was good at learning the *surahs* and he noticed that when he talked about the mosque his father paid him more attention; from time to time, when he correctly recited a *surah*, there came down a nod of approval. He asked his father if he could be sent to religious school for secondary education and his father agreed.

As Ahmed grew up his ambition was to become an imam, to advise people about Islam and to answer their questions.

No, Ahmed shook his head, he was not interested in traveling.

"Perhaps to Mecca?"

Ahmed nodded solemnly.

"*Inshallah.*"

During Ramadan Ahmed was at home more often and several times when I came he sat with me and we discussed differences in belief. East and West, believer and infidel. Ahmed smiled. "Everyone has their different opinion and we respect it. But one of us is wrong!" Ahmed liked to talk to me about his faith and the example of Mohammed. I had a thousand questions about heaven and pork and women and *jihad*; Ahmed always had an answer. Islam was as clear to him as a crystal pool in paradise.

A day or two after Saddam was captured, after a few pro Saddam demonstrations in Adhamiya had been broken up by the Americans, I asked him:

"What did they teach you in religious school?"

"They taught us that we should say *salaam*, peace, to everyone, no matter who they were. They taught us that we should forgive someone who had harmed you."

"But this is difficult."

"Yes, even in the Koran it is written that not everyone can have this kind of patience."

"Do you hate Saddam?"

"Yes, I still hate him."

"Should you hate him? Or should you forgive him?"

"Forgiveness means that if he fell into my arms I would not kill him. I don't care what happens to him now."

"What about the Americans?"

"Ah, with the Americans, it's different." Ahmed said that those who came as fighters should be fought.

"But it means only more death, as if death could wipe out anger or right a wrong—"

"Do you mean revenge?" Ahmed asked me.

"Yes, perhaps, revenge."

"It goes back to our roots, to the Arabs before Islam. If you kill my brother I will have to kill you. My conscience would not let me live while you lived. Mohammed put rules around these traditions. In Islam if you kill my brother I cannot kill you. The government should kill you and take my revenge for me. There are three choices: I can either go to the government and tell them you have killed my brother, or I can agree to accept blood money from you, or I can forgive you."

"Which option does Mohammed most strongly recommend?"

"If it is an accident the best thing to do is to forgive; but if a murder happens in a criminal way, you cannot forgive those murderers who kill others. In fact you will prevent more deaths by killing them."

"So what is an accidental death, when is it alright to kill? Why is it acceptable to blow up the Red Cross?"

"*Jihad*, you know, is only permitted against other fighters. But these bombs—it depends who's inside the building."

"It's often a mixture: Iraqis and foreigners."

"Well, if there is an American VIP in a hotel and he is staying the night there, maybe there are other innocent people in the hotel, but in this case it is OK to kill innocent people so that you don't lose the opportunity to kill the American. Perhaps you kill twenty innocent people, but if the American VIP was not killed he would kill a thousand innocent people."

"Is this written in the Koran?"

"In the Koran it doesn't say you can kill innocent people to achieve your goal. But each Islamic leader has his own group and his own view; he takes it from the Koran. Maybe it is right and maybe it is wrong."

"But the Koran is very definite about war and how to manage war. How can different interpretations be allowed?"

Ahmed had certainty. His eyes shone with the clarity of his mission and his smooth brown brow never knitted at my recalcitrance. His fingers were elegant and slender and he would gently press their tips together to define a certain emphasis or to gesticulate frustration. Every question had an answer, the answer was revealed through God and Ahmed kept his patience while explaining such obvious truth to me.

"The Koran is detailed about *jihad*. These differences in application are not very large. In the end it is only about how they achieve their goals and the Koran leaves some things to individual assessment."

"But surely killing innocent people has definite parameters? Israelis on buses are not fighters."

"Israel is different. The Israelis came and lived in our land, there are no innocent Israelis when a Palestinian suicide bomber blows up a bus."

"But suicide is *haram*!"

"Suicide is a sin, yes. But *jihad* is a special case. A suicide bomber is exploding himself but he is benefiting his religion."

"Do you think he is benefiting his religion in the eyes of the rest of the world?"

"Let them have their opinions! He is going to heaven as the highest rank of martyr."

"So what did you think about September 11th?"

Ahmed blinked. "The attacks on New York?"

"Yes. When the two great buildings were destroyed."

"Yes, it was *jihad*." Ahmed smiled. "I was very happy."

"But why *jihad* against America?"

"As long as it is attacking any Muslim country there can be *jihad* against America."

"But what Muslim country was it attacking in 2001?"

"Many different countries." Ahmed insisted. "But especially in Bosnia-Herzegovina, they slaughtered most of them."

I patiently explained that America had not slaughtered

Bosnian Muslims and had in fact defended Kosovar Muslims against the Serbs. Again, I asked Ahmed directly: so where was America attacking Muslims in 2001?

Ahmed bent his answer in a different direction. "It fights Islam in an indirect way. I don't know exactly. But America puts pressure on Muslims. It's a lot of countries. Specifically I don't know."

"So were there innocents killed in New York?"

"If it is true that al-Qaeda did this then it is a very big hit to the American economy."

"Ahmed," I told him, bit of Western superior fact between my teeth, "it didn't make any real difference to the American economy!"

Ahmed's logic twisted again.

"They say al-Qaeda hit it but I personally think it was the Americans themselves. Those two planes made a huge media propaganda against terrorists. After that, they could attack any Muslim country under the cover of freeing a terrorist nation. Afghanistan. Iraq."

AT THE END of 2002 I was working in Tehran, living in the heart of Bush's axis of evil and watching, with my semi-legal satellite receiver (and an amused smile at the surreality of juxtaposition), Fox News ratchet the rhetoric for war in Iraq. I went to the poorer districts in southern Tehran and talked to Iraqi exiles—almost all Shia—who had fled Saddam's terror and I went across the border to Iraqi Kurdistan and listened to the stories of the Anfal, chemical attacks, razed villages and mass graves. Every Iraqi story was a tortured horror. Old men lifted up their *dishdashas* to show me the circular scars of manacles around their ankles; toothless women described watching their sons being dragged away by soldiers, their houses burned; the Kurds told me that the gas smelled like apples and garlic, that it burned their lungs and that they had held their children in their arms as they died.

I was naïve then. Saddam was a bad ruler who repressed and killed his own people and, if force were needed to get rid of him, I thought, like Ahmed's innocent bystanders, this was probably a price worth paying. I believed in the principles and assumptions that I had grown up with, half American, half Brit, a mix of decency, might, right and democracy. In Iraqi Kurdistan, in March 2003, waiting for war, I watched Tony Blair argue, impassioned and with full moral fervor, the case for invasion in front of parliament. I watched Colin Powell detail intelligence on weapons of mass destruction at the UN. I believed in my governments, not literally, but I believed they were the good guys.

When the war came I went to the Kurdish North, where there was not so much mayhem: mostly we watched the Americans bomb the Iraqi front lines while we waited for Baghdad to fall. When the statue of Saddam was pulled down it was the signal for Mosul and Kirkuk to follow suit. We drove across the internal border into the husk of post-Saddam, along with thousands of Kurds over-excited to be reunited with relatives, pillaging weapons stocks and trashing whatever Baathie symbols, police stations, offices they could find.

I remember two or three days later the looting had died down and I went to the big Saddam hospital (quickly renamed *Azadi*, which means freedom in Kurdish) and found a young man lying in a hospital bed. He had the misfortune of a February birth date and on his eighteenth birthday, five weeks before the American invasion, he had been given a uniform, but no weapon, and drafted to stand in a trench. One day a

B52 dropped a bomb which cut off his right leg and his right arm. He was fit and handsome, he tried to smile, he said his stumps ached, but he had some medicine and he could listen to the tape machine his parents had brought him from home to distract him from his sleeplessness. Of all the ragged bits of violence I had seen, thin dead bodies, the wounded baby, death rattles in a blood-spattered emergency room, this image bothered me the most. I don't know why. He had been a soldier, a legitimate target, but now he was just a maimed boy, body and prospects ruined. It seemed a terrible price. His mother worried for him: How would he have a job? Who would marry him now? I held her hand and told her it would be alright, that help was coming, that in a few months there would be Western aid workers and health programs all over Iraq, that there were new technologies and special prosthetic limbs made out of titanium that worked with electrical impulses and were miraculous and bionic, "as good as new," that her son had a future. I think at the time I believed what I was saying.

The war did not end oppression in Iraq but continued and worsened it, killing and suffering; each year dragged a greater weight of misery behind it. The mistakes and miscommunication of the occupiers and the exile parties who set up shop in Baghdad were legion; their ignorance and ignominy were raked into a heap in the GreenZone and covered with a bit of tarpaulin. When I went back to London or New York, I could barely stomach the TV pundits-politicians-party chit-chat, which ran together as a mash of opinionated blandishment and lies. A year and a half into the disaster, George W. Bush was re-elected.

Ahmed's conspiracy theory was wrong, but maybe no more trite than its opposite: that democracy could be imposed by force. It was only the inverse of an opposite set of beliefs, scorn

and reaction, like two presidents calling each other "evil." All
of us grow up in a community, a society, a country that feels,
to us, safe and familiar; outside, across the sea, somewhere else,
reside the dragons of the other. Ahmed had absorbed the mores
and opinions of his community: family was honor, Islam was
right, the larger world was a conspiracy that kept Muslims and
Arabs down. He was subject to self-serving information and
the odd sticky gobs of propaganda like the rest of us. He might
have been cynical or depressed except that he was young and
angry and he had, in this condition, as my father used to call it
when he was talking about the youthful idealism of the inter-
nationalists in the Spanish civil war (Orwell, Koestler, Robert
Jordan and other heroes), "caught an ism." Ahmed had latched
on to an ideology—salafism, jihadism, nationalism—that, like
all ideologies, offered him clear concrete answers in an unjust
and confusing world. It was a one sided view, bent through a
prism; facts refracted accordingly. I would argue with Ahmed
and call him to order with countered, reasonable explanations, but anything contrary bounced harmlessly off his shiny-
armored certainty.

ONE DAY AHMED showed me a video made by one of the
resistance groups, Ansar al-Sunna.

> *The opening scenes were of the brutality of the occupation. Ameri-*
> *can soldiers kicking in gates on hard-knock night raids, a group of*
> *Iraqi prisoners, wrists bound, heads cowed, loaded in the back of*
> *a truck, American soldiers dragging a man, barefoot and shirtless,*
> *along the street, American soldiers firing their guns into a civilian*
> *crowd. An over-dubbed voice, screeching and hoarse, asked, "How*
> *can you be quiet when such things are happening!"*

Cut to a sermon of clerical intonation: "God loves those who fight for the sake of religion. Be patient, have faith and do not participate with the enemy. Jihad in Iraq has become the duty of every Muslim and those who are fighting are the true Muslim people. Everyone in every neighborhood should be called for jihad . . . to protect our nation. These enemies have come here to stop the religion of God. We must eject the occupiers. The Americans have come here with their interests and they are being backed up by the Jews . . . You must fight against all those sinners from north to south and rise up with one hand and fight in an organized way according to our religion."

Then there were scenes of mujahideen resistance. Pickup trucks at night, faces swathed in kuffiyehs, traditional headscarves, carrying homemade rockets. Shaky footage of Humvees exploding from remote-controlled bombs hidden along the road. Close-ups of the passports and documents of assassinated collaborators.

In the final sequence a group of mujahideen were positioning a mortar at night. The scene was lit with a handheld torch, a wobbling circle of green white in the dark.

Ahmed added his own commentary: "They hit the hotels with these."

"Thanks Ahmed, I live in a hotel."

For ten minutes or more the camera recorded luminous hands splicing wires, arranging mortar tubes in an atmosphere of concentrated urgency. One of the mujahideen began to try to light one of the rockets with a match, but the match flared and went out in the wind. He lit another, which flared and extinguished, and another, which burned and died, and another. Five or six failed matches. They were repositioning the mortar tube, whispering, "Move it, move it, just a little, just a little." Then finally the fire caught the match and the hand lit the fuse and the rocket whooshed into the night like a firework and hit nothing.

AT THE END of March 2004, four American contractors were hauled from their SUV in Fallujah, hanged, burned and dismembered. The latent insurgency blew into open flame and warfare. The streets were empty, it was a holiday weekend to commemorate the one year anniversary of the liberation of Iraq. I drove out to the Western suburbs one day to get a sense of what was happening and saw a tank on fire on the highway, and two Black Hawk helicopters, like flies after carrion, circling above. Ahmed had stopped going to his religious university; Ali's wife had been attending classes at the Ibn Haithem University, but a bomb had gone off on campus. Now everyone was home, coordinating rumor and news between friends and mobile phones and waiting.

Ahmed had friends from the mosque who were taking supplies to the people. It was a siege. Fallujah had been surrounded by marines and the road to Jordan cut. The marines kept attacking, driving into the town in armor, getting rocketed and withdrawing again.

"They've hit houses and mosques and hospitals."

Ahmed had spoken to a friend of his from the religious university who lived in Fallujah and who had told him what had happened when the four contractors were killed. The *mujahideen* hit them and then pulled back; it was the people of Fallujah who strung up the bodies. Ahmed shook his head and then related the gory details: there was a butcher among the crowd and he cut the bodies and distributed the meat.

Ali and Ahmed were excited by the Resistance, there was a flash of pride and fire in their eyes. Ahmed told me, "They are not terrorists. They are defending their country."

"According to *sharia*," Islamic law, Ali explained, "we cannot have a foreign force coming in and planning elections for us. In *sharia* it is said that each one called to *jihad* has to fight."

"The issue is the fighting now," said Ahmed, determined and resolute. "Many innocents will die, but they will be replaced, when Americans die they will not be replaced. People who are killed are given a next life and those who are wounded can ask from God anything they wish. This raises morale. But if an infidel is killed what is his benefit? If I carry a gun and I am killed, I benefit both ways. If I am killed I benefit and if I am victorious I benefit. The other side has no compensation. They have no reward of heaven because they are sinners."

I protested: more death? I could no longer believe in its exigency.

Ahmed, always patient, again explained: "The *mujahid* is protecting his country, his honor, his religion."

"But they are destroying your country and your religion is not under threat."

"In Iraq the Americans have taken all the names of those who perform the *fajar* prayer because they are mostly *mujahideen.*"

"But you are free to practice your religion! No one is stopping you studying the Koran or preventing you from going to the mosque!"

"I think they are pushing Muslims all over the world. Iraq is a Muslim country."

"But the Americans do not think they are fighting Muslims because they are Muslims."

Ali cut in to our debate: "The soldiers are just obeying orders. Their leaders understand very well what they are doing."

"So it's war."

"We have been waiting for this day," replied Ali, pulling his patriotism upright. "The Americans attacked us in 1991 and destroyed our army. They attacked us again in 1998. They attacked us from the air, with bombs, we could not see their faces. But now they are next to us in the streets; the people who were killing us are very close."

"With all their power and their planes and tanks and bombs, the worst they can do is kill you," said Ahmed. "But we're not afraid of death. It is a shameful thing for a Muslim to be afraid of death. God is on our side and Allah has promised us victory."

I understood that for Ali and Ahmed death was good: martyrdom, paradise and honor. But for an atheist like me it was the nihilistic severance of a future that might allow understanding, regret, forgiveness, compassion and solace.

Ahmed addressed my dismay. "What you have is only the life you are living now and to lose it is very difficult. But we have a replacement, the next life. This life is cheap, *inshallah*. I would wish my brothers to die fighting, rather than at home and in their beds. They would die with honor. We do not believe that fighting can delay or hasten death. It is already written. It is called God's will and it solves a lot of problems."

"Yes," I answered, "Islam, submission."

Ahmed concurred: "If you choose to be a Muslim you should obey and not argue."

A FEW DAYS later I went south to Kufa, to see the Shia uprising under the "firebrand cleric" Moqtada al-Sadr and when I returned I told Ahmed about the RPGs in the mosque and how they had shot up an American Humvee patrol. I asked him how he felt about what was happening.

"On one hand happy, because it's *intifada*; on the other side sad because so many of them are dying."

Ali came in and sat down: "And now the Sunna are taking advantage. There was fighting in Adhamiya last night."

"So it's beginning."

"*Inshallah*," said Ahmed,

"What will you do?"

"What I can do I will do."

"Do you want to fight?"

"What needs to be done, I will do it."

"Do you have a gun?"

"Yes, from before the fall of Baghdad we have guns. And we've been taught how to use them."

"I know, your father taught you all."

"We used to have air guns." Ahmed went back to his childhood with a smile. "I used to take it and go hunting, sometimes without my parents' knowledge. I even injured myself in the stomach once—"

I laughed, "How?"

"I was pointing it at myself."

"How old were you?"

"About nine."

"Well, that's one lesson. Don't point your gun at yourself."

Chapter 7

"ARE YOU SURE
IT'S NOT KUT?"

T HE SUMMER OF 1990: A LACUNA OF PEACE. DR.
Hassan had just returned to Baghdad from a sabbatical in
Munich (it took years of petitioning to get an exit visa), hope-
ful that things would now settle and relax and re-establish and
that he could resume his practice. Kamel Sachet was writing
training manuals for the Special Forces and winning intra-army
shooting competitions. On July 25th Saddam Hussein received
the American Ambassador to Iraq, April Glaspie, who told him
that the United States had no particular interest in a border dispute over slant oil drilling and debt repayments between Iraq
and Kuwait. Meanwhile, oblivious to all these people and their
concerns, Sgt. Mohammed Jobouri of the Special Forces Parachute Regiment, just another soldier in an army between wars,
was locked in the stockade under penalty of death.

Sgt. Mohammed Jobouri was then twenty, young and in
love. He had been at home for two weeks, sneaking out at
night to crawl into his love's bedroom window and sleeping
all day and not thinking about the consequences of desertion.
"I am on leave!" he lied to his disapproving father who rolled
his eyes at such youth and laziness. And what was there to get
up for? Barking drills in the parched heat; the repetitive order

of barrack life? Even in the retelling of the story, after ten years of exile in Syria (he had got out of Iraq in the mid-nineties), Mohammed Jobouri seemed unimpressed by the duty and discipline required by his regiment. He gave himself up to the long nights that eked toward dawn, absorbed in his love and his own sweet apathy; until a military patrol found him AWOL on the street and took him to the Military Prison No. 1 where he was beaten with extra ferocity by military policemen happy to exercise their schadenfreude at a Special Forces paratrooper stripped of his stripes.

He stretched out his index finger and I saw that it still trembled with old traumas. He rubbed his wrists in memory of wire and raw tendon and touched his jaw where it had been whacked with rifle butts. "In the cold weather it aches and hurts so that I cannot eat sometimes."

He told me that he had been sure he would be executed. He had been missing from duty for fifteen days. He was only a sergeant with no *wasta*, influence, to trade or intervene and he expected to be hanged. One day he was being transferred along with several other prisoners. There were eight or ten of them in the back of a truck, they were not blindfolded or handcuffed and there were only two guards. The truck stopped at a red light, the driver was lost in the streets around Adhamiya, and one of the guards got out to help him look at a map. Mohammed thought quickly, punched the remaining guard in the face, grabbed his rifle clip and threw it into the traffic and leaped out of the truck shouting at the other prisoners: "Run! Split up!" But the rest of the prisoners were struck dumb and paralyzed by the authority of the system in which they found themselves shackled (although unshackled) and did not move.

Mohammed ran as fast as he could until his lungs burned but the neighborhood was full of villas surrounded by high walls and after several blocks a police car cut him off and he was tackled, kicked a little for good measure and sent back to Military Prison No. 1.

"Why did you think differently from them?" I asked him as he sat opposite me in his down-at-heel office off the main street in Seyda Zeinab, the suburb of Damascus where many Iraqi exiles and refugees had settled. "The others stayed sitting on the truck, perhaps waiting too for their own death sentences and dared not run; but you ran."

Mohammed Jobouri scratched his head and said he did not wish to seem as if he had left them there: "I don't want to give the impression that I don't like to do things for other people."

"No, that's not what I mean," I reassured him, "I mean you thought independently."

He nodded.

"I don't know whether you will take this as flattery or as an insult," I said, "but you are the first Iraqi soldier I have talked to who has admitted disobedience."

He smiled a little at this.

"Where did it come from?" I asked, "Was your family well educated?"

His father had been a mechanic, his grandfather a simple farmer, his great-grandfather had died on the boat during *Haj*. He could see nothing special about his family background; but then he plumbed a little into his childhood and remembered that it was his grandfather that he had always revered and looked up to. When he was a child his grandfather had often taken him aside and led him through his fields and farm chores. There was something in his calm deliberation, his attention to his work, the careful way he tended to his crops and his cattle; he was a man who preferred listening to talking, but his words, when they came, held old wisdom. The example of his grandfather was buried deep inside him: common sense, arbitration—his grandfather was the great problem-solver of the family—and grace. Perhaps, he thought, that is why he behaved differently to most of the other soldiers.

By the time he was delivered to his regimental brig at the barracks next to the airfield at Abu Ghraib, pending tribunal (Special Forces soldiers were dealt with in their own units) he had been beaten so badly his head was swollen like a watermelon, his ribs were broken and he could hardly move. He lay on a straw pallet chewing small handfuls of rice, passing in and out of the healing oblivion of a coma sleep. When he woke one morning and managed to sit up he asked his guards if he could be taken to the shower. The guards were men he had served with and knew, but he was marked as an escape risk and they dared not let him out, so instead they threw buckets of water through the top of the door while he sat on the other side rubbing his wet body clean.

In the dark he suffered flashbacks from the beatings, shards of silver life and pain. He rubbed his wrists again; "There were times when I cried. I asked God to help me, not to free me, because I had brought this trouble on myself, but just to let me see my family one last time—"

These last words were wrenched from his closing throat and he fished in his pocket for a pair of sunglasses, which he put on. He looked somewhat ridiculous, hiding his gathering tears so obviously—suddenly he found he could not hold himself back any longer, and acutely embarrassed, he rushed out of the room.

When he returned, I told him he did not have to—

He said no, he wanted to continue, he wanted people to know. His voice was hoarse, a torn cadence stretched thin and blocked by tears as his words returned to his cell and took up his prayer. While he prayed softly, unbelievably his small brother Raed, then just a boy of six, appeared beside him, smuggled into the camp by his friends and pushed through the bars of the window, "like an angel." He crawled over to Mohammed and told him all about his adventure, wide-eyed, quite pleased with himself and without any fear or pity or reprimand.

I let this miracle rest for several heartbeats. "What happened to the angel Raed?"

Mohammed looked down and sighed, "Raed went in a different direction."

Raed had joined the Saddam Fedayeen units and become part of Uday's murderous entourage. Gripped in the eye of the madness. "He was transformed into a ruthless Bedouin, like Saddam." Mohammed was disgusted and sad. "He knew nothing but what they told him, he was indoctrinated."

One night, after the fall of Saddam, when Mohammed had returned to Baghdad for a visit, he sat up with Raed watching an American movie. Raed didn't believe that the skyscrapers were real. He had never been outside of Iraq and for him they were legends of invented foreign propaganda.

"An innocent child turned into a beast. I don't blame him, it was his surroundings."

MOHAMMED'S TIME AWAITING the due process of sentence of death was helped by his friends who brought him fruit and bottles of frozen water. In his end days he felt the joy of his family's love and he read the Koran straight through for the first time and began to feel as if God was testing him as he was testing God. He learned patience in prison, for what else was there to learn but inward strength and tropes of survival?

Still he tested the system; somehow God was not the solace

of fate to him, but will. He borrowed ink from a soldier who was a calligrapher and drew a picture of disembodied eyes looking toward a figure that had a crown like the Statue of Liberty and held a weighted balance in her hands. For that piece of sarcasm he spent the night standing outside as shifts of soldiers threw buckets of filthy water over him. When he was put back in the cell he took a nail and scratched on the wall a picture of the punishing officer as a devil being stabbed by an angel, like St. George with a sword. For this he was made to stand at attention outside all night under a glaring burning light bulb so that the mosquitoes came and ate him.

As long as the Koran lasted, his patience held, but when he had finished it, he ran out of patience and prayed for his own skin. If this was a parable, salvation would have come the next day with a cracking bolt of lightning. But instead of God, it was Saddam who was omnipotent, and it was the fickleness of his whim, not God's, that rescued Sgt. Jobouri.

The next morning he was woken by the Red Alert trumpet and a commotion of frenzied activity as everyone hurried to muster. A friend of his ran up to his cell door, calling his name, "Mohammed," out of breath with the news. "I remembered you, Mohammed!"

"I hope that you remember me when you do good deeds so that God might save me!"

"We were in the canteen last night, it was on the radio—it is a general amnesty!"

All day the barracks were full of noise and clamor and scurry. A helicopter took off ferrying the Colonel to a meeting at the Republican Palace, leave was canceled, officers recalled, soldiers rushed to and fro, equipment was counted, checked and packed. Drill or exercise? No one knew, rumors flew about, but the Colonel's summons to the Republican Palace and his

agitation on his return kept the usual excitement of mobiliza-
tion to a grimmer hum.

In the late afternoon, a sergeant major of the regiment, a respected man, came across Mohammed in prison: "Are you still
here? You should have been released!"

"No one dares to ask the Colonel to countersign the
order—"

The sergeant major, braver than two lieutenants and a regimental secretary, got the order signed and told Mohammed
to gather some borrowed kit, double-time, because they were
jumping that night.

They were dropped after midnight, seventy-five paratroopers on the first drop and then the plane turned around and
seventy-five were dropped on the second pass. Mohammed felt
himself fall out of the large white noise of the plane into the
pure dark of an unexpected night. He had missed two training jumps and was as nervous as if it was his first time. The
lurching fall sucked his spirit upward from his toes to the tin-
gling roots of his hair, the wind rushed in his ears and his eyes
streamed tears because he had no goggles. When the canopy
yanked open with a jolt and a split-second terror of tangle and
malfunction, his heart stopped and then his spirit re-entered
his body in reverse, as if he was returning to himself. He settled himself in midair and lit a cigarette, cradling the match
flame in his shirt collar against the wind. Small spark in the
middle of the hanging night, surrounded by a silence as dense
as water.

He floated for a few moments, inhaling the smoke and the
quiet. He looked down at his feet—it was always hard to judge
the distance to the ground at night, their parachutes were of an
old Russian design and unsteerable and they carried no altime-
ters—the black earth flew up toward him unseen but some old

instinct kicked in as he hit the ground and he managed to roll and gave quick thanks that he had not broken anything.

He took stock: he was weak and thin from his injuries and his confinement, when he ran his hand over his face his cheekbones felt sharp and alien. But he had his uniform on again and he touched, a little in disbelief, the Special Forces badge on his shoulder, and felt the outline of a parachute suspended above an ox head with the words "Sacrifice Martyrdom Glory" embroidered beneath. His equipment was meager but weighed heavily enough: helmet, Kalashnikov, three extra clips of ammunition; a further seventy-five bullets and four grenades were strapped to his vest. Below that he carried a bed roll stuffed with food for two days, cans of cheese and stew (they used to open the cans with the sharp edge of an ammunition clip), tea bags and sugar, a razor, shoe polish, a gas mask, a roll of bandages, a change of underwear and dog tags. He carried no personal items, rings, jewelry and money were forbidden, but he had a tattoo on his inner forearm so that his body could be identified. It was the name of his love, "Sabrina."

The unit gathered in the desert. He could see the lights from a town some way off, but there was little traffic on a nearby road. The Lieutenant opened the envelope containing his orders, it was a handwritten note with no official stamps or signatures (for plausible deniability) and it commanded the unit to take control of their area, capture any passers by, avoid shooting and wait for one hour before they turned on their radios.

There was nothing in the vicinity but a few shepherds, these they duly captured. When the Lieutenant finally made radio contact they were ordered to proceed south to support the Republican Guards in their capture of Kuwait City.

Saddam's invasion of Kuwait was a classic Bedu desert raid. After the war with Iran, Iraq was crippled with debt, a big

chunk of it, upward of $10 billion, owed to Kuwait, who to-
gether with the Saudis and the Americans had pumped money
to Saddam as long as he was fighting Khomeini's Shia revolution. Saddam had hoped to raise money by getting some kind
of discount on the debt and by cashing in on rising oil prices,
but Kuwait's Emir proved recalcitrant on debt negotiation,
upped Kuwait's oil production, which depressed oil prices, and
ignored Iraqi complaints about Kuwaiti slant drilling under the
border that tapped southern Iraqi oil fields. Originally Saddam
had discussed a limited incursion into Kuwait, but the few generals that he confided in did not dare to try to temper his ambition or his hubris. Saddam was goaded by Kuwaiti arrogance
and encouraged by the apparent uninterest of the Americans,
confirmed, for him, during his meeting with their ambassador April Glaspie. History—and people's lives—are so often
reduced to the whim of a bully and some stupid bit of crossed-
purpose misunderstanding.

IN THE COOL desert night, the soldiers listened to their
orders and looked around at each other in conspiratorial aston-
ishment.

"Are you sure?" Mohammed asked his Lieutenant. "It's
Kuwait, really? Not Kut?"

One of the soldiers laughed. "It's Saddam's gift! He wants to
make it up to us, after the war with Iran when we never left the
country! He wants to send us on a trip!"

No one was very worried: the Kuwaitis would run away,
they were known as bad fighters, they were not the Iranians,
after all. . .

They were right about the Kuwaiti army. It did not fight
much. Kuwait City was taken by surprise. The palace was sur-

rounded, the Emir fled with his family to Saudi Arabia in a convoy of SUVs. There were small firefights by night guards and alarmed traffic police, the Minister of Sport came out onto the street brandishing a sword and was shot dead, Kuwaiti army barracks and arsenals were seized and raided. By the morning the vanguard of Iraqi paratroopers, Special Forces and armored columns that had driven down from Basra were manning checkpoints, some wearing stolen Kuwaiti uniforms, and arresting anyone driving to work in a car with official plates.

The Iraqis looked at the rich fat Kuwaitis with their huge American cars and their fancy newfangled car phones and laser discs and microwave ovens and their supermarkets stuffed with frozen pizza and Argentine beef and mangoes from India and spat with disrespect. They did not deserve their country (which in any case was a historical province of Iraq) if they did not defend it. The Kuwaitis looked at the Iraqis as rough frightening cousins and stayed indoors. An order was given that officials, police and workers should return to their offices and factories, those that continued to sit at home—particularly policemen—were rounded up as resistance.

The surprise invasion shocked the world. Under a UN resolution, the United States organized a coalition of more than thirty countries to liberate the emirate. Television news went 24-hour with pictures of terrified Western families held hostage in Iraq, SCUD missile attacks in Israel, smart bombs hitting the cross hairs of the targets and reports of Iraqi atrocities—some real, some, like the famous story of Iraqi soldiers tossing babies out of incubators, sheer Kuwaiti fabrication. Under the weight of outrage, Saddam, so recently an American ally, was demonized. Saddam had overreached and now his hand was stuck in the cookie jar and there was nowhere to maneuver.

Saddam postured, declaimed, proclaimed, and installed a triumvirate, his half brother Sabawi, his cousin Ali Hassan al-Majid and Aziz Salih Numan, to govern Kuwait as the 19th Province of Iraq. Tanks and infantry were deployed and entrenched in the desert. He sent Kamel Sachet to command the Special Forces in charge of the security and defense of Kuwait City. Kamel Sachet's deputy was General Barakh Haj Hunta, a close friend of his, a man all Kurds remembered for his helicopter from which he had inspected Anfal operations and thrown captured *Peshmerga*.

Sgt. Mohammed had no great opinion of General Kamel Sachet; once he told me, "He was just like the others." A hard instrument of the regime, simultaneously cowed and exalted by his position and concerned with the politics of reports and the whispers in Saddam's inner court. He did not think he was a particularly bad man—Barakh had the more ruthless reputation—but he considered Kamel Sachet just another one of them. There were plenty among the ranks who derided the Kuwaitis for their softness and assumed the propaganda that Kuwait was a left-over part of Iraq for the taking, but there were plenty too who felt uncomfortable about the whole invasion. Sgt. Mohammed could not know, for example, that when Kamel Sachet had heard (*fait accompli* on the television like everyone else) of the invasion of Kuwait he had turned to his wife and said, "This is mad; he has created a disaster that will destroy us all." Disquiet, in an army ordered by discipline, is undisclosed.

IT WAS THIS disquiet that I was searching for, these flickers of conscience. This army, as instrument of the regime, did monstrous things but it was made up of ordinary men who did not seem monsters to me nor that abstracted and overwrought Hollywood word, "evil."

Some time into my investigations I read Philip Zimbardo and then I read Stanley Milgram and then Hannah Arendt, Albert Speer, Gitta Sereny, Primo Levi (again). These were psychologists and writers who had tried to address the well-springs of evil in the aftermath of the ash and the final reductive horror of the Nazi concentration camps in the Second World War. Man's inhumanity to man. WHY? How do ordinary little human cogs make up a torture machine?

Philip Zimbardo was a young psychology professor at Stanford University in 1971 who devised an experiment to test the psychological results of incarceration. He wanted to understand what happened to prisoners when they were locked up. Little did he expect that the more interesting results would be the psychological effects of prison on the *guards*.

He set up a mock prison: corridor, cells, punishment closet, shower block, in one end of Stanford's Department of Psychology. He advertised for volunteers for a social experiment and weeded out applicants he thought were somehow unstable or smoked too much dope (it was California in the hippie age) and separated, by random lot, the eighteen young men into prisoners and guards. He noted, with some amusement, that in that era of youthful anti-establishment rage, no one really wanted to be the guards.

He gave the prisoners numbers and dressed them in a kind of short tunic with no underwear permitted. The guards were kitted out in crisp military style uniforms, handcuffs, whistles, truncheons and mirrored sunglasses. He separated the guards into three eight hour shifts and told them it was their responsibility to create "a psychological atmosphere that would capture some of the essential features characteristic of many prisons," although they were not permitted to physically harm the prisoners.

Zimbardo had planned for the experiment to last two weeks. But he was forced to call a halt to it after six days; the guards had begun to physically, verbally and sexually demean the prisoners to such an extent that two prisoners had already broken down and had to be removed. Zimbardo's girlfriend at the time (later his wife), a psychology Ph.D. student who was not involved in the experiment, walked in one evening and saw a line of shackled, hooded prisoners being led down the corridor for their toilet break. She felt chilled and sickened at the sight and she confronted Zimbardo about her misgivings. He said she was letting her emotions get in the way of the research, but she would not back down. Finally he agreed to suspend the experiment the following day. She had told him what he previously, caught up in the unfolding drama and the logistics of organizing it all, had not noticed: "What you are doing to those boys is a terrible thing!"

The "guards" never hit the "prisoners" but they used every other trick of intimidation they could, at their worst they became caricatures of the nasty POW commandant, the sadistic Southern warden, the mocking sarcastic jackboot. Prisoners were made to sing their numbers during roll call, if they were out of tune they were forced to do push-ups: ten, then twenty, then an indefinite number until the guards told them to stop. Pointless chores were invented, such as picking burrs out of blankets or polishing boots or remaking already perfectly hospital-cornered beds. Orders were barked, sticks brandished, prisoners singled out for ridicule, stripped, confined to the punishment closet for increasing amounts of time, left naked all night or chained to a bed. On the final evening prisoners were lined up for roll call and ordered to "hump the camel," by simulating sodomy with a prisoner bent over in front of him.

The shock of the experiment was how quickly and completely the arbitrarily assigned roles had transformed the volunteers into brutalizing enforcers and cowering inmates. Of course, as Zimbardo observed, not all the guards were equally aggressive and not all the prisoners equally passive. There were plenty of degrees and incidents, power plays, reactions, countermeasures—but ultimately, there was no defiance. Neither the guards who (as some admitted afterward) were uneasy about the humiliating punishments meted out, nor the prisoners who suffered them, ever asked to quit.

Zimbardo noted that among the guards there were roughly three different categories. There were the leaders who invented the routine and the punishments and grew into their roles, devising more ingenious ways of breaking the prisoners down. There were the followers who seemed to look up to these leaders, reinforce their actions and curry favor. And then there were the guards who did not like to participate in the excesses. Those in the third category never spoke out or stepped in to counter the authority of the other guards; instead they often absented themselves, found something else to do. In their dealings with the prisoners they were fair and reasonable and sometimes, when the other guards weren't looking, friendly and helpful; they let them cadge a cigarette or an extra few minutes in the shower.

SGT. MOHAMMED WAS deployed on the streets of Kuwait City in a mobile unit overseeing checkpoints. He saw the gangs of Baathie cohorts strip factories of plant, libraries of books, ministries of computers. Kuwaitis were forced at point of gun or threat of kidnap to "sell" their house or the contents of their warehouse or their cars. "Of course we were under orders to shoot looters," he said with a rueful smile, but the thieves often carried *laissez-faire* documents signed by Uday, and there was nothing anyone could do to stop them. As America and her allies massed in Saudi Arabia, the pillaging peaked nefariously and insecurity among the ordinary Iraqi soldiers, moral and physical, grew. "The human side was the most difficult," Sgt. Mohammed recalled, "the animosity from the Kuwaitis, cursing looks. If you went into a store for a sandwich people would avoid you." He said he believed Saddam had appointed Kamel Sachet and Barakh, tough fighting men of solid reputation, to lift morale.

Part of Sgt. Mohammed's job was to provide support for Istikhbarat (military intelligence) units who were hunting resistance cells. Informers, 3 a.m. raids, radio transmitters and networks of Kuwaiti policemen. One night his unit stopped two Kuwaitis out driving well after curfew. The Kuwaitis were distraught and said that soldiers had come into their house, smashed the place up and raped their Philippino housekeeper. Sgt. Mohammed went to the scene and verified the smashed cupboards, woke up the sergeant at the nearest checkpoint and made him account for his soldiers, toured other checkpoints in the area and asked if there had been any patrols. The Istikhbarat interviewed the Philippino housekeeper, but when she was brought to make an identification from the soldiers who were on duty in her area that night, she was frightened and refused to point anyone out. But still several Iraqi sergeants were imprisoned for two days for negligence and their soldiers lashed.

One night Sgt. Mohammed accompanied a lieutenant (a decent officer he respected) escorting a military driver caught

AWOL to the Istikhbarat headquarters that had the name, Orwellian enough, The Department of Investigations and Following Up. When they arrived, the lieutenant and Sgt. Mohammed brought the driver into an interrogation room; as Sgt. Mohammed understood it, the lieutenant wanted to scare the AWOL driver into talking. In the interrogation room an infamous Istikhbarat captain was at work. A Kuwaiti man was tied up naked and blindfolded on the floor. One of his legs was broken and in a plaster cast. The captain's "executioners," as Sgt. Mohammed called his assistants, were beating his other leg with sticks. This was much harsher than Mohammed had ever seen before; it seemed to be of a different level of cruelty, deliberate and unlimited. The tortured Kuwaiti was screaming, "For the sake of Saddam leave me alone!" The captain called over a soldier whose name happened to be Saddam and taunted him, "You wanted someone called Saddam! Here is Saddam! You will talk now! God is in heaven and he's not coming to help you!"

"For the sake of Mohammed!"

The captain called a soldier whose name was Mohammed.

"You wanted Mohammed? Here's Mohammed! Say it, now! Tell it, now! Say it!" He put a gun to the Kuwaiti's head, close to his ear so that the click of the released safety was magnified. He gave him an empty bottle and told him to hold it and then screamed back at him, "I'm going to shove this up your ass!"

"It was a horror film, they were cannibalistic, they were zombies." The captain's eyes were dead and crazed. "They were like animals gathering around a piece of prey."

The decent lieutenant touched Sgt. Mohammed's shoulder and said quietly, "Let's leave."

But the captain had noticed their arrival and jerked his head at their cowering AWOL driver and ordered, "Bring him over."

At this the driver fainted. The lieutenant stepped over him and put his body between his prisoner's and the captain's.

"I'll get you the full story," the captain told him.

"I brought him just to let him see—he is not yet formally charged—"

As the lieutenant remonstrated with the captain, Sgt. Mohammed and the driver were led away by one of the "executioners" into a farther hall. In this hall there were many prisoners, tied and chained. Some were handcuffed to metal hooks in the wall, others, Sgt. Mohammed saw, with bowel clenching horror, were nailed by their ears to wooden planks.

ONE NIGHT SGT. MOHAMMED was with a unit of Istikhbarat when they arrested several members of a family in one house as part of a resistance network. The youngest son was only eighteen years old and had been apprenticed to the police for just two weeks, with no official position except a leftover ID card. He was a weak skinny kid called Abdullah and when they arrested him he stammered and became hysterical. The arresting Istikhbarat officer slapped him and dragged him past his aunts who were pleading, "He's too young!" An Istikhbarat corporal raised his hand as if to hit the wailing women who were thrusting a Koran at Abdullah to cure his hysteria, instead he caught one of them by the forearm, twisting his body, rubbing himself against her. There was nothing Sgt. Mohammed could do but accept the pair of shoes one of the women gave him for Abdullah as they pushed him into the car, handcuffed, and forced his head between his knees.

They took Abdullah and the other relatives to the prison on the base; it had been built by the Americans and was of a modern design with electric sliding doors. The supervising guard checked the new prisoners in and told them they could choose a mattress, a blanket or a pillow. Sgt. Mohammed had taken pity on Abdullah, who was still shaking, but at least was no longer barefoot, and managed to get him all three, as well as bringing him a bowl of yogurt and some tea, and to leave him a few cigarettes and a box of forbidden matches. Later he badgered his decent lieutenant into interrogating Abdullah himself, so that he would not get beaten for stammering.

Sgt. Mohammed was Zimbardo's third category of guard.

"When it was possible I would help, when I could avoid the problems."

One night he found himself alone on the street. He was heading back to the barracks to persuade his quartermaster friend to issue him with a box of extra bullets. It was December or January; the Americans were bombing. A couple of the soldiers in his platoon had shot off their rifles under cover of the bombardment to test the barrels—firing without orders was forbidden—and it was to replace these spent bullets that he had gone back to get a new box. On his return, not far up the road from the Istikhbarat office, he saw a Kuwaiti sitting in a car. Just sitting in his car, alone, looking in his rear-view mirror as if he was watching the entrance. Mohammed came up from the other side unobserved, opened the car door and pointed his gun at him.

The Kuwaiti put his hands in the air. "I am waiting for my wife," he tried to explain.

"Which house is she in?"

The man pointed, but the house he pointed at was dark and looked shut up and empty. Mohammed shook his head at the man's story. "I will have to take you in for questioning."

The Kuwaiti became alarmed and started to beg him not to hurt him.

Mohammed looked about him to see if anyone was around, and when he was sure there was no one, he shut the car door and waved at the man to go.

"Yes, he was probably a spy," Mohammed told me.

"Why did you let him go?" Now I was Zimbardo.

"Because the Kuwaiti resistance were too weak, they weren't much of a threat, and I didn't want to harm him."

"But he was your enemy."

Mohammed shrugged. "It was his right to defend his country."

"But you let him go, it was against your orders and your duty—"

"After what I had seen in the Department of Investigations, I didn't have any good faith in the legitimacy of the occupation. After I had seen them raid Kuwaiti families and detain people . . . I knew arbitrary arrest from Iraq, perhaps I wanted to limit the spread of this disease."

"Did you feel good afterwards, having let him go?"

"I was relieved. I felt as if I had saved my soul and done something my family could be proud of."

But he never told anyone he had let a spy go, not even his family.

In Baghdad in 2004 we used to observe cynically that American helmets were the same shape as Wehrmacht helmets; it is bland axiom that all occupying armies end up behaving the same way: aggressively and badly. This is the empiricism at the heart of Zimbardo's experiment: a certain environment creates a certain response. But Zimbardo also wrote that he could never have predicted which volunteers would have turned out to be abusive in power or who timidly erred toward compassion. It didn't seem to have anything to do with obvious qualities like personality or confidence or height. I don't know if we should forgive the "leaders" or the "followers," the captains or their executioners, or the angel-demon Raeds, but the onion peeled, these layers of anecdote and happenstance and incident, at least to me, began to reveal an understanding of them.

KAMEL SACHET HAD no jurisdiction over the Istikhbarat and their enthusiasms, but he made it very clear to his soldiers that he would not tolerate looting or violence against civilians and that transgressors under his command would be shot. There was a case of a Lebanese woman married to a Kuwaiti who claimed she had been raped by an officer of the Special Forces. Because the lieutenant in question was Special Forces the investigation was carried out by his regiment. There was mitigating confusion: the lieutenant it seemed had in fact been having an affair with the Lebanese woman while her husband used the connection to get stolen cars through checkpoints. Kamel Sachet was unmoved by the details. He told the disgraced lieutenant, "The Iraqi position and reputation is now under a spotlight, what you did could trigger a crisis; we will not tolerate looting or rape and anyone involved is a traitor and should be executed."

Sgt. Mohammed happened to be on base when the lieutenant was executed.

Two lines of ten men were drawn up on the parade ground. One was the firing squad, the other witnesses, each man drawn from a different Special Forces unit. General Kamel Sachet and General Barakh stood on a small concrete platform, overseeing the event. They wore camouflage uniforms and red berets and had pistols at their hips. The lieutenant was tied to the basket of the ladder of a fire truck and the ladder was raised up high. Kamel Sachet repeated the formal judgment of the tribunal and asked the Lebanese woman if she wished to recant her story. Sgt. Mohammed noticed that she was wearing a blouse that showed her cleavage and that she was heavily made-up. She shook her bare head of hennaed hair. The execution squad then raised their guns to their shoulders, elevated the barrels and shot the lieutenant tied above them.

At the sound of the volley the Lebanese woman began screaming. Kamel Sachet stepped off the podium and went up to her and slapped her hard across the face. He was furious. "Do you think we do these things cheaply?" he demanded of her. "Why are you screaming now?" The Lebanese woman slumped sobbing, the body of the Lieutenant was winched down and a mercy shot delivered to his forehead, although it was clear he was already dead. The Lebanese woman said she didn't think they would shoot him like that—Kamel Sachet hit her again in disgust. "We knew he was innocent, but your allegation became public—this is your doing!"

There were others who were hauled aloft on cranes and shot. A colonel who was smuggling gold out of Kuwait in a coffin was executed and his body left pinioned in the sky for a week.

SADDAM DECRIED RETREAT or negotiation. Kamel Sachet organized the defense of Kuwait City as he was ordered. But the reality and the rhetoric disconnected. Two weeks before the Americans and allies initiated their ground attack, Kamel Sachet lost a whole battalion from Kuwait City, and pulled back into the western Iraqi desert to guard against a coalition invasion of Iraq. With less than eight thousand men to defend the city he deployed his soldiers into small eight-man teams scattered throughout the residential districts, where they would be safer from bombardment. Sgt. Mohammed spent several weeks fortifying a nest in the corner of a residential block. They built embrasures in the windows and concealed them with exterior wall paint, and stockpiled food and ammunition for six months. It was from the observation point on the roof that he watched through his binoculars the American marines landing in helicopters at the airport. The other soldiers in his team saw it too—when he climbed down from the roof he found they had already disappeared.

Sgt. Mohammed, now alone, called his headquarters. Kamel Sachet himself answered the telephone. Sgt. Mohammed reported that American marines had landed, that his unit had gone to headquarters and not returned and that he awaited further orders. Kamel Sachet asked him how far away the Americans were. Sgt. Mohammed replied that they were on foot without vehicles and he estimated they would reach his street in fifteen minutes. Kamel Sachet asked him if he had a vehicle. Sgt. Mohammed replied that he did not. Kamel Sachet ordered him to make his way, as he was able, back to headquarters.

Sgt. Mohammed found a bicycle on the street, but by the time he reached the HQ of the 65th Battalion, Kamel Sachet had already left for the other battalion headquarters to assess and organize. Instead he found General Barakh in discussion with several other officers. He gave his report on the American marines at the airport. The commander of the 65th Battalion suggested regrouping the soldiers who had been deployed in the eight-man teams into a striking force for a counterattack. Barakh asked him how long this would take. He was told, "About an hour."

"One hour?" Barakh exploded with tension and fury. "One hour is enough for us to lose Kuwait. We don't have one hour!"

Barakh had a crop that he kept under his arm, an affectation that recalled his days at the officers' course at Sandhurst in England, and he whipped at the walls in frustration as a unit of soldiers came running in disarray: "We have lost contact with everyone, the Americans are coming and it's impossible to stop them!" Barakh dismissed them and railed, cursing Saddam in the clouds:

"Your plan was the cause of our destruction!" He smashed a window with his elbow, *"Ila an ili khala Saddam!"* and threw his crop away in disgust. Wheeling around, he issued orders for the administrative papers to be burned and the ammunition destroyed: "Burn everything and leave!"

Saddam ordered the retreat from Kuwait City too late, later than the panic, and the streets were a mess of flight as everyone scrabbled to get out and back over the border to Basra. Sgt. Mohammed hot-wired a school van he found on the street and left in a loose convoy of stolen cars. They drove up the coastal road because the main highway had been bombed into the highway of death and was impassable with craters and the charred carcasses of men and vehicles. They were bombed on the coastal road too; it rained cluster bomblets that popped up as if on springs and went off like grenades. The van wasn't made for off road driving; at some point they abandoned it and walked the rest of the way in the dark.

Chapter 8

EUPHEMISMS

AFTER THE SPRING UPRISINGS IN 2004 EVERYONE in Baghdad began to spend more time inside than outside. Inside there was some sanctuary, although the windows banged with concussions and the gunfire was constantly intermittent; outside there were bombs and columns of black smoke, the sudden low veering clatter of helicopters and armored dragons patrolling the streets. Dr. Laith, a friend and colleague of Dr. Hassan's, in fact the one who had spoken up for him when he had been arrested in '83, and was now active in one of the new secular political parties, was shot at on the overpass near his home. He abandoned his car and ran down a side street to escape. When he went back he counted seven bullets embedded in the bodywork, but he couldn't be sure if he was the target or if it was just crossfire.

Behind the wall ("call me on your mobile phone when you are turning the corner into my street and I will come and open the gate; the buzzer is not hooked up to the generator and I don't want you to get out of the car and knock, we are near Adhamiya, some of the neighbors, I don't know them—some people could see you"), Dr. Laith's home was large and well appointed. The living room was grand seventies open plan, sofas, side tables, gray velvet and gilt. There were pictures of his children, grown up and safe in the West, in silver frames on a polished coffee table. His wife, Bushra, wearing a chic long house gown and a matching headscarf, came in from the kitchen with a glass of orange juice for me. I was tired and ill and she was sympathetic. She nodded, everyone was tired and ill these days, and sat in the armchair opposite to join in the conversation. Dr. Laith and Bushra's brother, who had been a general, were looking through a pile of family photographs. I had asked them about the old days, and the memories had come out.

PHOTOGRAPH: *Black-and-white, an old and timeless Arab Bedouin, with a checked scarf wrapped around his deeply lined face, sitting on a donkey minding a small herd of sheep.*

Dr. Laith came from the same poor southern Shia background as Dr. Hassan. His father was an illiterate farmer. He joined the Baath Party in 1961 as a schoolboy; their socialism seemed to assuage the injustice of his poverty, their Pan-Arab nationalism gave him pride. In 1963 his village was hooked up to electricity. The family had a gramophone, but it was broken. Dr. Laith, like Dr. Hassan, joined the army in order to gain sponsorship for his medical studies.

PHOTOGRAPH: *Three young Iraqi men in dark narrow suits and narrow ties of the sixties. They are sitting, laughing, three bottles of beer on the table, three trim mustaches.*

"I think I bought my family their first radio after I graduated from military college. And then their first television in the early seventies."

PHOTOGRAPH: *Officers graduating from military intelligence school, Dr. Laith among them. The young men are sitting in rows*

in civilian clothes, sports jackets and checks, underneath a banner:
"1977 The Good Soldiers are the Sons of the Revolution and its
Party."

Dr. Laith specialized in psychology; during the Iran-Iraq war he and Dr. Hassan collaborated on psyops, the mechanics of morale, speeches and slogans and songs. Together they had designed leaflets dropped over Iranian positions.

"Oh, these old things, these old memories!" said the general. He wore a dark suit and had gray hair and an aquiline profile; his manner was grandfatherly, distinguished, friendly, melancholy. He once told me he had commanded a unit during the Anfal campaign against the Kurds in 1987, ordered to clear villages with artillery and small arms harassment. He carried the image of one woman, who had lost her baby in the panic, running in circles and screaming. Her terror, he confessed, long haunted him.

PHOTOGRAPH: *A family picnic in summer Technicolor, children in*
swimsuits, deckchairs, Tupperware filled with salads, paper plates.
Bushra is wearing a sundress and her feathered blonde hair falls
to her bare shoulders. She is stretching her arm toward her small
daughter toddling in the grass.

Dr. Laith quietly shuffled his past. The general lit a cigarette and wiped his eyes, "The seventies. The Golden Years. I'd like to have a bottle of whiskey and cry now."

"WE STARTED FEELING something was wrong," Dr. Laith began, as we reached the eighties and the descent. "There was a kind of chaos. I felt the lie, but I could not say anything or they would cut my neck. If you were executed your disgrace went back to your family, your sons could be killed, your property confiscated. It was as if I was living two personalities. I would do my best as an officer with my duties and then I would come home and speak against the regime. All Iraqis have two or more characters. It was the only way to survive under pressure for such a long time."

At the time I nodded, but I still pushed him to explain his own involvement. I had spent six months straight in Baghdad and every week worse, more bombs, more assassinations, more shooting. The violence had crept incrementally so that I did not notice I was scared and the fear sublimated into hangovers, fever, knotted shoulders and a dull numbness in my mind that I did not even have the wit to notice; I had not been able to read a book for two months. I was tired and tried to focus my blur into black and white: "Why?" I asked bluntly, stupidly, "did you go along with it all?"

"You are talking as a Westerner," said Dr. Laith, unfolding his professional assessment like a partition. "You have not lived the Iraqi experience. Iraqis use excuses as a defense mechanism. If I am a general and they tell me to invade that village, I will invade the village and kill everyone on the way and I will come back home and I will make my prayers. It has nothing to do with honor. It is fear. There were two kinds of Iraqi officers. Those who would carry out their orders and tell themselves, "I have no power, it is not in my hands," and go home and pray. And those who obeyed their orders and went home and said to themselves, "I have no power, it is not in my hands," and drink half a bottle of whiskey. Both will sleep a deep sleep."

When Dr. Laith wrote his reports on the psychological conditions of the front-line troops, his first and greatest effort was to protect himself. "We bent the truth. There was fear to say anything." He carefully checked every line for nuance, he rewrote, weighed and inveigled. Each sentence had to balance a pretense of fact with an analysis that sounded acceptable but was essentially meaningless. "How could we give them bad news?"

IN JANUARY 1991 Dr. Laith was recalled from his research into cognitive therapy for phobias for his Ph.D. thesis and sent to the front in Kuwait to report on army morale.

He remembered a conversation with a friend of his who was a unit commander, dug into the desert waiting for the Americans to come. The officer spoke to him in a monotone: "I expect to be attacked tomorrow. In this extended desert, in front of a superior army, how can I ask for help? I am certain all communications will be lost. I have supplies for only a short time. I am responsible for my men. How am I going to prevent the loss of their lives? Already I have the mentality of loss, and most of the other officers are the same. We are thinking: *How can we stay alive?*"

Dr. Laith wrote in his report: "The morale of the soldiers is not what we would wish."

In the evenings, discussions in the Officers' Club in Basra belied the undertow. The world was watching. The Arab League leaders seesawed between their realpolitik diplomacy and pandering to the anti-Western outrage of their repressed populations. Colonel Gaddafi made a public declaration from Libya about destroying American hegemonic aggression. Dr. Laith commented to his fellow officers, in general conversation, that Gaddafi's pronouncement was farcical, hollow rhetoric cast so many thousands of kilometers away from the battlefield, and added sarcastically, "As if he would screw himself trying to fight the Americans, like our own leader has done!"

As soon as he said it, he regretted it. A small silence formed like a bubble around his comment. He dared not glance up at Brigadier Bari to see if he had been paying attention. There was already an argument between them. A couple of months before, when the Americans had first threatened war and the petrol stations in Baghdad were closed and the fuel supplies paralyzed, Dr. Laith had arranged for twenty liters to be delivered from some official source to his home but the brigadier had intercepted them for his own use.

The general conversation resumed but Dr. Laith sat apart from it, when the group broke up he tried to remonstrate with Brigadier Bari, but to no avail. Dr. Laith knew a report would be made, it was inevitable, but he hoped that there was a chance the report would get lost in the paperwork: it was one small thing and there was a war on and there were so many things. . .

Dr. Laith watched the soldiers, the remnants of an army of almost 800,000 men, come out of the killing desert of Kuwait hungry, wounded, in disarray, lost. The retreat was like a wildfire Chinese whisper: messengers that deserted, scrawled desperate communiqués; radio static. For several days the Iraqi army slowly trudged, bewildered, sad and angry. Thousands of soldiers on foot, their legs swollen from walking, took off their chafing boots. Their officers ripped off their rank insignia; they had lost their soldiers and had no idea where their units were. The morgue in Basra was full, bodies were piled up on the streets; there were abandoned corpses on the roads. Soldiers sat in shops, in cafés, lay down in the parks and slumped on pavements, it was raining and it was cold and the misery in their eyes was visible. The bridges over the Tigris were bombed, only the narrow, single-lane, pontoon bridge was passable and it was stuck with traffic. There was complete loss of control. Soldiers were cursing Saddam openly.

In the confused disillusion, Dr. Laith saw Special Forces General Kamel Sachet and a senior colleague pacing the empty basketball court at the Officers' Club. Kamel Sachet had left Kuwait City thirty-six hours before, driving his white Mercedes himself, leading a convoy of jeeps and trucks along the highway of death with no comms except the short-range hiss of walkie talkies. They had weaved through bombs, black smoke, wreckage, as F16 jets glinted like silver in the high drawn dawn. When they reached the Iraqi border, dust rimmed and adrenaline spent, Kamel Sachet brushed his uniform carefully and told his driver (who had, on this occasion, traveled in the back seat) to wash the car. He said he would not carry even dust from Kuwait as dishonor.

On the basketball court of the Officers' Club he strode and snarled. He was furious and his fury was without fear. "Everything was lost because of them! I was told there would be no retreat and then suddenly they ordered me to retreat!" He talked openly, angrily, extraordinarily, shockingly. Dr. Laith kept quiet and listened. General Sachet excoriated Ali Hassan al-Majid, Saddam's Viceroy of Kuwait. His orders had been absurd! One day they were ordered to arrest everyone with a beard, another day they must arrest everyone driving a certain kind of car, another day men who wrapped their red-and-white scarves around their heads. The idiocy, the excesses, the crassness . . . General Sachet continued, seething with the blackness of defeat furled, like the smoke from the bombed retreat, in his lungs. He was usually a taciturn man but now the words flew out of his shame and lacerated the atmosphere like shrapnel. "They killed them as if they were animals!"

DR. LAITH INTERVIEWED soldiers in the city. Many openly blamed Saddam. On the night of 1 March 1991, the day before the *intifada* flared, Dr. Laith delivered an oral report on the state of the morale of the army to the Minister of Defense, Saad al-Jobouri, and his deputy, Sultan Hashem.

He chose his words carefully. He told them the soldiers were displaying signs of clinical hysteria and that they were using bad language. He did not tell them that the soldiers had begun to heckle Saddam, because cursing the leader was a capital crime and if he had heard the leader being cursed and had not informed the Amn, then he would have been considered an accessory.

DR. LAITH GOT out of the city only hours before the uprising against the regime erupted. He went home to Baghdad, put his head down and took up his research again. The events in Basra took a few months to catch up with him. On 26 October 1991 two men from the Military Amn called at his house at about 4 p.m. They told him that General Khazem wished to see him. General Khazem was a friend of his and he thought the summons was routine. He changed into his army uniform and got into the waiting car. The windows of the car were tinted black and this was not usual. There was a driver and an officer and a bodyguard in the car and this was not usual. Still, Dr. Laith did not want to alarm himself. They arrived at General Khazem's office, which he knew well, and the two men left him at the reception to make telephone calls. It was only then Dr. Laith felt something was not right and within minutes he was blindfolded with a piece of rubber and taken to the Istikhbarat office in Kadhamiya and thrown into an isolation cell for one month.

Dr. Laith stopped his retelling. He looked up and told me he thought he had seen the former Brigadier Bari on the street a few days before.

"Did he see you?"

"Yes, I think so. I wanted to confront him, I wanted him to admit that he made a mistake. Some people who were imprisoned are now asking for compensation from their persecutors—but I think Iraq needs some measure of forgiveness and this forgiveness should start from people confessing their mistakes."

Dr. Laith was in solitary confinement for one month and then his case was brought before a judge. The judge was, by chance, a friend of his and did not want to be placed in the position of passing judgment and so he referred the case to a revolutionary tribunal, citing the political content of the case and arguing that his court had limited jurisdiction over such matters. Dr. Laith was moved to a prison in an old barracks near Ramadi which had been used to hold Iranian POWs. The commandant of the prison was also a friend of his, and he had an air conditioner in his room, books to read and visitors on Fridays. After three or four months of legal confusion his file was referred back to the original judge who saw that it was not a case in which any powerful players had a direct interest and now found it politically safe for him to sentence Dr. Laith to time served. Afterward the judge tried to apologize in a way that would encourage Dr. Laith to be grateful to him for his leniency to a friend. But imprisonment had changed Dr. Laith. He refused to play this game. He reminded the judge that if he had been tried as a political case in a revolutionary tribunal he could have been sentenced to death.

He went home, re-evaluated, thinking, eyes open. After a few weeks, old friends and colleagues came to him with offers of jobs, promotions, extra salaries—the head of the Baghdad Amn came personally—but he turned them all down. He found himself outside the circle, isolated, afraid, unable to sleep. But still he resisted. He saw that the resumption of rank and status, after being arrested, cowed a man forever.

"It bears a very complicated psychological explanation." Dr. Laith had examined himself over several years. Why had he resisted the pull of his old Baathie life? "I have had to answer these questions: Why had I been with these people? What had I done?

"I go back to the circle. From 1979, from the beginning of the time of Saddam Hussein, the circle was closed completely and my thinking was limited. It became a matter of fear. It was impossible to go outside the circle because then you would be an enemy and your life would be under threat. Those that left the circle, most of us, were pushed or shocked out. It was the philosophy of Saddam Hussein. You would be shocked out of the circle and then he would pull you back in and it would be worse because there would be more fear than before. If you went back you would live under fear and become the perfect obeyer of orders."

His unwillingness to return to the fold allowed him some moral solace.

"It was only in this moment that I behaved a little bravely." He did not sleep; he expected to be re-arrested, but this defiance saved him. He managed to leave Iraq in 1996. His life in exile, in Libya, Syria and finally London, was demeaning and difficult, he had lost his position and his money. His wife Bushra had to live separated from him in Damascus. She started to wear the veil.

"I felt lost," she explained, "I felt lost and I went to the Koran."

PHOTOGRAPH: *Laith and Bushra at a party in the seventies. Laith had wide pinstriped lapels and a big kipper tie, Bushra is wearing a feathery strappy satin evening gown. They are wearing party hats on their heads and smiling. There is a bottle of champagne on the table.*

"I have not changed inside." Bushra continued, "I talk to people, laugh with them. I go to parties and dance. These things are not prohibited. But my outside look has changed."

"I am against the *hijab*," said her husband ruefully.

"I don't like it either," agreed Bushra, shrugging, "but God has imposed it upon us."

"It is something Islamic," Dr. Laith tried to explain. "My wife now puts on *hijab*, she feels the religion of it. Even though her father was a religious man and he never made her wear it as a girl, in fact he used to buy her fashionable clothes. In the sixties and seventies we used to walk in Baghdad and come across maybe one woman in a whole day who was wearing the black *hijab* and we looked at her as if she was retarded. But the Arab nation and the Islamic nation have been under pressure, they began to see that the ideologies of the world, communism or Baathism, didn't solve their problems. They looked for mercy, they went back to their religion to look for a safe haven. They are searching for a solution."

"A solution to what?"

"This region has been a trap for us since the fifties, sixties, our economic status is deteriorating. There is no security in the whole region. The issues have no solution, like Palestine, like security in general, like the administrations . . ."

PHOTOGRAPH: *Laith wearing a clean white dishdasha in Mecca on* Haj *in 1973.*

"I believe Eastern society has had a kind of breakdown and gone back to their religion."

"A crisis of confidence? A moral retrenchment?"

"Definitely."

Dr. Laith sat back in his chair and showed me pictures of his children, in Germany, in America, graduating and thriving, but far away.

"But I kept this thing," he told me, as if reminding himself, and later I was reminded of Sgt. Mohammed and the other officers who had managed to get out of Iraq and re-learn some measure of perspective, "this one good thing, this moment," continued Dr. Laith, "I refused."

Chapter 9

UPRISING

S ADDAM HAD GATHERED ALL HIS MIGHT AND SWOLLEN
pride into a great wave that crashed, shattering its kinetic
tumult into spurts and spray of white noise, fizz and confusion.

Kamel Sachet was in Basra. Tired soldiers milled, senior
commanders stalled, the mob vented and seethed. On 1 March
1991, the day after President Bush declared a cessation of hos-
tilities, an Iraqi tankist shot a tank round through a portrait of
Saddam: a gaping hole in the wall of fear. Kamel Sachet was in
his white Mercedes with official government plates. His usual
driver, his nephew Abdul Qadir, was driving; in the front seat
was a loyal lieutenant. They were close to the shore of the Shatt
al Arab when they were confronted by a knot of rioters, stones
cracked the windshield, shots were fired. Kamel Sachet shouted
to abandon the car and led their flight, shooting his pistol as
meager covering fire. They made it around a corner, down a
side street, over a cross roads, to the gate of the Republican
Palace complex. But the palace was still under construction,
there was no garrison inside. They banged on the locked gate,
shouting to open! open! The guard on the other side hesitated,
Kamel Sachet shouted, "I am a general, for God's sake, open
the gate, we are under attack!" But by the time the guard un-
locked the gate, the crowd had caught up with them. Suddenly,

grinding around the corner, by some miracle, appeared a tank column. The rioters dispersed, running into the side streets; the tank commander hauled the three of them up onto his tank. He looked at Kamel Sachet for an order.

"Back to your headquarters. We'll get more information there." They could hear gunfire and see thin columns of black smoke between buildings. The tanks crunched slowly back through the empty streets; they listened, trying to locate the source of a distant clamor, but the noise was fragmented, like a bouncing echo. They passed their white Mercedes, windows smashed and gutted by fire.

The first days of the uprising were a genuine spontaneous expression of rage and frustration, a grass roots free-for-all, the angst of the demobilized soldiers mixed with pent-up resentment of the southern Shia (those Tikriti bandit cousins lining their own pockets with the old smug Sunni elite), which spread, Basra to Nasiriyeh to Amara to Kut, Kerbala, Najaf. Party headquarters were burned, hated officials strung up, offices looted; a rush of foaming fuck-you. And then posters of Ayatollah Khomeini began appearing over the anti Saddam graffiti, the exile Shia Badr Brigade showed up in black shirts, mullahs exhorted from minarets, and Iranian soldiers crept over the border and manned checkpoints.

The uprising was all over Basra but it never took complete control of the city. Basra had been the center of operations for Kuwait and there were too many bases in town and around it, as well as the presence of the defense minister and the chief of staff and several senior commanders. In the first days Kamel Sachet stayed at the headquarters of the 10th Battalion. The base was safe enough, defended by high walls and a thousand fresh troops who had not been in Kuwait. Abdul Qadir told me they found an empty office room with a broken window and the three of them holed up there. He cooked rice and scrounged cans of soup. The gunfire continued, intense and sporadic. Kamel Sachet was quiet.

Hamdani had been wounded in the retreat (a flesh wound in his leg; shrapnel from an American bomb) and found himself washed up at some overrun base in the desert, a staging point in the general flight, before he made his way back to Baghdad. "Incidents evolved . . . It was an action and a reaction . . . There was no coherent strategy, everyone asked each other, 'What's going on?'" He said he thought many would have been like Kamel Sachet at that moment, perched on a fulcrum, frozen between pit and pendulum.

President George H. W. Bush had broadcast his encouragement of the uprising over the Voice of America, urging "the Iraqi military and the Iraqi people to take matters into their own hands." Overhead American jets flew reconnaissance sorties; on the ground scout units and vanguard armor chased the fleeing Iraqis through the desert and then stood by as the Iraqi army shelled its own towns. But as the Iranians began to take advantage of the situation and show their hand among the Shia in the South more openly, the Americans dared not risk an Iranian takeover of the South. They pulled their forward armor back and tacitly allowed Saddam to fly his helicopters. Better the devil you know, they thought, better the devil than the Iranians. If the Americans had left their forward units in the southern Iraqi desert, if they had intervened more directly, the uprising might have had a chance—but there was no political will to push on to Baghdad. As Donald Rumsfeld, then defense secretary, later explained, "I would guess if we had gone in there, I would still have forces in Baghdad today. We'd be running the country. We would not have been able to get everybody out and bring everybody home."

I don't know what was going through Kamel Sachet's mind in those days of insurrection. Abdul Qadir told me his uncle sympathized with the uprising; certainly among the rebels were many of his own soldiers, but as angry as he was at the destruction of the army, the shame of the defeat and the blunt stupidity of it all, he could not countenance desertion. He had seen soldiers—even officers—in the melee pulling their chevrons from their battledress and exchanging their uniforms for *dishdashas*. "I would never take my rank from my shoulders," he said. And he could not countenance anarchy, whipped up among the Shia by Iran—it became a matter of national security. Hamdani told me, in his opinion, "If it wasn't for the uprising and the Iranian interference there would have been a huge movement against Saddam Hussein by the army, even the Republican Guards."

OFFICERS WERE SCATTERED, walked home through the desert, took off their uniforms, sat at home and drank or prayed, hid in relatives' houses, ignored recalls to arms, conferred in whispers and unease. Saddam used those closest to him, Ali Hassan al-Majid and his cousin and son-in-law Hussein Kamel, to put down the uprising. They gathered what officers they could and mustered clots of Mukhabarat thugs and bodyguards to rally contingents where they found them. They said, "This is not a civil war!" Fourteen of Iraq's eighteen provinces had blown into rebellion; party offices and garrisons in every major city except Mosul and Baghdad were overrun. They called it "Treason! Backstabbing treason!" The uprising was an American-Iranian plot and those who participated in it were traitors.

IRAQIS OFTEN TOLD me, only half joking, that Iraqis were an unruly mass of *shirugi* (a slang word for thick-headed Marsh Arabs) who needed the rule of the rod, a strongman, to control them. Saddam was a murderous bastard, but he was effective, he was respected. He compared himself to the conqueror Saladin, he carved his initials into Nebuchadnezzar's palace at Babylon, and during the uprising he smashed his fist on the table and unleashed his wrath.

Once in Baghdad I met an instrument of this fury. Emad was a square brick of the regime, he had been in Saddam's bodyguard regiment. He was a reflection of his overlord: "They call me the murderer!" he boasted. "They call me crazy . . . They call me Mr. Mustache!" To Emad, Saddam was mighty, second only to God.

"I used to love him a lot, and I still love him as a character. He was a good man inside. It was only the Tikritis who were bad and they were everywhere. When he was captured I cried. They never would have caught him like that; in a hole. It was something else—a drug, a trick." He looked down at his lap. "On the second day we heard that it wasn't him, I was fooling myself, I shot so many shots in the sky, five magazines!"

He told me how he had once seen Saddam summon one of his relatives who had angered him by divorcing his wife and taking up with a younger girl. Saddam commanded him to take his wife back but the relative refused. Saddam pulled out a gun. "He took a decision in one second, like that!" Emad admired such decisiveness, he called it brave. "And shot him between the eyes."

That March Emad went with a posse of Special Amn under Hussein Kamel to put down the uprising in the Shia shrine town of Kerbala. They had bags of money and paid the street kids as runner-spies to tell them where the traitors were hiding. They went from house to house, killing. In one place, Emad recounted, he cut one man's throat with his knife and shot another man sitting on a sofa. He was ordered to fire an RPG into a house with a mother and her children inside, but he refused. His officer was furious and called Hussein Kamel to report him.

Hussein Kamel pointed, "Come here, Mr. Mustache! You think it's up to you? I am the President's cousin!"

Emad saluted him.

"Why do you not obey orders?"

Emad's knees were trembling. He had seen people shot for less. But Hussein Kamel agreed that it was a waste of ammunition, and he was only sent to prison.

In prison they beat him and lashed him raw for several days and pushed him into a vat of urine. When he was released they sent him to a special Amn hospital to recover and then he was put back on duty as if nothing had happened.

Emad was not an educated man, he was not given to self reproach or much emotional analysis, but he guessed enough at his "badness" to try to balance it with an effort to proffer his own humanity. He told me that he had a recurring nightmare in which he was given an order that he couldn't complete, that the bloody image of the man he had stabbed in Kerbala came back in his dreams. A religious sheikh advised him to pray for forgiveness and sacrifice a sheep, and he had done this, but it had not helped. If he became angry, he admitted, he could beat someone "without control"; he said he had felt numb and indifferent when his father had died, but that a small instance of suffering, like a child begging on the street, could move him to tears. In the nineties Emad had been assigned to Uday's bodyguard: cars, girls and violent mayhem; once he saw Uday split a man's head open in a restaurant in front of his wife and children, once Uday had tried to drown him in a swimming pool as a joke. Emad had wanted to quit but it was impossible. He told me he had broken his own arm to gain time off and wrapped the fracture with a fish so that it would heal slower.

The human cogs of the torture machine seemed as unhappy as their victims. Which meant, as I scribbled down in a notebook, "*there's no rational explanation for the machine's existence at all.*"

KAMEL SACHET'S FAMILY heard nothing from him in the three weeks since the retreat from Kuwait. He appeared one evening, toward the end of March, unannounced, tired and drawn and sad. When he arrived he kissed each of his children in turn. He sat on the floor in the reception room, Um Omar brought him food, his children ranged around him. When he talked his eyes reddened. Out of the checked tears came the anger. He criticized Saddam in a way they had never heard before. Saddam had told him there would be no withdrawal, and then, at the last minute—*after* the last minute—he ordered the retreat. "We could have held out six months!" But now everything was lost: "The military power we had is now finished." His troops were all gone, the same men he had led through the Iran-Iraq war and he knew how brave they were. His favorite daughter Shadwan had never seen him come home from a defeat. She had never seen him criticize Saddam so directly. "He felt shy from us," she told me, "he did not look us in the eye."

The next morning he left for Mosul. In the North the Kurds

had also risen up, but after a few days the *Peshmerga* were pushed out of Kirkuk and Erbil, and the population fled, terrified of gas reprisals, into the mountains and were trapped against the Turkish border.

I don't know what Kamel Sachet did in Mosul and where he was over the previous month of *intifada* is disputed. One of his old bodyguards (who heard it from a cousin who was in a unit near the area at the time) told me he had been sent to Amara, close to the Iranian border, to put down the uprising there. Abdul Qadir maintained that he spent the entire missing month of uprising in Basra but that he did nothing but sit in the room with the broken window.

HAMDANI WAS PROBABLY right about the level of mutinous feeling in the officer class after the Kuwait fiasco. There were certainly plenty of stretched necks in the weeks after the uprising had been bulldozed into mass graves. Saddam leveled his senior command: those who had criticized the order to withdraw, those who did not display the fullest loyalty during the uprising, those who hid at home, made excuses. Kamel Sachet's deputy in Kuwait was shot. Barakh was shot. The Special Forces were disbanded. After 1991 Saddam effectively ignored the army, instead investing in his elite Republican Guard and the Saddam Fedayeen and paying his favorite loyal commanders with Toyota pick-up trucks and bricks of devaluing Saddam smooth-faced dinars. On Army Day the infantry marched past the Iran-Iraq Victory Memorial holding bulletless guns (lest someone take the opportunity to shoot their president) with white socks on their hands in lieu of gloves.

Kamel Sachet was called for a meeting with the Chief of Staff. He was lucky; he was given retirement. His colleagues

waiting uncomfortably outside for their own fate, congratu-
lated him and he smiled back at them, relieved. He got into
his new Mercedes and drove out along the highway past Abu
Ghraib, accelerating. He liked to drive very fast. Deep in the
desert, he fashioned a small pyre with newspaper and gasoline
and burned his uniform. Kuwait had washed any pride in it
away and he felt himself reduced to this painful futile gesture,
out in the middle of nowhere, and it made his eyes smart and
his nostrils curl as the acrid smoke billowed sideways.

After this he spent much of his time on his farm near Hilla,
sometimes he took his sons with him, but more often he was
alone. He put on a simple *dishdasha*, pruned his fruit trees,
walked along the small river that fed the irrigation ditches,
prayed and often visited the mosque he had built nearby.
He applied for permission to go on *Haj*, but an exit visa was
denied. He liked to work with his hands, he tended his land
and withdrew from the machinations of his former life. Several
people told me this was the most relaxed and content they had
ever seen him.

His idyll in the country was short-lived. On Army Day in
January 1992 he was invited to the Palace.

VIDEO. *A white and gilt formal state room in the palace full of
generals in dark green dress uniforms decorated with medals. Hussein Kamel is visible among them, his chest covered in gold braid.
Kamel Sachet appears incongruous in a pastel blue safari suit. He
walks forward to shake Saddam's hand. You can see how physically
powerful he is, the extended hand reveals sinewy wrists mapped
with veins. There is strength in his grip; he leans in and clasps the
President's shoulder in a warm display of affection and then pulls
back and puts his second hand over Saddam's to make a double
handshake of fealty.*

Saddam asks him, joshing:

"Kamel! Why are you wearing civilian clothes? We are not used to seeing you out of uniform!"

Kamel Sachet replies that he was retired now.

Saddam coughs his jackal heh-heh-heh laugh, "I don't like seeing you in civilian clothes!"

Shortly afterward Saddam appointed him Governor of Maysan Province.

Chapter 10

THE GOOD CALIPH

I WENT TO MAYSAN IN FEBRUARY 2005 ON A PRESS junket organized by the British Embassy in Baghdad. We took a succession of bone rattling aircraft: Puma helicopter from the GreenZone to the airport, C–130 transport plane from the airport to Basra, Sea King from Basra to Abu Naji, the British base outside the provincial capital Amara. To say this was the long way round would be an understatement. A year before I had driven through Amara on my way to Basra; it was only two hours by car from Baghdad. Now it was too dangerous to drive down any highway anywhere in Iraq (except Kurdistan), two friends had been kidnapped in the summer and foreign journalists had a price. Even in Baghdad it was too risky to drive into most of the city's neighborhoods (resistance gunmen on corners, interviews as lures, sudden gun battles, car bombs, pick-up truckfuls of motley camouflage, balaclavas and Kalashnikovs—police, commandos, Iraqi army, Mehdi army, militia—who could tell?). I always wore a big black tent *abaya* as disguise in the back of the car, texted my whereabouts to a friend every hour, and took care never to walk down the street.

When we arrived in Amara we were put on yet another helicopter and hopped south so that we could see the good news

story of how the marshes were being reflooded and villagers returning. From up high the scars from the Iran-Iraq war and the
bandit skirmishes of the decade of sanctions were still visible.
The land looked like an abandoned battle map of criss-cross
cicatrices: ditches, trenches, horseshoe embrasures for artillery,
berms, fields scraped for shallow graves, tire tracks, single file
paths meandering between scrub; a land plowed by guns up to
a flat-line horizon. In places salt dregs glimmered like pow-
dered bone. We touched down in a cloud of dust, loaded into a
convoy of Land Rovers and were shaken past a row of mud villages filled with buffalo and ragged children with flies in their
eyes. The villages ran like a ribbon along the edge of a great
wide lake; I remember watching a fragment of extraordinary
beauty as a flat bottomed canoe piled with bright green rushes
glided through the azure water in the golden sun of the late
afternoon—before we were herded back onto the helicopter,
flown back to the camp, fed beans on toast with little packets
of Marmite, and deposited in a press conference, our brains so
rattled we could hardly form a coherent question.

The next day we were escorted by a platoon of Welsh Guards
through the narrow streets of Amara's market. We wore obligatory body armor; the traders watched our alien white faces
and our guardian phalanx with a mixture of suspicion and
reticence. Moqtada's face, black turban, black beard and black
scowl, bisected by his trademark pointing accusing finger, was
posted up all through the market lanes. We tried to stop and
talk to people but our escorts held their submachine guns in
the ready position and discouraged any lingering.

It was a couple of weeks after the first elections for the Iraqi
parliament that had been characterized by Shia smiles and
indigo fingers, stained to prevent re-voting. Moqtada's block
had won control of the council in Amara and the British Em-

bassy press woman kept trying to tell us that they were nice technocrats really, despite the fact that Moqtada's Mehdi army had attacked the Pink House, the municipal governorate building, the previous summer and besieged the British garrison inside. The British officers who briefed us gave the impression that all was progressing well with phrases like "focused and dedicated," "fair and fair play," "precise surgical operations" and "the elections actually went incredibly smoothly." They were keen to show that they were reasonable in an unreasonable situation and not like those trigger happy Yanks, but it was spin all the same.

We were given an audience with the governor in an office that was gilt edged and decorated with plastic flowers. The governor had a broad jowly face with the requisite mustache above a shiny tie and played the concerned politician. He was flanked by a British official from the Ministry of Defence and Colonel Ben Bathurst, the commander of the Welsh Guards in Amara. We journalists asked desultory questions about democracy and the local elections. The governor replied with non-committal diplo-utterances like "It is the first step" and "the political process is very, very long."

At some point I stopped copying these useless quotes into my notebook and looked over at the British colonel. He had a clean-shaven boyish face that had sagged a little in middle age but remained frank and open. Everything in his upbringing and his experience of life had taught him the superiority of reasonable civilized behavior, even-handedness, temperance and fair-mindedness. I looked into the governor's eyes, dark and burned black with a viscous mobility about them. He kept his hands carefully in his lap, as a show of outward composure. We were all stuck in the deference and the formality of the charade.

After the interview various local dignitaries and council members arrived to see us. Moqtada's councilors were young, ascetic and unsmiling with carefully trimmed beards, and talked about regeneration projects; the local sheikhs swirled their robes, complained about the Americans and gave ponderous pronouncements, the religious men in turbans studiously avoided my female eyes and talked courteously about respect. I asked one councilor, more jolly and independent than most, how the election had been conducted. He rolled his eyes and mentioned certain "Shia groups" and "ballot stuffing" and cast a careful glance over his shoulder in case someone had overheard his remarks. I smiled back to reassure him. He said he had been a professor in Amara for many years; I asked him if he remembered Governor Kamel Sachet. "Yes, of course!" He smiled warmly. "He was very much popular in Amara, yes, of course! He did many things for the Shia poor in Maysan!"

IN BAGHDAD, SPRING of 2004, through the network of former Special Forces officers, I found Major Nejar, sometime adjutant and close friend of Kamel Sachet. Major Nejar was the stereotype of the Sunni officer class: tall, well-built, fit, neat hair cut short, well pressed shirt and trousers, mustache. He hectored and puffed, direct and emphatic. His eyes bored, his finger jabbed, his arrogance inflated and then he would exhale with exaggerated bonhomie. He laughed to provoke me: "You might call me a terrorist if I tell you what I have done!" He proceeded to tell me that the previous year he had fought the British alongside Ali Hassan al-Majid, Saddam's supreme commander in the south. They had made their way back to Baghdad together, a long drive through tank country, sandstorms and shot up highways, skirting the American advance on back roads, spitting at the lack of resistance. "Ha!" he roared his audacity at me. "They said to me when I got to Baghdad, why don't you kill him? But I would never betray him. No!"

Nejar explained, drawing a line across his throat, that Kamel Sachet could not refuse the appointment as Governor. His family would stay behind in Baghdad; he must take up his post immediately. But as he had burned his uniform (after 1991 provincial governors were formally military governors), he and Nejar drove to the row of military tailors the other side of the Thieves' Market in Baghdad and ordered up a new uniform in an afternoon. "We needed a maroon beret and we couldn't find one." Nejar remembered, "I had to go back to my house in Diala and get one for him."

They arrived in Amara in the evening of 28 April 1992 and Kamel Sachet informed the Mayor that he was relieved of his duties, moved into the Governor's compound, billeted Nejar in the guesthouse and posted two guards at the gate. A few days later Kamel Sachet carried out the orders of Saddam to execute two senior Baathie officials who had assassinated a third Baathie official on his doorstep in front of his children. Saddam wanted them shot in the exact place of their crime as a revenge show for his aggrieved family, and this was done. Afterward, Nejar told me with a tight smile, "Things went more or less smoothly."

Kamel Sachet inherited a difficult province. Maysan's people were poor Shia, cowed by the *intifada* crackdown; the borderland was a smugglers' zone crossed with agents of the Iranian-backed Badr Brigade infiltrating sabotage; the highways were hijack alleys; and the outlaw Marsh tribes, led by the dashing "Prince of the Marshes," collected bands of deserters and ambushed army outposts. Saddam, long incensed by the lawlessness and rebellion of the Marsh Arabs, ordered the entire marshes drained so that their villages, hideouts, livelihood and heritage would be destroyed. Maysan was the buffer zone that absorbed assassinations and insurrection funded and fanned from Iran; Kamel Sachet understood very well that he must walk the line and hold it.

During the day it was safe enough in the city of Amara, but when he went to Kut or to an outlying town Kamel Sachet traveled in an armed convoy of six or seven cars and machine gun mounted pick-ups. At night the roads were treacherous despite military patrols, and party offices were sometimes broken into; odd bombs and arson. The Baathie head of an Amara city district was assassinated one dusk on his way home and there were other corner killings; none were ever publicly announced by the government.

In any case, the government, whatever was left of it, had been badly damaged by the American bombs and the uprising of 1991. The rubble was cleared, the bridges in Baghdad rebuilt and opened to much fanfare, but the country was divided into no fly zones, American and British and French planes patrolled the skies and continuing UN sanctions had razed the economy. There was no state to speak of, only one man, the Wizard of Oz with a trilby and a pistol, ordering vast palaces and giant mosques to be built, empty edifices and void facades. A quarter of Iraqis worked in the public sector and salaries fell to $5 a month. No satellite TV, virtually no Internet (a single government controlled server, under close surveillance and out of reach for most), no foreign literature, the airports were closed, imports were squeezed to a trickle and taxed, the economy sank inward and broke down, society was stifled, hermetic; families sat silent in sufferance and mistrust. The missing salaries were replaced by corruption, handouts, patronage, nepotism: passports were sold, exit visas bribed; prisoners paid for separate cells. There was only the will of the President surrounded by a brutal and nefarious inner court of Tikritis who turned mafia and internecine and shot each other at family parties. Saddam had ruled his republic of fear with a terror whip, now he was forced to harness the old systems of authority, tribe and religion, through sheikhs and imams whom he manipulated and killed as necessary to maintain the grip of his choke-hold.

In Maysan Kamel Sachet also relied on the local tribe structure. He rewarded sheikhs with weapons licenses, protected their tribes from army infringements and punishments, and excused their sons military service; in return they policed their own territory. Problems, as they arose, were negotiated within this alliance.

For example, about a year into the engineering works to drain the marshes—a military campaign that was not under Kamel Sachet's command—renegades, probably under the Prince of the Marshes, attacked a digging party and destroyed the bulldozers. The nearest forward army post twice sent units to retrieve the bodies and twice they came under attack. The commander then appealed to Kamel Sachet to intervene and help broker a deal that would allow the bodies to be recovered.

Abdul Qadir drove Kamel Sachet in his armored Mercedes at the head of a convoy of fifteen or so vehicles, bodyguards, pick-ups, an army unit in jeeps and elders from the Albu Eitan, the local tribe of the killed bulldozer drivers. They drove forty kilometers on rutted, dusty, summer-baked mud roads into the desiccated marshes. They passed collapsing reed thatch huts, abandoned villages, army tent encampments. The road was uneven and full of holes and the going slow. It was evening by the time they arrived, radios crackled static in the still uncertain gloam, several soldiers went to lift out the black burned shadows inside the charred yellow diggers. The truce was slight, the dried land open and exposed, Kamel Sachet watched the horizon with an expression of sadness on his face. He did not agree with the draining of the marshes, he said it was too hard a punishment to turn thousands from their homes and their sustenance, but the marshes were base and bridge for the rebels and the command could not let such insolence stand.

THE NINETIES WERE the decade in which the sadness bit into soul. The war with Iran had gathered bitter energy in a rolling swell, the wave had curled in Kuwait and smashed itself on the shore of Basra, flooded the South and the North until there was only an island left in Baghdad. In Baghdad there were fewer electricity cuts, more power to light the propaganda on TV, the all night arc lights over the construction follies and the marching parades on the President's birthday, but everyone understood now that it was only madness acting whim behind the stage sets. Kamel Sachet's pride in himself, his position, his achievements, his country and patriotism, was spent. His sense of duty had curdled. When he came out of Kuwait he had been angry and now, beginning a new chapter in Amara, he was full of something that he would not have known how to call remorse. He fell back to the Koran, truth and salvation, God's laws to govern his conscience, not man's. He tried, I believe, in his own way, to atone.

Kamel Sachet imposed his tenets of discipline, modesty and piety upon those around him and on the tone of his regime in Amara. His bodyguards, a separate (almost private) military unit made up of tribal relatives, were required to pray five times a day and he continually impressed upon them the need to adhere to the correct timetable for prayer. They grumbled about having to wake up for dawn prayer after a night on duty, but never to his face; his anger could extend through his fist in a heartbeat if he thought God's word was being mocked. His office was piled with newspapers, books, papers and letters and petitions and overlooked by framed verses from the Koran that he had hung on the wall. He kept a prayer mat unrolled in one corner where he prayed, even interrupting meetings and delegations to do so. The men who staffed his office (there were no women; if a woman came to a meeting he respectfully declined to shake her hand) also prayed five times a day. Kamel Sachet did not directly order them, he did not need to, his authority was enough to make it clear that anyone in his orbit must follow his example. Even one of his staff, appointed by the Mukhabarat as an internal spy, was careful to pretend to be especially devout.

Office hours ended at 4 p.m., but Kamel Sachet usually stayed until 6 or 7. Um Omar remained in Baghdad with the children, venturing to Amara only once or twice during her husband's tenure. Omar or Ali joined their father during the summer holidays, learning the lessons of leadership and authority and responsibility by his example. When the boys were staying, he would try to leave his office earlier. He taught them how to aim a pistol carefully, using bottles and targets in the back yard. Sometimes the bodyguards would join in, full of male bravado and boasting and prideful good shots, and sometimes in the evening, one of them would cook *kebabi* over a brazier and they would all gather round to comment how good so-and-so's *kebabi* was and how *kebabi* and *mazgouf* and *tika* were the barbecue province of men and that women were much better suited to the intricacies of *dolma*. Omar was a teenager when his father was away from town and he would take the car and drive around with girls in the passenger seat, vrooming and showing off. None of Kamel Sachet's bodyguards ever told on him—they were scared to, wary of Omar's anger as much as of Kamel Sachet's.

Kamel Sachet always discharged his duties with diligence. Twice a week he traveled to different towns and villages in the district and he would often stop his convoy to greet ordinary poor people and listen to their complaints. Once, one of his bodyguards recounted to me, they were returning from a visit to a certain village and came across an old woman lying in rags by the side of the road, waving them down. The convoy was stopped and Kamel Sachet himself got out and asked her what she wanted. It seemed that she was paralyzed and she asked for a wheelchair. Kamel Sachet wrote a letter for her which said that her family should come to his office and he would arrange for a wheelchair and a small pension.

His time in Amara was full of these small incidents. A doctor from Maysan who worked in the same hospital as Dr. Hassan in exile in Abu Dhabi told me he often used to see Kamel Sachet in the hospital in Amara. He suffered sometimes from blood in his urine, he said as a complication of a bilharzia infestation when he was a boy. He liked doctors and enjoyed sitting with them; sometimes he visited sick patients late at night after their families had left.

Abdul Qadir, his driver-nephew, told me that once his convoy had stopped at a red traffic light in Amara and the traffic policeman at the intersection halted the oncoming green traffic flow to let the governor's car pass. Kamel Sachet was furious, upbraided the poor traffic policeman, and reported him to the traffic directorate recommending that he be fined a month's salary.

A Janabi Istikhbarat officer told me he had asked Kamel Sachet, as a friend, if it was true what he had heard: that he had rolled up his trousers and taken a shovel and helped to clear the main storm drain in Amara when it was flooded and blocked one winter. When Kamel Sachet confirmed the story, the Istikhbarat officer asked, "But how can you, a general, stoop in such a way?" Kamel Sachet replied, "Here I may have rank but with God there are no ranks nor positions."

PERHAPS HIS GOOD deeds were recompense, but they were also, in no small part, credits to be counted with God, banked against his judgment day. So many points for observing the timetable of prayer, so many points for taking care of the sick or the poor. He practiced mercy on a Shia saboteur sent from Iran who handed himself in. He went to pay his respects at the funerals of the poor and insignificant. He gave money to the needy. He thought of Allah and his kingdom of heaven and compensated his guilt with humility. When he held the hand of a frail old man dying in a hospital bed he would say to himself, "Ten credits." He carried his own death very close. He was not afraid of it; his end, he knew and trusted, was already written and determined, but he must have guessed that the odds were against his own longevity. His system of credits, almost obsessive, was his preparation.

PHOTOGRAPH. *Kamel Sachet stands straight and impeccable in an elegant dark green uniform with a twist of red braid over one shoulder. His sleeves, however, are uncharacteristically rolled up to his elbow and he is holding out a carrier bag, in a gesture of charity and supplication, to a poor wretch wearing a filthy* dishdasha *with a clump of loose turban on his head and a twist of rag wrapped over his face. Several similarly limping, listing, disheveled figures are gathered in a disparate semi circle, hobbling, leaning on walking sticks, some apparently blind. Behind Kamel Sachet, several steps*

behind, as if recoiling in disgust, are a group of army officers and
health officials.

Kamel Sachet had learned of an old and long-neglected leprosy hospital in a far off place, near the Iranian border in a des-
olate region, forgotten under a wide spaced sky where eagles
flew. The staff had been drafted during the Iran-Iraq war and
never returned, the windows and door frames had been torn
out by looters. The lepers who remained, crumbling and suffering, begged food where they could and stacked their dead
in the basement because they had not the tools nor strength to
bury them.

When Kamel Sachet heard about the hospital he gathered
municipal and health officials together, including the bald
paunchy head of the Baath Party in Amara and the Head of the
local Women's Union (who he had insisted wear the *hijab*), and
led the convoy without telling where they were going. The
hospital had been so long abandoned none of them even knew
of its existence.

As the convoy arrived, the lepers came out to see this extraordinary sight but were afraid of the big cars and the important people and clung, timorous and curious, to the hem of
their ruined building. The appalled officials, in clean dark green
uniforms, stood out of obligation and dread and held their nose
against the ragged white apparitions that confronted them. The
outline of their humanity was blurred and deformed. Their
heads were wrapped in loose turbans like bandages. Faces were
concave, hollowed out, eaten blind, noseless. Some stretched a
withered stump across their face in shame and attempted modesty. The women squatted in the dry earth, enveloped in dusty
ragged tents of *abaya*.

Kamel Sachet delved into the carrier bag he carried and

walked forward and gave clean clothes to the patients with his own hands. He asked them how they lived and who they were. One man was a Kurd. Kamel Sachet asked him when his family had last come to visit. He said he had been at the hospital since 1957 and since that time he had received no visitors nor knew anything of the outside world.

Kamel Sachet and Nejar helped to put the new clothes on the lepers who were too weak to do it themselves. The health officials recoiled and refused. The patients chanted *surahs* from the Koran because no illness can be caught if it is not God's will. Soap, food and blankets were brought out of the cars. Kamel Sachet went into the building accompanied by Abdul Qadir.

They found a woman bedridden in a room. She had been put there because she was contagious. Kamel Sachet pushed opened the creaking door. Abdul Qadir told me he had been scared and he stood in the doorway and retched. The room was dark because the glassless windows were boarded up with cardboard and a terrible smell came out, the strong sour stench of unwashed rag. It was a summer day, the roof was corrugated iron, the heat beat in the room and was trapped there. Abdul Qadir inhaled the stagnant disease and it stuck in his throat. The woman was of indeterminate age and lay in a heap of straw with a cloth over her hair on a filthy rickety bed. Her whole body was swollen and her face, while untouched by leprosy and neither spotted nor collapsed, was a strange engorged dark blue color. Kamel Sachet greeted her respectfully, "*Salam Aleikum,*" and handed her food and clothing.

Afterward Kamel Sachet redirected part of the healthcare budget and ordered a new hospital to be built for the lepers in Amara. He ordered the nurses who worked there to be paid double and the doctors who went once a week to check the patients to be properly remunerated. He persuaded army volunteers to clean the place, saying it was for the sake of humanity and for God.

In Amara they called him "al-Calipha Omar Bin Abd al-Aziz," after a great and famous eighth century caliph who shared a mix of Kamel Sachet's monikers—Kamel Sachet was known as Abu Omar, father of Omar, to those close to him and his full name was Kamel Sachet Aziz, after his father. The Caliph had ruled with piety and munificence, refusing bribes, redistributing land, canceling taxes for converts to Islam, forbidding the practice of "cursing Ali" to foster greater unity between Shia and Sunni and humbling himself with simple cotton clothes and manual work—and so rebuffed the greed of the nobility that they had him poisoned.

At home, Kamel Sachet wore a simple *dishdasha* with a red and white headscarf draped over his head without the honorific black band, the *agal*, in the manner of a simple farmer. In his right hand he held a plain string of black plastic prayer beads. He did not absently thumb the beads, as most men did, a calming tactile rhythm to play away the days, but automatically and meditatively counted each bead and stretch of gap between each bead, each one an individual prayer followed by a breath of respect. As governor, he paved roads, ordered a canal to be dug to drain the flooding rainwater into the river and repaired the sewage system that had been damaged since the Iran-Iraq war. He made sure that the profits from the big state farms in Maysan were directed into accounts for the refurbishment of mosques and into a fund for the *zakat*, the fifth pillar of Islam as prescribed by the Koran, a charitable tithe to be distributed to the poor. He set up a committee to listen to petitions from ordinary people and offer stipends to students for university and the disabled. He distributed land to war widows and local civil servants and when he toured villages he took sacks of grain and rice for poor families. He set up an office where women could make complaints of violence and drunkenness against their husbands. He kept an open office on Tuesdays so that ordinary people could come with their concerns (although in practice the office manager often turned people away); once an old man came in to plead for his four sons who had been sentenced to execution, and Kamel Sachet looked into the case and had them all released. He was always careful to couch his orders with reference to the President. He would say, "Saddam says that we must increase the salaries for teachers because too many teachers are leaving our schools for the private sector."

And, most infamously, he closed all the bars and liquor shops in the province.

Arshad Yassin, Saddam's cousin, brother-in-law and former chief of the presidential bodyguards, came to Amara for a semi official visit. Kamel Sachet tried to avoid these Baghdad Baathies and any kind of official frippery—once he refused to meet the head of the Iraqi Association of Art (he had no time for the arts or entertainers) who had come expressly to see him. Arshad Yassin, however, was too close to the President to put off, no matter how distasteful he found him. Kamel Sachet met him in his outer office. Tea was poured by the office manager; outside two sets of bodyguards sized each other up.

Arshad Yassin chided Kamel Sachet, "Abu Omar; you've created a mini Islamic state here!" Several officials from the Amara branch of Uday's Olympic Committee as well as the head of the Baath Party in Maysan, a toady drunkard called Aziz Salih Numan who Kamel Sachet knew and disliked from the time in Kuwait, had complained of his religious excesses in presidential earshot. Arshad Yassin had come to broker conciliation.

"Let them at least keep the bar that's still open on the Baghdad road, Abu Omar—"

But Kamel Sachet answered him, "There is a bar that remains open? Well, I will close it immediately!"

For the time being Saddam backed him, but inevitably those
Baathies who had expected to be automatically awarded large
tracts of government farmland and construction contracts felt
their toes pinched and bitched at Kamel Sachet's welfare measures and his religious zealotry. Aziz Salih Numan was his most
prominent adversary.

No one I ever talked to had a good word to say about Aziz
Salih Numan, who apparently suffered from diabetes, gouty
legs and a terrifying temper. He had been one of the triumvirate ruling Kuwait and he and Kamel Sachet had already
established a mutual dislike. He was an apostle of Saddam, a
facsimile with a smug jowly grin, black military beret and mustache, a Mini-Me tyrant who groveled in front of his master, a
Shia who compensated for this political insecurity by making
himself a trusted implement of Saddam's torturous crackdown
of the Shia South. His brother had been assassinated, and he
maintained a reasonable paranoia of the same fate; it was said
that there was a Kuwaiti bounty on his head. He spent most of
his time in Kut, but kept a house in Amara that was built like
a castle fortress with towers surrounded by a high fence and
covered in marble. It was rumored there was a prison in the
basement. Kamel Sachet refused to give contracts to Numan's
relatives, but insisted on putting them out to public tender, and
would not allocate his business interests to certain government
buildings that he requested. Numan complained to Ali Hassan
al-Majid and to Hussein Kamel, spread rumors in Baghdad,

called Kamel Sachet a Wahhabi, and wrote reports accusing him of leniency against those who had cursed the President.

Kamel Sachet and Aziz Salih Numan avoided each other as much as possible but an incident occurred on a feast day held to commemorate the date of a previous visit by Saddam to Maysan. Aziz Salih Numan arrived and due to a mix up in timing and communication, was kept waiting for fifteen minutes before Kamel Sachet came to greet him. He was furious at such a failure of protocol and disrespect and he shouted at Kamel Sachet in front of several other officers:

"Why were we not greeted properly? Are we fools?"

"If you know what you are, why are you asking?" Kamel Sachet retorted, angry, and reached for his gun. Aziz Salih Numan bristled and moved his own hand over the holster on his hip and continued to rant.

"You don't deserve such a position. I am the representative of the President! I will take my measures after this insult!"

The following day an informal peace meeting was held between the two at which Nejar (sometimes bodyguard to Aziz Salih Numan) officiated. There was tension and three Pepsis on the table.

Aziz Salih Numan leaned forward and asserted himself as a lecturing superior:

"You are the Governor. You have a high rank in the army. Your relationship with Saddam Hussein is strong. But listen. Nejar is a witness to what I will say to you: Don't behave like this, whether something is right or wrong—Your trust in Saddam Hussein is 100 percent, but Saddam needs the party more than he needs the army. He needed you as an army commander during the Iran-Iraq war, and he gave you cars with golden keys and he needed you in Kuwait. I know you are honest in your dealings with Saddam. But don't trust him 100 percent. We know that if I told Saddam that I, as his representative, was kept waiting and Kamel Sachet did not greet me, it's an insult to who? To him! You would be executed!"

Kamel Sachet knew what he said was true, but kept his pride: "I have done nothing to be executed for. It was an administrative mistake."

KAMEL SACHET SPENT a little over two years as Governor of Amara before the reports piled up against him, too many complaints from too many different quarters, and he was reassigned back to Baghdad, back home, to an administrative position in the Presidency in Baghdad, selling government cars. He was recommended for the job by Khalid al-Janabi, the sheikh of the Janabi tribe and then Mayor of Baghdad. It was a position which suited Saddam, it sidelined this recalcitrant and independent extremist, while keeping him occupied in a useful position, close by. Indeed, to Saddam it was a good fit, the office of selling government cars was always fraught with nepotistic deals but he could trust the unimpeachable reputation of his war-hero general to act without favoritism (Kamel Sachet would not even allow his own sons to buy one of the government cars he was responsible for—a piece of incorruptibility which greatly frustrated his sons) while detaching him from any military duties and separating him from the officer corps who revered him.

NEJAR WAS EAGER to describe Kamel Sachet's great qualities, his bravery and his goodness. But he made it clear, slanting his gaze, that he would protect Kamel Sachet's memory and reputation. "Don't go into personal details," he warned me. "I came up with Kamel Sachet, he did me many favors and I am loyal to him and I tell you to avoid these things. Many times I was in his house, many times, and I never met his wife or his daughters." He looked me straight in the eye, trying to discern if I knew about the scandal. I returned his stare. Eventually he broke off his drilling and resumed the general's résumé.

"Kamel Sachet asked for retirement several times. I advised him not to take his request directly to the President, because the President would calculate this request and suspect it. This was one of his mistakes." Nejar paused. "He wasn't afraid of Saddam Hussein. He was honest with him, he believed Saddam was his friend and trusted him and did not believe that he would betray him."

The next time I saw Major Nejar we met in the coffee shop of my hotel. He seemed distracted and nervous. His swagger had sharpened into aggression. It was now mid April 2004 and Fallujah had blown up and Moqtada's Shia were revolting in Kufa and no one could pretend any more that the violence was just teething problems at the beginning of a new era of democracy and prosperity. Nejar no longer wanted to reminisce about incidents from Amara and talk about Kamel Sachet's achievements there. He had been driving a taxi to make ends meet but he was running out of money and the situation was not good enough for his pride or his pocket; he needed something that conferred a certain status. Without much preamble, he asked me if I could help him get a position in the new Iraqi Mukhabarat.

"Working for the Americans?" I was incredulous.

"I know things," he hinted darkly. "I want a job. For my future." He said he had put his name on the list but they had not called him. Some former colleagues of his had already been called and he was worried he was being ignored. He wanted me to put a word in with someone, to get his name moved farther up the list. I told him I had no particular contacts with the Americans in the GreenZone and no way to do this. He went cold and repeated his request. He told me that any further conversations were connected to this favor. I repeated that I was only a journalist and powerless. He sneered, leaned back in his chair and clicked his fingers for the waiter to bring the bill. We never spoke again.

Chapter 11

MOSQUE

JUST AS HE WAS PUBLICLY EQUANIMOUS AS GOVERNOR, so Kamel Sachet had no choice in his appointment to his new position in the Presidential Office. He had long rescinded his pride in such matters and did not care about the outward appearance of demotion, but the constrictions and suspicion of Saddam's court strained his conversation and his mood. He went to his office every day, competently organized the sale of government cars and other extraneous items—an attempt by the government to raise some cash in the strapped time of sanctions—and spent the balance of his time building mosques.

The first mosque he built was in Baghdad, in Saidiya, not far from his home, on a plot of land which Sheikh Khalid al-Janabi helped him to purchase. He built a plain concrete cube without a minaret—he did not believe in wasting money on decoration—and named it after one of his victories, which had also been the name of one of the divisions he had commanded, the Sadiq Mosque.

The mosque was pared back to the utilitarian; Kamel Sachet insisted on simplicity and reverence. He made sure that the gate was separated from the door of the mosque by a path, so that people could spend a few moments contemplating the distance from the earthly street and their quotidian cares to a clearer-headed godliness. He did not allow shoe racks inside the mosque, as was usual; he said that shoes had no place in the mosque at all, not even carried in by hand, but must be left farther away by the entrance. Inside, the walls were unadorned except for a few *surahs*, the carpet was industrially woven and there was no air-conditioning which might have required the additional cost of a generator. Harith al-Obeidi, the young Islamic scholar Kamel Sachet hired as the imam, suggested he plant a small garden, something green and serene, but Kamel Sachet said he did not want to spend money on something that would be a distraction.

"His military character imposed itself on his religious behavior," Harith al-Obeidi told me, complaining. I met him in Damascus in the summer of 2007 for tea on a restaurant terrace in the old city. He had become an MP in the post-Saddam era and he explained the state of political disintegration in the Baghdad that he had just left. The Sunni political tide had turned against pretending cooperation with the Shia parties and his Sunni faction had pulled out of the Maliki government. He threw up his hands, exhausted with cynicism at all the bombs, the militias and Iranian ambition and American short-sightedness. . .

"An officer will always be an officer," he said of Kamel Sachet, reverting, more comfortably, to reminiscence. "I saw him once throw the shoes a man had carried in to pray outside the mosque. And he was obsessive about cleaning the mosque himself. He came every Thursday evening to wash the floors on his knees. Sometimes he brought his elder sons with him. And about paying for the upkeep. He did not like to receive donations. He would say, 'We're not in need; I wont accept charity!' He didn't even like to replace worn-out furniture. The only important thing for him was to fulfill his religious duty."

Harith al-Obeidi had studied at the Baghdad University School of Sharia, completed his MA in Islamic Science and Comparative Philology and written his Ph.D. thesis on the Rules of a Traveler According to Sharia. He described himself as a moderate, a man who preferred dialogue and who found the dictations of Kamel Sachet's extremism confining: "He was practically *Salafi*!" God was the only sanction, the Koran the only guide. Kamel Sachet would not allow him to counsel those who came for advice or with domestic troubles. According to him, a mosque was for prayer, not for pastoral care and community projects. He attached great importance to the memorization and recitation of the Koran and classrooms were set up to teach young boys, but he didn't allow the mosque to sponsor a youth soccer team, as some mosques did: soccer had nothing to do with the worship of God.

The Sadiq Mosque existed within the lines of Kamel Sachet's own design. It was the place he felt most at peace and relaxed. The moment he stepped across the threshold a smile spread across his face: grace of autonomy or God's space, free from any autocrat. He was, perhaps, even happy. Those around him knew that in these moments, anything they asked for, he would give.

I ALWAYS IMAGINED Kamel Sachet's relationship with Islam was personally defined, a private solace, interior world, retreat. Although he was more extreme than most he was not alone in his reversion. During the eighties and nineties there was a general trend toward the practice of conservative Islam in the Arab world. Women donned headscarves, bars were closed, public immodesty frowned upon and vilified. In some ways Islam seemed to become a shelter from reckless and unjust dictats of rulers and corrupt officials: a reaction against the secular regimes—of Jordan, Iraq, Syria, Egypt, Saudi Arabia, Tunisia, Morocco, Indonesia—as well as a rebuttal of the Western examples, of either communism (which had collapsed under its own weight) or the democracies of Europe and America which preached human rights and supported the monarchs and dictators who oppressed them. This upswell of Islam became a new kind of Pan-Arabism, a way to reclaim culture, morality, values, identity.

Dr. Laith's wife, Bushra, had taken up wearing the *hijab* late in life, but she could not explain exactly why—it was something sunk deep out of explanation. She said it just felt more comfortable. Um Omar had grown into her thirties following Western fashion and hemlines, but had bowed to the wishes of her husband and the justifications of her belief. Whenever I asked to see Iraqi family albums, the pictures would illustrate this progression: miniskirts to seventies feathered fringe and floaty sundresses to a headscarf and a full length coat; over two decades women had retracted into the safety of the enveloping *hijab*.

Saddam himself was always sensitive to his costume. In the seventies he had been known for his fine tailored suits and Italian shoes, the international man of sophistication; in the eighties he was rarely out of uniform (which he wore plain and unadorned in the manner of Napoleon and Stalin, other rulers who understood the necessity of theater), by the nineties his portrait, rendered in ceramic tiles, paint, plaster, ink screen or sculpted in bronze, wore whatever the scene demanded: a mortar board outside a university, a stethoscope outside a hospital, rich tribal robes on the highway to Amman, battledress next to a parade ground, even, apparently without irony, Kurdish dress, complete with baggy pantaloons, at the entrance to Kirkuk.

Saddam went along with the new wave of religious conservatism, crafting rhetoric and ordering props in line with the tenor of the times. He initiated construction on the Mother of All Battles Mosques in Baghdad to be the largest mosque in the world, he redesigned the national flag to include the inscription *Allahu Akbar*, God Is Great, and had a Koran written in blood, which he claimed was his own. But it was as if he were trying to have dominion over the sea. Prayer is collective and Friday sermons occasions for opinion. As much as the new religious mood washed the public shore with a soothing lap, it also swelled into opposition. Islam politicized, became an ism, into Islamism. And mosques were the natural meeting places.

Young men came to Friday prayer to listen to imams preach an Islam that was enshrined in Sharia godliness and therefore purer and higher than that of man-made secular authority. During the week they went to prayer after work and then hung around in the courtyard until the final evening, talking among themselves. They discussed Islam and *Sharia* and studied the Koran and the Hadith, the life of the Prophet that accompanies the Koran, grew their beards, wore the traditional *dishdasha* instead of foreign modern trousers; some even wore it deliberately short, above their ankles, in the fashion of the early followers of the Prophet Mohammed. The security services sent undercover agents to infiltrate congregations. Obeidi laughed, "But everyone knew who they were because they were the ones wearing short *dishdashas* but on their face they only had a mustache."

During Ramadan in 1993 Kamel Sachet asked a famous and controversial cleric to lead the prayers at the Sadiq Mosque. Banners advertising his arrival were put up all over the neighborhood and on the appointed Friday the mosque was full and the streets around overflowed with hundreds who unrolled their prayer maps on the tarmac and squatted by the curb to listen to the sermon through the loudspeakers. The cleric, from the same tribe as Kamel Sachet, had been recently denounced by the government and removed from his position on the Islamic Committee; and his popularity was in proportion to his dissidence. His tannoy words were clarion and boomed across the nodding crowd: One day the end would come for secular regimes! Islam was the only right and correct way! *Sharia* was every man's obligation before God! It was the duty of the youth to stand up, to obey their religion and their God and to follow in the example of the Prophet Mohammed (Peace Be Upon Him)!

Harith al-Obeidi said he himself also began to use the pulpit as a challenge. He stopped leading with a prayer for the life and health of Saddam Hussein and often took the risk of delivering sermons without first receiving the required permission from the official Islamic Committee. "If I was preaching at another mosque I would arrive just before I spoke and leave directly afterwards to avoid the Mukhabarat." But it was always risky; several times Mukhabarat agents came to the Sadiq Mosque with questions and intimidations.

"Why do you not offer prayers for the President?"

"Come to the office to answer some questions."

"Why do so many young men come to your mosque?"

"Does Kamel Sachet know there are so many?"

"Who are they?"

"The mosque should not be open between sunset and evening prayers."

When al-Obeidi told Kamel Sachet about their visits, he cursed their intrusions and called them dogs.

It was difficult to tread the line between the accusation of opposition and the justification of the sanctity of worship; but it was an equally hazardous balancing act for Saddam: the fatal car crashes and ambushes by "unknown assailants" of popular imams blew into riots. Kamel Sachet never allowed his outward mask of fealty to slip, but in court circles, among men like Aziz Salih Numan, Hussein Kamel and Ali Hassan al-Majid, Kamel Sachet was openly called a *Wahhabi*. Reports were written accusing him of having treasonous Saudi connections and receiving Saudi funds for his mosques.

After a couple of years Harith al-Obeidi resigned from the Sadiq Mosque. Perhaps he felt too exposed, perhaps, as he said, he had grown tired of Kamel Sachet's interferences and his iron stricture. "I don't like radicalism," said Obeidi. "Kamel Sachet imposed too many of his own personal opinions on me and on the mosque." The imam who had spoken during Ramadan fled the country not long afterward and was sentenced to death in absentia. Unfavorable reports piled up in the file of Kamel Sachet.

Chapter 12

HIS SHEIKH

I N THE PREHISTORY OF ARABIA, BEFORE THE DAWN of the Prophet, there was a Christian tribe of Yemen called the Kelbi led by a poet called Zuhair bin Janab. As Islam established and spread victorious, the Kelbis migrated north and merged with the Muslim conquests of Syria. Mo'awiyah, the fifth caliph, founder of the Umayyed dynasty, conqueror of Syria and Egypt, had a Kelbi wife. His son, Yazid, victor of Kerbala, slayer of Hussein, the martyred grandson of the Prophet (and thereby villain of all Shia), also took a Kelbi woman as one of his wives. Yazid died without issue in 683 and the dynasty passed to another branch of the clan; the Kelbi ran out of favor and retreated south along the Euphrates.

Lost in the vagaries of desert life, sand blown over gaps of dry centuries, over a thousand years the Kelbis became the Janabi tribe. Nomads, sheep herders, camel traders, they settled where they could find grazing and moved according to topography and war. They stretched from Ramadi and Fallujah to Hilla; and south, Mahmoudiya, Latifiya, Iskandariya, to Jurfa Sakr, west of the Euphrates. Some settled in Baghdad and wrote Janabis into documents and records, some settled near the shrines of Najaf and Kerbala and married and converted into Shi'ism. In the nineteenth century they sold food to the

Ottoman armies, in the early twentieth, they dug canals for the British, in the time of Saddam they filled the security services and the official ranks of the Iraqi state. The Janabis grew in number until they were a quarter of a million.

History came down in epics and poems, battles and heroes and feuds, folklore, shadow plays, the whispers of old men and grandmothers. A son was always taught ten generations of ancestors. Adnan Janabi, Sheikh of the Janabis, recounted to me fourteen with ease, his name long with antecedent:

"Adnan Abdul-Munim Rashid Ali Khalaf Ouaid Khattab Mohammed Alloush Mohammed Noufal Mohammed Ali Ougab . . ."

He remembered the death of his grandfather's last camel. It was 1945; he was five years old—he didn't remember why the beast died, just that it was the last camel, long useless, and its carcass made a shadow on the ground. Afterward his grandfather used the saddle to rest his elbow against Bedu tradition during tribal assemblies in the *mudhif*, the traditional meeting house built of reeds.

He told me about a vast bronze tray that he had inherited, 200 years old, capable of holding 250 kilos of rice, 4 whole rams and a baked bull. Adnan liked to use it every year at the Eid of the *Haj*, the time when sheep were slaughtered as festival sacrifice and their meat distributed to the poor. He had it re-plated with chrome because untreated bronze could react poisonously with food. It needed fifteen men to carry it so he had a special trolley made so that it could be more easily maneuvered.

Adnan laughed. "I mechanized it," and he bobbed his head back from inhaling a long draught of *narghila* to watch Tunisia score against Spain in the World Cup. It was June 2006, we were sitting in a café in Beirut, marble and aged mirror,

clattering backgammon, TV screens for the soccer, glasses of
milky arak and plates of pistachios. Adnan had moved to Beirut
because Baghdad was too dangerous; he was a moderate and
therefore found himself condemned by both sides: Sunni insurgents linked to al-Qaeda in Mesopotamia and Shia reveng-
ists and their Mehdi army militias. "I am on all the best death
lists!" Adnan did not look like a sheikh, he lacked the usual
Iraqi belly, dyed black hair, mustache and swagger. Instead his
frame was slight, his head was bald, his face clean-shaven and
he carried the intelligent air of an ancient sage as he considered the soccer players sprinting up and down the green pitch.
"Now Spain will come back, you see the Tunisians were lucky
too early, the Spanish are stronger and they will win." Adnan
had a glass of wine before him, its level had fallen and he ordered another bottle and mocked his own indulgence: "And
forty years ago I was a communist!"

In fact Adnan was, practically, an Iraqi anomaly, a leader
without agenda, ideology, prejudice or hatreds. He felt an
almost overwhelming helplessness in the surge of violence in
Iraq; he tried when he could to broker kidnap deals, protect
journalists investigating atrocities; he urged restraint, alliance, negotiation—but the bloodshed was out of control, the
contents of Pandora's box had been tipped into hell. Every
day the newspapers printed arbitrary statistics: 23, 42, 59, 130,
168—so many that the figures of the dead were lost in the
numbers. The car bomb scenes of black smoke, white am-
bulance, red blood pools on the tarmac became as if by rote
and went increasingly under-reported. Headlines were spiked
with gore and vile innovation: decapitated heads wrapped in
black garbage bags, bodies dumped by rubbish heaps with
their hands bound and their skulls drilled, a daring kidnap
raid that took over a hundred employees out of a ministry, a

new type of car bomb that released clouds of poisonous chlorine gas.

Adnan analyzed the situation perfectly correctly: he said law and order only existed when the central authority, the government of the state, maintained its monopoly on violence. In Iraq everyone had a gun and every political leader, sheikh and neighborhood don had an army/bodyguard/militia. This anarchy was the result, and as long as neither the Americans or the Kurds or the Sunna or the Shia were willing to cede to a monopoly, the anarchy would continue. "I am a realist. What I've learned from this life is to be realistic."

During the World Cup Beirut was decorated with multinational flags: each household had picked a different country: Brazilian banners, the English cross of St George hung over balconies next to French tricolors and pizza places daubed in red, white and green. At night, when the bars let out after the matches, it was a carnival, cars streamed through downtown fluttering blue and white Argentine colors or the red flag of Morocco or green for the Sunnis who liked to support the Saudis. It was a parody of divided Beirut, a weird blast of irony, as a tooting cavalcade drove past the window while Adnan and I discussed the sectarian fighting in Baghdad. I told him I remembered the black Shia flags hung up in Baghdad to commemorate Ashura in 2004, the month of mourning, which were then never taken down so that they became, in effect, territorial markers.

We paused. It was very stark and clear. We shook our heads, drank more wine. How could this be stopped? It could not be stopped. We were sitting in a city where the pock-marks of bullet holes of fifteen years of civil war were still visible. Chaos could not be controlled; it seemed it had first to exhaust itself. After the soccer was over and the Spanish had indeed won, a band played old Lebanese songs and everyone became sentimental, singing laments of love and war, clapping to encourage two red-lipsticked, full bodied Levantine women who got up to dance with sashaying hips and pathos, plucking the sweet melancholy rhythm from the smoky air with their fingertips. We applauded unknowing, as the last easy moment of a happy drunken corner of the Middle East slipped past midnight. Three weeks later Hezbollah and Israel went to war. More bombs, more death.

ADNAN HAD KNOWN Kamel Sachet well. Kamel Sachet's family hailed from the Albu Hassoun subdivision of the Janabi tribe, a clan with a hardscrabble history of marginal land and minority and a reputation of pride and aggression—Adnan told me that as recently as the fifties the Albu Hassoun had fought the fierce Garaghul over land that had been reconfigured by the meanderings of the Euphrates. There was killing on both sides but in the popular imagination it was the Albu Hassoun who cowed the Garaghul. Janabis liked to marry their daughters into the Albu Hassoun for the protection the alliance afforded. It was said a Janabi should always employ an Albu Hassoun bodyguard or else he would be robbed. "The Albu Hassoun were not to be meddled with!" Adnan laughed. "But Kamel Sachet was a great hero for all Janabis."

Kamel Sachet's farm near Hilla was close to Adnan's father's land and Adnan got to know him in the eighties when he would often come to the *mudhif* and sit, a glass of tea in one hand, his red beret at his elbow, and wait patiently while the other guests dispersed. He preferred to talk to the Sheikh in a private audience, and Adnan perceived that he was independent, almost a loner. Adnan was impressed with his careful, frank manner of speaking and his tone of responsibility leavened with self-deprecation. Kamel Sachet liked to talk about his farm, irrigation and crops, date harvests, water rights. The Sheikh would tell him of tribal matters, the minor scandals of Janabis, who had positions in the presidential apparatus, and they would discuss people they knew, commanders, anecdotes, trouble and promotions. Kamel Sachet always offered to help any Janabi when he could. He paid for the daughter of an executed officer to go to university and study to be a pharmacist, he gave soldiers leave to attend funerals or weddings, or, if they had gone AWOL, an official note of excuse that could save their lives. This was the tradition of *wasta*, connections, the patronage of tribe.

Kamel Sachet's deepening religious observance was obvious. He read many religious books and often listened to religious sheikhs, but Adnan noticed that he did not follow any one in particular. He fasted when the calendar required and prayed according to the timetable, but he deplored extra fasting or praying through the night as mystical indulgences. Even when his father died Kamel Sachet did not attend the funeral; he said such gatherings were distasteful to him and not true Islam. In the Hadith it is written that burials should be quick and simple without pomp and fuss. Adnan's elder brother Khalid, then Mayor of Baghdad, who had succeeded his father as Sheikh, had to send a car for him so that Kamel Sachet would be able respectfully to receive the envoy that Saddam was sending.

Kamel Sachet acquiesced to this political nicety, but he made it clear to his brothers: "This is your right to receive condolences if you wish. But I am here as my social duty, I am not here to receive condolences."

I suggested to Adnan, during one of our conversations, that Kamel Sachet's religiosity was, in some measure, a moral retrenchment. Adnan nodded.

"His battle was internal, to reconcile himself with the state. He was exercising his duty as an officer, as a general. He did not become a recluse or a rebel. He did not become Osama bin Laden or a saint. He was not a weak person who did good deeds in order to go to heaven. But he needed this rock to hang on to as he tried to navigate his moral compass in a corrupt state in which he was an important person."

Kamel Sachet became trapped by his position and his duty to his position. Adnan had spent much of his life recusing his own position. In the sixties he had studied economics in London and been part of an Iraqi exile group that monitored human rights abuses and political prisoners during the short lived Baathie takeover in 1963. In the seventies he had returned to Iraq and accepted a position in the new oil ministry helping to organize the nationalization of Iraqi oil, long a dream of his. But he soon ran foul of Vice President Saddam Hussein. In 1973 OPEC announced the oil embargo in response to the October war with Israel; Adnan discovered that Saddam was involved in selling oil in breach of the embargo, behind the back of the Baath Party regional command. Somehow (*wasta*) he survived Saddam's anger and managed to retire to the country.

"I put on a *dishdasha* and became a farmer and I had the biggest fish farm in the Middle East and I became a very rich man with that fish farm."

He did all that he could to live apart from the regime and its entrapments. His brother Khalid was the opposite. Khalid became close to Saddam, he often went hunting with him, and rose through the Party ranks to Mayor of Baghdad—Adnan admonished him, tried to reason with him, but to no avail.

Part of the reason that he was left alone in his country exile, he knew, was that Khalid had brokered an understanding with Saddam. But after many years excused, he found himself pulled back into the morass. In 1995, Khalid died in Rome, possibly poisoned, possibly on Saddam's orders; Adnan became the new Sheikh of the Janabis and was duly summoned.

A car was sent to his house in Baghdad. He did not know where he was being taken nor could he ask. On arrival at a government building he was shown to a room and told to wait. After a while, perhaps half an hour, he was taken in a second car, escorted through a checkpoint into the grounds of the Republican Palace. He was shown into an anteroom where his identity documents were re-checked and his name uttered into a telephone. The officers there smiled and were respectful and asked him politely if he had waited long, if his family was well, *inshallah*, it was hot today, more hot than usual! They asked him to take everything out of his pockets, wallet, house keys, a small notebook, which they took and placed in a pouch. Then a doctor in a white coat came into the room and asked him to open his hands facing up and traced his palms with his fingertips like a fortune teller. He was told to take off his watch. He was told to take off his clothes. The two attending officials remained polite. He took off his vest and his underpants. The officers checked his clothes thoroughly and ran their hands over every seam and looked carefully inside his polished shoes. This naked humiliation—Adnan pursed his lips with distaste and shame as he remembered—induced a measure of self-recoil.

He was asked to put his clothes back on, and when he had dressed, he was shown into an office guarded by two soldiers on the door. Mr. President, Saddam Hussein, sat behind a large but ordinary desk. Adnan stood before him; there was no chair to sit on. Saddam leaned back in his chair, cleared his throat and chortled what he imagined was a friendly greeting. "Heh heh heh."

Adnan's position as Sheikh was both precarious and protected. He tried to avoid the functionary requirements, the summons of all Sheikhs and the hand-outs of envelopes of money, "a pathetic amount, less than $1,000; I took it only once, because a Janabi in the Presidency advised me I must, and I gave it away to charity." Like almost all Iraqis, he maneuvered the best he could manage and hoped for an Iraq after Saddam.

THE END, WHEN it came, was a foreign invasion. The Americans! Operation Iraqi Freedom! Weapons of Mass Destruction! War on Terror! Mission Accomplished! Tank columns streaming through the desert, shock and awe exploding palaces. For the Iraqis there was a chink of hope amid all the destruction and the conundrum of how to be free under occupation.

On 10 April 2003, the day after Americans pulled Saddam's statue down in Firdous Square in Baghdad, Adnan convened a tribal meeting in Latifiya, a town south of Baghdad heavily populated by Janabis. He asked his elders, the tribal judges and leaders of smaller affiliated tribes, what they wished to do. Many said that the dignity of Iraq was being trampled and they should fight. Adnan listened and replied: "If we all agree to fight then I will fight with you and we will fight together. But first think of the consequences. This is the Americans, they have their annihilating bombs. If we fight, they will certainly retaliate against any resistance. I do not think the Americans come to take our land; they have no imperial will or ambition. I believe they want to install a government over which they have some influence—and where in the world is there a government over which America has no influence? Perhaps it is better to wait and co-operate and we will be better able to protect our families and our communities in this way."

At the beginning the tribal elders agreed and resistance was petty. Once a week the American commander in Hilla came to see Adnan in his *mudhif* for consultation. Adnan was able to discover which Janabis they were targeting for arrest and in some circumstances get some detained Janabis released. But after six months the arrests and night-time hard-knock raids grew more frequent and indiscriminate, false witness and vested interest; even tribal dignitaries were being arrested and sucked into Abu Ghraib without process or paper trail, denied lawyers, interrogated, ignored, lost in the system for weeks while their families petitioned locked gates. The American commander in Hilla rotated and Adnan found he had no influence with his successor. In Baghdad he could not gain access to the local commanders at all.

People grew angry, unsettled. A Janabi imam denounced Adnan at Friday prayer: "Our sheikh: a collaborator!" The imam was banished by tribal council, barred from preaching by other imams, and Adnan sought out a meeting with him to confront his views. The preacher said to him, "I concede you are trying to help. But all these tribal leaders are useless. We have a new situation here. They are only looking after their own goats."

One night, a few months into the occupation, Adnan and his wife and his two grown sons were at home in Baghdad watching television. They heard a loud banging blast and rattling and then shouting. His home was being raided. Several American soldiers, oversized, bulked up with armored vests and combat webbing, helmets like storm troopers, night sights like metal mandibles, burst in. Adnan stood up to remonstrate but he was pushed by a shoving, gloved hand at the back of his neck, face down into the carpet.

We were sitting in Beirut, talking in a quiet bar, Adnan was drinking whiskey. When he told me this story he did not look at me, he looked down into his glass, at bitter brackish memory.

"They don't understand anything about our culture, nothing."

I said something sympathetic. I understood, I told him, about curdled pride—for the head of the family to be dishonored this way in front of his wife and sons—not the fear (no Iraqi ever admitted to fear), but the humiliation of it.

Adnan cut me off. "No. It is not the same." He was not any ordinary man suffering the indignity of occupation. He was a sheikh, a leader. "It was unacceptable," he insisted, "completely unacceptable."

Adnan never told anyone what had happened. He bent his pride and went on trying to work with the Americans within the framework of the ongoing political process, the efforts to write a constitution and prepare for a sovereign Iraqi government. He joined the government as a minister without portfolio, and allied himself to Ayad Allawi, who the Americans were positioning as a secular unifying Iraqi leader. At the end of March 2004, after four American contractors were attacked driving through Fallujah and the Americans surrounded the town with tanks, Adnan tried to negotiate between the Americans and a local insurgent leader who was a Janabi. The insurgent leader agreed to evict the foreign fighters in return for a ceasefire, but local *jihadi* firebrands called him a traitor and denounced any compromise.

"The moderates always lose after a while," Adnan lamented. He tried to talk to the "hotheads," but admonishment and reason were deflected with ideology. The tide had already turned, violence crashed into press conferences, and the insurgency made any political process moot, although no one yet admitted this. The Shia exile parties, the Dawa and SCIRI (Supreme Council for the Islamic Revolution in Iraq), the latter an Iranian protégé, held the ascendancy, local Shia factions (mostly the Mehdi army) armed themselves by joining the police force, then feuded and blew into revolt; and the Sunnis became embittered and enflamed and complained rancorously, to no apparent effect, that the Americans were taking sides.

IN JANUARY 2005, just before the first elections, I went to see Adnan in Baghdad at a house he rented in a guarded ministerial compound adjacent to the GreenZone. He said he would send an escort car with two of his bodyguards, and we arranged to meet them in a flat space of cracked asphalt underneath the Jadriyeh bridge. In the past it had been a place where husbands came to teach their wives how to drive, now it was an open-air speakeasy in defiance of Shia vigilantes who firebombed the alcohol shops. It was twilight, a guard-gunman waved us in. Men sat on the concrete parapet along the river with cans of beer in their hand or a small flask of arak in front of them, watching the purple dust dusk settle, sunset over the Tigris smudged with the black smoke from the Dora power station.

Adnan's bodyguards found us, signaled to follow them and we drove around the edge of the GreenZone, twelve foot high concrete blast walls on one side. At some point there was an opening and we turned right into a concrete canyon and stopped at a checkpoint. The bodyguards in the car ahead of us showed their passes and we were waved through, around another bend, slowed into a tank jack chicane, and waited behind another car being checked at the second checkpoint by Iraqi army soldiers. The two men in the car ahead held their arms out to be padded down. Above us was a watchtower on stilts fortified with sandbags. We got out of the car to show our identification and present our bags to be searched. I looked up, the concrete blast walls made a trench of narrowed sky edged with filigree razor wire. The soldiers finished searching the two men in the car ahead of us and handed them back their guns, a Kalashnikov to one, a pistol to the other, who stuffed it back in the waistband of his trousers.

The searched us perfunctorily. One of the soldiers excitedly pointed at his chest, making a joke.

"Saddam Hussein. Me Saddam Hussein!"

"Bah! Your mustache is not big enough!"

And he pointed to his ID, which showed that his name was indeed Saddam Hussein.

We found Adnan in a fury. He had just resigned from the cabinet.

"Oh the D.o.D. has its own ideas, they trample over everyone's heads. Practically everything that could go wrong happened. They actually made every single error they could have. What they say is correct. We *are* stooges of the Americans."

He had resigned in protest at all of the mess and manipulation and because the day before he had been arrested by a sneering and officious American sergeant at an entrance to the GreenZone where he was going for a meeting with the Deputy Prime Minister. The sergeant had looked at his pass and said it was no longer valid. Adnan asked to see his commanding officer, the sergeant became even ruder, Adnan asked his name and unit. The sergeant looked at his men, irritated and nonchalant, "I think he's gotta be arrested." So they pinned his arms behind his back and tied his hands with plastic flexi cuffs and showed no interest in his protestations.

Now he cursed his participation. Several of his relatives had been kidnapped and killed. He was used to driving himself, without bodyguards and unarmed. Now he traveled in a five car convoy with thirty gunmen, "And," he added, in sheer frustration rather than fear, "I am never safe!"

FOR A LONG time the civil war was called sectarian violence. It was piebald, bandit, vicious, hard to fathom and impossible to contain. Baghdad neighborhoods became cantons, separated by vigilante gunmen groups, berms, roadblocks, checkpoints, ID killings. Families (many of whom were mixed; it was common for Sunni to marry Shia) were labeled and then forced out of their homes at gunpoint. South of Baghdad Sunni and Shia were historically mingled around Latifiya and Mahmoudiya, Shia were hauled out of their cars on the roads and shot, reprisals, revenge, intimidation flared through the villages. Al-Qaeda in Mesopotamia mixed with local insurgent groups, the reconstituted Iraqi army, such as it was, seemed full of Shia thugs or Kurdish mercenaries. The area became known as the Triangle of Death.

Adnan was exhausted by the violence. "The Americans are murdering Janabis and the Janabis, whether they are Sunni or Shia, are murdering each other!" He swallowed a gulp of whiskey.

"And the Janabis are the worst!"

BEIRUT, ISRAELI BOMBS and its own civil disorder notwithstanding, was respite. By the summer of 2007, when I saw him, Adnan had relaxed into his exile. I met him in Paul for coffee and we sat surrounded by the Lebanese grandee class with its peacock women: high lacquered hair, arched eyebrows, lip liner and bronzed cleavage, Cartier watches looped around their wrists and Prada bags dangling from their fingers. Adnan and I laughed a little at the display; I noticed he himself had adopted resort wear: he was tanned and wore a crisp beige linen safari suit with no tie.

"I would rather be *chic* than sheikh," he joked, showing off his new sunglasses. "You see I am relaxed these days, I am doing practically nothing!" He handed me a business card with the name of the new think tank channeling technocratic expertise into policy and legislation suggestions for the Iraqi government. He shrugged, he said it kept his mind ticking over, his efforts engaged.

The civil war had entered the warlord phase. The news was consistently atrocious. Adnan admitted he could no longer bring himself to watch it; I said I could not either. There was no point even talking about it any more. Instead I asked him about his son Salam. He looked at his watch, not for the first time, I realized.

"He's at the airport. He should be getting on a plane to Amman soon—but, you know, always delays. Sometimes you have to spend all night at the airport if there's a security alert."

"But he's at the airport," I confirmed to encourage him, "so he got through the road alright."

"Yes, yes," Adnan nodded, "but this morning I was very nervous about it."

Salam had been in Baghdad for the previous four months, waiting to get a new G-series passport that would allow him to travel. The new G-series passports were gold dust in Iraq then, it was a year of exodus, hundreds of thousands of people had left their homes, many fled across the easiest border, to Syria. Salam had sensibly bribed someone in the passport office, but that person had been arrested and so they had to worry about Salam's name showing up on some blacklist and then they had to find other people to bribe. Finally, he had got the passport just three days before. Adnan said he didn't think Salam had left the house more than three times in the whole past four months.

"It's an Iraqi mess," I ventured. "Now it seems like an Iraqi mess even more than an American mess."

Adnan nodded. I widened the discussion. I said I had been reading to try to understand—the breakdown of society, moral collapse, barbarism, totalitarianism—not the books written now, in the contemporaneous maelstrom, but books from another time and place, from Stalin's Russia and the aftermath of the Nazis: the old school history trick of compare and contrast. I mentioned Solzhenitsyn.

"You know I could never finish *Gulag Archipelago*," he said.

I told him I couldn't either. "I mean I read it. But I could not read it as a whole beginning to end. It was too long, too terrible." We discussed parallels and insight, but the mirror was too sharp to be able to look at directly.

I said to him, "You know, what I always remember from the *Gulag Archipelago* is the beginning, when he describes how most people, officials, mid level men who knew what the system was because they were part of it, who sat in those new apparatchik apartment blocks in Moscow and watched their neighbors disappear and the apartments around them empty, sat at home and simply waited to be arrested, they did not flee or hide or disappear into some small town somewhere. Even when the knock came, they did not try to run or jump out of the window or get away . . ."

"Yes," said Adnan, "in '74 you know what I did when I had that call from Saddam? After I wrote the report about his oil selling deals during the embargo. I had a call from Saddam and he threatened me directly. Afterwards I left the office immediately. I collected my wife from her university campus, we collected Salam, he was small then, from kindergarten, and I drove around for several hours. My wife told me: whatever you decide I am with you. I had the possibility to go to the countryside or to Kurdistan because I had friends in the resistance there, and there was a mutiny in that year and you could get to an area which the government did not control—but I went home." He paused, evaluating. "It was a subconscious submission. I cannot rationalize it, even now. I went home and I stayed at home for two weeks."

Adnan explained that he found his own behavior all the more mystifying because he had plenty of experience of the consequences of a Saddam threat. He had been in the Communist Party, he had taken part in the violent demonstrations in Baghdad in 1956 and been shot at. In 1963, while the Baathies were having their first coup in Iraq, he was in London taking witness accounts of murder, rape and torture; Saddam's name had come up in conjunction with the execution of a Janabi who was a Communist friend of his. He knew the Iranian opposition to the Shah, he had connections with the Algerian NLF, in Iraq in 1961 and 1962 he had met Kurds in the North.

"So I knew the game. I knew the underground and its violence. But in '74 when I was threatened I went home. I don't know. I really don't know why. I used to try and rationalize this behavior, but I don't think it's useful any more."

In trying to comfort him, I began to tell him about the Stanford Prison Experiment and Stanley Milgram. In the early sixties Stanley Milgram, then a social psychologist at Yale, had devised an experiment to test for the human hardwiring of obedience to authority. He gathered unsuspecting volunteers from the nearby town of New Haven, working class men, middle class women, a priest, a few students—a random enough mix— on the pretext of gathering research on how punishment affected learning. The volunteers were shown into a room with a board of electrical switches and a man in a white coat who oversaw and explained the procedure. In the next room was another man, ostensibly a volunteer, strapped into a chair. They were to ask him questions from a sheet of paper they were given and if they received a wrong answer they were to administer an electric shock to the subject. The board displayed a series of switches labeled from 15V "slight shock"; beyond 375V, "danger: severe shock"; to 450V, marked only "X X X." With each wrong answer the subject was to receive an incremental increase of voltage.

The subject was portrayed as a volunteer, but in fact he was in on the experiment. There was no real electricity applied to his fingertips and he had a careful script to follow. He began by producing a few wrong answers and suffering the resulting "shocks." As the shocks increased, he acted out more and more discomfort. He yelped and cried out, then screamed, then begged to be let out of the chair, then sobbed and let it be known he had a heart condition and that he was worried, then screamed agonizingly, then went silent and eventually, at 350 volts, became inert and unresponsive.

The purpose of the scenario was to see how far each person would agree to go along with the experiment. Most people (although not all) voiced disquiet at some point. Then they would invariably look over to the technician in the white coat and ask what they should do since the man was obviously in pain. The technician was scripted to assure the volunteer that the shocks, while undoubtedly painful, would cause no permanent tissue damage and repeat four sentences in order: "Please continue," "The experiment requires that you continue," "It is absolutely essential that you continue," and, "You have no choice, you must go on."

In these empirical scenarios, there was no coercion, nor sanction if the subject refused to continue to shock the "learner." The subject was told, for example, they would still receive their small stipend for participating. Over several weeks Milgram recorded that more than 60 percent of good and ordinary folk from New Haven continued to administer increasing amounts of clearly painful electric shocks, even as the subject appeared to lapse into unconsciousness, until the end of the switches and 450 volts had been delivered three times.

Milgram tried different set-ups and conditions for the experiment: he varied the proximity between "teacher" and "learner"; he put another, more sympathetic, person in the room with the technician and the subject; he moved the whole thing away from the auspices of Yale University, in case its hallowed reputation was influencing compliance. Each variation brought a slightly different set of results. A greater percentage of people found it easier to shock the "learner" the farther away from him he was, i.e., behind a wall or in a soundproof room. If other people, "peers," in the room also questioned the necessity of continuing the experiment then a greater percentage of volunteers refused to continue and refused to continue earlier in the process.

Milgram found that the social context, the effect of "peers" creating a group reaction, could counteract the general determination to obey authority, but over the years the experiment has been repeated in different countries and cultures with different age and socioeconomic groups. Most people, when asked in polls, don't believe that anyone would continue shocking a civilian "learner" just because they were told to do so by someone wearing a white coat. In fact New Haven's 60 percent compliance rate in the experiment at Yale turned out to be, in global terms, on the low side. Philip Zimbardo, picking up on Milgram's research in his own efforts to understand "The Lucifer Effect," made another point. He noted that none of Milgram's volunteers refused to do the experiment from the beginning, all of them began the process of pushing switches which delivered increasing voltage to the "learner" and that even among the subjects who stood up and refused to continue because they felt they could not be part of something which was causing pain to another person, not one went to the aid of the shocked learner or attempted to intervene by going to higher authorities to demand that the whole experiment be stopped.

When I read Milgram, I was very impressed with the idea that obedience to authority was a learned cognitive behavior that ran through almost every society.

"It seems empirically clear," I told Adnan, "that most people do what they are told for no other reason than they are told to do it." He listened, amazed, and nodded.

"This idea is helping me on some soul searching!"

"I am beginning to see that perhaps Iraqis are not crazy Arabs after all—imagine!" I said laughing, "They might be just ordinary human beings!" Adnan laughed back, "Yes, but all the same, they *are* crazy Arabs!"

"Solzhenitsyn said that there is a line separating good from evil that runs through every man."

"Yes," said Adnan, more serious now, but uplifted, as I was, by the emerging sunlit thought that there was perhaps, a universal morality, as there was a universal condition. "Human nature is the same," he said. "People are not good because they are taught in school to be good, there is a cultural impact over generations to make people comply, certain things are not acceptable, these norms are sanctioned under authority . . . Iraqis are repressed and exposed to violence; it's not strange to see what is happening now. The Americans don't represent authority and the Iraqis perceive them only as representing random violence."

He told me that two days previously his house in the safe VIP compound adjacent to the GreenZone in Baghdad had been raided by American soldiers looking for one of his men who was not there. The soldiers took laptops and documents and stole $7,000, the life savings of one of his bodyguards who had kept them in the office because he thought they would be safe there.

"I think," I told him, "that the Americans are no more uncivilized than the Iraqis are uncivilized." Adnan smiled and took my hands in gratitude across the table.

"Yes," he agreed, tenderly holding the thought, "I think we are all the same."

Chapter 13

SHAME

ADNAN'S ELDER BROTHER, WHO HAD BEEN SHEIKH before him, was called Khalid; Kamel Sachet also had a brother named Khalid. No one ever spoke well of him. Most people dismissed him as living off his elder brother's uniform, a marginal, inveigling, figure.

"He drank a lot," a Janabi Istikhbarat officer once told me, shaking his head. "He was totally unlike his brother. Khalid was crazy."

At the end of 1999 Khalid fled to Jordan and made a public defection, claiming he had been an officer in the Mukhabarat (according to the Janabi Istikhbarat officer he had only ever been a driver) and offering information against Saddam's regime to the Jordanian intelligence services and Western journalists.

One day, during a Google trawl, I idly typed the name Khalid Janabi, hoping to understand a little bit more about Adnan's brother's death in Rome—Adnan had information from senior figures, rumors, bits of witness and suspicion, but he didn't like to talk about his theories—and instead came up with the transcript of an interview given by Khalid Sachet calling himself, more anonymously, by his tribal moniker, Khalid

al-Janabi, to Radio Free Iraq, part of the American government's Liberty Radio Network.

"Khalid al-Janabi" told how he had been part of an exterminating force ordered by Qusay to kill 2,000 prisoners in Abu
Ghraib in the spring of 1998 to relieve overcrowding. He recounted how the prisoners had been hanged one after another
in the five execution chambers; there were so many that they
delegated a group of specially designated prisoners to shoot
some in a separate room. He also described in detail how the
Mukhabarat blackmailed senior army officers by sexually com-
promising their wives and daughters.

> *Khalid:* . . . When the officer leaves the house, they go
> in and plant a camera in the chandelier. You know of
> these things of course. It is like the head of a pin called
> the fish's eye, which can photograph the whole room.
> Or they plant a recording device, very small of course.
> This is very sensitive, and anything said in the room, we
> hear it and record it. The voice is altered. On the video,
> we of course see and record everything with his wife, his
> moves, everything. This of course when the woman goes
> to the house, if the [officer's] wife goes along with it,
> fine. Otherwise, she is forced. We have the kidnapping
> operation. Her daughter leaves the house. We have a car
> to pick her up. We have special houses with swimming
> pools in Al-Jadriyeh, Al-Habbaniyah and other places.
> Each is prepared with a room fully loaded with video
> equipment. They violate the daughter if they are able
> to get her, or the wife, and a complete documentary is
> recorded. Then they tell her that they have the movie.
>
> *Q:* They tell them!

Khalid: Yes, yes. I will tell you later how they threaten the officer. And they tell her that if she does not cooperate, they will show it to the officer and that would tell the officer that his wife is such and such and then they show him a cassette. You know, an officer whose face is covered with layers of battle dust does not submit to someone telling him his daughter called so and so! You know that we are raised on manners and honor. He does not take it. So, they keep such tapes. This process begins when the person becomes an officer until he becomes a commander.

Q: What is the objective? What is the goal of this entire process?

Khalid: The objective is when the person becomes an officer. When I and other officers told my brother, the general, in 1982, he of course did not believe it.

Q: Did you tell him?

Khalid: Yes, yes, I told him, my dear brother, true, you are in a high position and big commander, but we at the intelligence system have pulled the rug out from under your feet. He said that there is no such thing. I told him, fine, I will prove it to you. One day when I was duty officer at the Technical Branch, I pulled out a movie of one of the officers who is still in the state apparatus. I cannot tell you his name. We had a video at home and told the . . . general.

Q: You mean Major General Kamel?

Khalid: Yes, Major General Kamel Sachet, my . . . brother. So, I told him I wanted to show him a video. I played the tape, and he saw only a part, and told me to turn it off.

Q: Did he see?

Khalid: Yes, he saw the officer, the daughter, and what they did to her. This was not a matter of a composite video or any thing. The act of rape was very clear. He said turn it off.

Khalid is not a reliable witness, but I quote this interview to illustrate the invidious techniques devised by Saddam's regime to terrorize and marshal its own officers. There were three concentric walls built to defend the fortress of obedience. The innermost wall was crenellated with the consequences of torture, imprisonment and execution. The middle wall was built of heavy threat bricks against family members. "We will kill you whatever happens, but you can spare her by confessing," they would tell some bloody, beaten, shocked man forced to confront the scene of his wife or sister or daughter whimpering under the black and blue grip of a squad of lascivious Amn thugs. The outer wall was made out of videotape and photographs, eavesdropped transcripts and dossiers, and was designed not to repel so much as to ensnare, and by binding and entangling, disable any further assault on the dictator-keep.

Violation, blackmail. The disgrace of a female family member is the greatest dishonor an Iraqi can endure. The shame could stain an entire family. Sisters would be refused by eminent suitors, perhaps the best they could hope for in the shadow of a scandal would be some ugly, poor cousin willing to debase himself for a cash enticement. Brothers would be humiliated, their positions within their tribe and community compromised and sullied. It is a wound that we in the West, long unbonded from the idea of the extended family as a collective of social, financial and moral responsibility, cannot really understand. But dishonor remains, for many Iraqis, a nasty flesh wound, a laceration that suppurates and scars and takes a very long time, sometimes a generation or more, to heal.

Chapter 14

PRIDE

ABOVE ALL KAMEL SACHET TRIED TO PROTECT his family.

By the mid nineties, the net was closing. The Sachets' phone was bugged—this they took for granted—and there was often a car parked outside with two men watching. When he rose early to drive to the mosque for dawn prayer an agent on a bicycle followed him. The surveillance permeated the house and kept the family under protracted strain. Sometimes the telephone would start ringing at one or two in the morning but when it was answered no one was on the line. One day all the keys to the house disappeared; they changed all the locks but it was chilling to think someone had stolen into the house to take them. Their back gate neighbors moved out and were replaced by an odd household of men who seemed to be spying on them. Kamel Sachet warned his children there were microphones in the house and informers among their close friends. Fewer visitors came and when they did there were ellipses and sideways remarks and superficial pleasantries instead of conversation. At night Kamel Sachet instituted a system of watches, just like he was on a battlefield expecting an enemy attack, so that someone in the house was always awake. It was difficult to sleep through the tension, any noise or voice would make them sit up in their beds, waiting for the knock. Um Omar suffered from headaches and insomnia.

"I could tell by his face that he was angry," she told me. "I said to him, why are you angry?" But he would only answer, "How do you know I am angry?" and refuse to discuss anything further. Kamel Sachet kept his face in a mask and tried to brazen it out with his self belief that was in fact only his belief in his trust in Saddam.

More than once he saw a white sedan in his rear-view mirror and riled, stopped his car and walked back to confront the agents. He even dared to complain to Saddam's secretary: "Why am I being followed?"

Saddam's secretary blithely told him that it was for his own protection.

One morning Dr. Hassan spotted Kamel Sachet's Mercedes ahead of him on the highway as he was driving to work. He did not want to drive up alongside him and wave, it would seem rude and brief, so he hung back and tried to drive slowly. For several kilometers Kamel Sachet also drove slowly, he had noticed the car following him. Dr. Hassan decided to end this awkward chase by pulling into a petrol station for a few moments, but when he drove off again he soon caught up with Kamel Sachet. Finally he ended up drawing alongside him at a traffic light. Kamel Sachet turned and recognized his old friend and when Dr. Hassan explained his embarrassment the two of them laughed like boys with relief.

But the shoulder hunch knotted. Dr. Hassan said that in these years the only times he was able to talk openly with Kamel Sachet was when he came to his office and Kamel would release his driver from waiting so that he would have an excuse to ask him for a lift home and they could chat in the car. When they arrived at his house, Kamel no longer invited him in. Dr. Hassan said once or twice he tried to urge him to leave the country, but that he always refused to consider flight. "Let them arrest me. I have nothing to be afraid of because I have done nothing wrong."

He drew his family close under siege. He would not let Ali join the army although national service was obligatory. Ali admired the strutting officers he saw visiting his father, he envied their pistols and their new cars, their privilege and superiority. He asked his father if he could enroll in the Military College, but his father refused, stating unequivocally the inversion and negation of the value of the entire patriotic effort of his career: "Those who become close to them become criminals just like them." To get Ali out of conscription Dr. Hassan wrote a report stating that Ali Sachet was suffering from depression and was mentally unfit for service. The Amn came to ask him questions about this, but he defended his diagnosis and the investigation lapsed.

Shadwan had gone on to university after completing high school, but Kamel Sachet forbade it for his younger daughters. He said that the universities were not safe places, especially for girls, that male students would try to befriend them or lure them—they were the daughters of a man in his position—and he could not allow it.

Amani was tall and pale and wan and she limped slightly when she walked. I saw her several times at the Sachet house, she would smile shyly in greeting, but she never spoke to me directly except to nod *Salam aleikum* and she never came down to sit and chat as the other members of the family did. Something had happened that could not be talked about. Whatever it was—or wasn't: I have no desire to repeat rumor and falsehoods here—it should have been a private family matter. But Kamel Sachet had made too many enemies in the regime who wished to exploit his discomfort, undermine his position, provoke his temper with conspiracies and cast suspicion on his loyalty. In that ratting atmosphere, a scandal splintered into stabbing mirror shards that reflected the shadows and searchlights, some real, some spectral: Mukhabarat agents, Iranian Shia spies, Saddam himself.

"What happened with Amani was the major thing that destroyed Kamel Sachet," Dr. Hassan told me, sitting in his Abu Dhabi office. "For something to happen with a daughter is a very big thing according to Arab mentality. Even if his son Omar had died it would have been easier for him. The thing with Amani was a catastrophe."

Kamel Sachet was in torment over it. When it first happened, Dr. Hassan found his friend sitting in the dark alone, unshaven. The atmosphere was bitter and funereal. He saw that the general was close to tears, white with anger; his shock seemed to be beyond bereavement. He saw his strong brave friend crack.

"It would have been better if she had died," said Kamel Sachet simply.

Dr. Hassan saw the danger of his retribution and reasoned with him, "Think of your duties as a father before Allah, believe in your own mercy and trust in the will of Allah."

Sheikh Adnan, like Dr. Hassan, tried to calm him, to rationalize and soothe.

"The wisest thing to do, Kamel," he told him, "is not to blow up the issue. As a believer, you know sometimes things happen to test the moral mettle of people. Allah would not ask you to shoulder something that you could not manage."

Kamel Sachet found little solace in his words. The kingdom of God was a far dream, in the meantime he had to navigate the social fall out, weft and warp, tribe and party.

"I need not only to pray to God, I need the understanding of my people," he said.

Adnan offered him the advice of wise men, he exhorted his friend to "handle the situation humanely." He reminded him that death was not sanctioned by the Koran, it was an older Bedu salve, it was an anachronism. . .

AFTER SEVERAL MONTHS of public and private anguish Amani fell out of a second-story window and into a coma. Her legs had absorbed the brunt of the fall, her feet were broken up, a femur was cracked, she had internal bleeding, a ruptured spleen and a fractured skull. Suddenly, all of Kamel Sachet's bitterness was washed away with the crisis. He went from hospital to hospital summoning doctors and specialists for second opinions and he became again just a father who wanted to help and protect his daughter. He asked Dr. Hassan to talk to doctors to help him understand the complications of her medical condition. For a long time it was not clear that she would wake up and if she woke up whether she would be brain damaged and if she had her mind intact whether she would walk. Kamel Sachet prayed hard for her survival. He did everything he could to get her the medical care and attention she needed. Dr. Hassan was surprised. "He was not angry. I saw him as a kind father. He was anxious. He did not betray any guilt; guilt would have been an alien emotion to him, but this was the other side of the coin, the worried parent."

He stayed by her side for many days and after two weeks, when she finally came out of the coma, he made sure her mother could visit her often. Dr. Hassan tried to explain to me the trauma he observed in his friend, but he said he was not a social psychiatrist and his English could not master the technical terms.

"Honor is very important for any Arab man. For a good man. And for Kamel Sachet, a famous general, a hero, it was something even more. Honor included his whole family. These are the kind of men who would not even tolerate talk about their daughters . . . it is the structure of the Arab personality, it depends on honor and on the honor of their women."

Kamel Sachet never really recovered his old self: even after Amani had returned home and learned to walk again in convalescence, the episode seared him like a brand that was stamped onto the pages of reports that found their way to the desk of the director of Qusay's Special Amn. He withdrew from people and kept away even from those he had been close to. When his friends asked him why he no longer encouraged visitors, he told them, "to avoid the problems." Dr. Hassan saw less and less of him. When he went to his house one of his sons would tell him Kamel was away even though he could see his car parked outside. He thought perhaps Kamel wished to protect him, that association would bring him also under suspicion. Dr. Hassan had a cousin who was a neighbor of the Sachets and he told him that there was always a Mukhabarat car parked on the corner.

"One time," remembered Shadwan of that difficult period, "he was going to the farm near Hilla with his driver. He had fallen asleep and when he woke up, out of the blue he said, 'Qusay is going to kill me.' Maybe it was the end of a dream."

Chapter 15

WAITING

KAMEL SACHET'S APPREHENSION WAS BOUND TO Saddam's. Security was a noose that tightened into a garrote. The closer to the throne, the greater the risk. Dr. Hassan had described the atmosphere of fear in the later Saddam era, ever thicker paranoia, dread, a constant unbroken tension—suspicion, surveillance, cars in the rear view mirror, agents, eavesdropping, reports . . . But a general could never debase himself with fear. Whatever that stomach prickling feeling was, Kamel Sachet suppressed it.

It was a time of plots and plotters and the conspiracies Saddam imagined were real enough. The senior military commanders had never recovered their faith in him after the Kuwait disaster and the subsequent cull; Saddam knew this and was careful to keep their power in check. He kept the regular army in the provinces, diluted with conscription and pressed volunteers, effectively starved of weapons and resources. Even the Republican Guard found their status slipping in favor of the new regiments of Saddam Fedayeen, Saddam's men of sacrifice, commanded by Uday, who swore loyalty not to Iraq but to its president. These units were raised throughout Iraq but Saddam kept a cohort of them close, a personal paramilitary bodyguard death squad, and fattened their officers with bounties of cash, land, and Toyota pick-ups. Throughout the nineties, the years of constriction, a steady stream of disgruntled senior commanders, men who had fought through the Iran-Iraq war, who had survived Kuwait, left, walked through minefields, smuggled in the boots of cars into Kurdistan or bribed exit visas and drove across the desert to Jordan. The defector-traitors told and sold information (real, exaggerated and bullshit) to the CIA and the Jordanian General Intelligence Department, UNSCOM (United Nations Special Commission) and the IAEA (International Atomic Energy Agency) or to the Kurds or Saudi agents or Iranian middlemen in exchange for cash, stipends, backing, visas, residency permits, passports for their families and protection.

Saddam was penned between two no fly zones, militarily emasculated by the teams of UN weapons inspectors destroying missile stockpiles and any nuclear and biological capabilities he may have hung on to, and impoverished by sanctions. Meantime machination abroad: exile groups and parties, the Shia militias backed by Iran, the Kurds in their rivalrous, but *de facto* independent northern crescent, the old scions—Chalabi, Allawi, various pretenders to the throne—mingled with the new defecting arrivals, set up think tanks and committees, wrote political manifestos and reports, went to conferences, lunched chummily with their friends in Washington, smoked cigars with the mandarins in Whitehall, entertained journalists with their own agendas. Each boasted of networks and support within Iraq; much of it was power dreaming, they could say anything when there was no voice to contradict them; those who remained in Iraq were locked in isolation and no one could ask their opinions.

⟨◆⟩

ADNAN JANABI HAD told me to look up Nabil Janabi when I was next in London. Nabil Janabi was a Janabi acquaintance of his; "He has some television program now, he is kind of a player, he knew Kamel Sachet, he might be able to tell you something about him."

I found Nabil Janabi's number through a friend and we arranged to meet at a café on the Edgware Road. I recognized him immediately; he looked like the synthesis of his middle-aged exile demographic: dyed black hair (for the television cameras), beige suit, mustache, cigar. He wore a badge on the lapel of his suit: "I love Iraq" written across the outline of his country. He was helpful, genial, pleased with himself and talked in vague self-aggrandizing terms. He had reinvented himself as a presenter on an Iraqi cable news channel, hosting a daily show of interviews and views. He told me it was the most popular television program in all of Iraq. "All Iraqis, they love me!" He received thousands of emails every day, his mobile rang constantly from Baghdad, from Diala, Mosul, friends, contacts and well-wishers. "They call me the father of Iraq!" he declared, pumping his platform, "I have a great vision for Iraq . . . I am under pressure to return . . . I have told Prime Minister al-Maliki this: 'I know all of Iraq now.'—He doesn't hear as much of Iraq as I hear!" He revealed that there was a secret meeting convening in Iraq of "several groups" who wanted to promote him as a new leader of Iraq, someone who could negotiate with the Americans for them, "We will have a new general election, reconciliation! Not this false al Maliki reconciliation!"

He smiled, mock self-deprecating, as if to say, it was a long shot, yes, but who else could save the country?

His English was accented with a genial growl as he outlined his biography for me, careful to highlight the key self-mythologized episodes and characteristics that Iraqi men of his generation valued: poetry writing, intelligence, bravery, financial success, respect and popularity. I had listened to other stories like Nabil Janabi's; always roughly the same three acts: Life in Iraq, Prison, Flight.

He grew up in Baghdad well-off and well connected. In his youth he pursued intellectual passions and on 26 February 1976 he was arrested for writing a seditious poem entitled "Blue Democracy." (Iraqis often don't know their own birthdays, but they always seem to remember exactly, clearly and without hesitation, the date on which they were arrested, the date on which they were released, and the date on which they left Iraq; such are the real milestones of an Iraqi lifetime.) He told me he had laughed at the judge who sentenced him to eight years, been released after two years during a Presidential Amnesty, then set up a construction-import-export company ("I was so successful in that business. I became rich enough to help the sons of the needy!"), which the government subsequently closed, claiming he was using the premises for illegal meetings. By 1982 he was under almost constant surveillance when a Janabi cousin of his, who was an Amn Colonel, told him he had received the order for his arrest. Because they were relatives, he said, he could "lose" the warrant on his desk for three days, but no longer.

Escape stories vary in their details, but they are usually abetted by conniving corruption and end in a heart stopping traverse, across a minefield or a checkpoint or a border. In the next forty eight hours, Nabil found another Janabi relative in the passport office to issue him with an urgent passport under his grandfather's name, managed to get an on-the-spot visa from the Lebanese embassy and bought a ticket to Beirut via

Amman. He asked his Colonel cousin to give him an Amn officer to escort him through the airport because he was worried Mukhabarat officers stationed in the terminal would recognize him. This Amn officer wanted his brand new Mercedes for payment. Nabil told him he couldn't give him the Mercedes because it was in his brother's name; the Amn officer then said he wanted money, $10,000. Nabil got him down to $7,000. 25 February 1982. His brother drove him to the airport and the paid-off Amn officer escorted him inside and then he waited, hiding in the toilet, until the last call for the Middle East Airlines flight to Beirut, his heart thumping, nerves taut. He carried only a briefcase containing $50,000 in cash and three kilos of gold.

He got off the plane in Amman, almost delirious with stress and exhausted with adrenaline. He could still see his brother waving through the terminal window and he could still hear the Amn officer telling him never to come back or they would kill him for sure. He went to a hotel and collapsed on the bed with his mind veering freedom. "And then I was the happiest man in the world." He stopped and caught himself; he had not told his wife he was leaving or said goodbye to his children. "But still not very happy."

The Amn officer who had accompanied him at the airport, Nabil added, as postscript, was executed some years later.

He was eventually granted asylum in Britain and he lived twenty years, the patched up half-life of the exile. Back in Iraq, his wife was forced to divorce him and his children were always denied exit visas. He settled in London, studied at the Open University and eventually gained a Ph.D. in linguistics from London University. In time he remarried an Iraqi woman and had two daughters. He kept in touch with the Iraqi community abroad. He saw Jalal Talabani, leader of the PUK (Patriotic Union) faction of the Kurds when he visited London and formed a connection with the Jordanian Royal family. "King Hussein was a close friend." He wrote articles for Arab newspapers calling for regime change and democracy in Iraq and passed on information heard through the exile network and those go-betweens who traveled in and out of Iraq, to the British intelligence service MI6 (on at least one occasion that he admitted to me) and the Americans and the Jordanians.

He was involved. He penned articles and letters, published bits of poetry, connected connections, phone calls, old friends, networks of dissidence and proto-politics. He tried to find links and paths between the outside and the inside, but it was always fraught. Phone calls were monitored, expensive and cracked by terrible lines, fax machines were in the ministries and subject to power cuts and paper shortages, email was virtually non existent. Messages passed friend to friend, cousin to cousin, ear to mouth, but communication of any real kind was slight. Everyone wanted to get rid of Saddam—kill or coup—but still he remained, as implacably absurd as a heavy stone at the center of a web.

In the nineties, Nabil recounted, he visited Sweden several times to send letters from a neutral postmark, part of a broad letter writing campaign, urging officials and officers inside the regime to organize themselves against Saddam. One time he posted three thousand pamphlets exhorting democracy from several post boxes around Stockholm. Nabil Janabi's grandfather had been Sheikh of the Albu Hassoun subdivision of the Janabi tribe, and it was through this family connection that he had known Kamel Sachet well as a young man. He told me that in July 1998 he sent, from Sweden, a handwritten note addressed to Kamel Sachet's address in Saidiya. He knew Kamel Sachet's reputation and standing among the military class from other exiled officers and he hoped to enlist his leadership. He did not write Kamel Sachet's name on the envelope, nor did he sign the letter; recipient and sender were thus anonymous, and no interlocutor was used. "Between two people there can be a secret," explained Nabil, "but between three?—No." Kamel Sachet, he hoped, he claimed, would recognize his handwriting and know, in turn, that Nabil, his old friend and relative, was close to the Jordanian Royal Family and lived in London and therefore his missive would carry the implicit support of these two governments. Kamel Sachet was undoubtedly too intelligent to fall for such a ruse. The letter asked, in general terms, to try to coordinate a cadre of opposition officers.

In August of 1998 Saddam expelled the UN inspection teams as spies. By November he had, under American pressure, allowed them back in again. In the interim he reorganized his national defenses in the face of expected air strikes. Kamel Sachet was appointed to an advisory role with Ali Hassan al-Majid's command of the south. Kamel Sachet never really took up this position, he either refused point blank to serve under Ali Hassan al-Majid, who he reviled, or he simply remained in Baghdad, attending strategy meetings in the Presidency as required.

In the early autumn of that year, Nabil Janabi went to Amman, on one of his regular trips. There he met a Janabi relative who brought him a message from Kamel Sachet. *He had the "amana," the thing he had given him to keep, was still with him.* By this Nabil understood that he had received the letter.

After this, Nabil had no further communication or news from Kamel Sachet. He heard only rumors, and it was hard to know which ones were true. He continued his exile efforts, kept his close connection to elements of the Jordanian Royal Family and befriended Khalid, Kamel Sachet's brother, when he was living in Amman in 2000 after his "defection." Khalid had his own theories and version of events, but these, Nabil knew, were also second-hand.

TIME PASSED, TIMES changed. When the American tanks rolled into Baghdad, Nabil was poised, like so many Iraqis, to go home. But he went home, like so many Iraqis, as a foreigner, backed by foreigners, with a foreign agenda. He carried a British passport and had money from a Jordanian prince to set up a monarchist party to push their own pretender candidate (there were several disseminated Hashemite princes floating around since the monarchy had been deposed in Iraq in 1958). He found Khalid in prison (on some kind of conspiracy charge) and had him released to his own custody and appointed him his head of security. They took several gunmen and a convoy of landcruisers and drove across the broken border garrisoned by a few uninterested American soldiers, passed the smashed portraits of Saddam, across that long featureless desert, fast down the highway through Ramadi and Fallujah—because there were always a bunch of bandits ready to rob travelers—to the airport outskirts of the capital, the empty sand-concrete military bases still painted with the Iraqi military flag entwined with the Palestinian flag, the blue and white striped traffic police posts, wreckage, black twisted burned cars, kids yelping, a tank impaled by its own turret.

For exiles the return was salutary. They knew it would be bad, they had talked to relatives and watched the news, but when they saw, with their own eyes, the extent of the collapse—Iraq reduced to third world; it looked like Africa! Rackety generators, lakes of sewage, ragged kids in the streets, mounds of fly blown garbage, lumpen empty tracts of construction scarred suburb, and so many women covered in black! And where were the old bars and the restaurants they used to go to? Where was the life? The park along the river where they remembered family picnics and fish restaurants was now un-kempt and blocked by two American tanks and coils of razor wire. And the people! What had happened to people? Iraqis used to laugh and tease each other and extend their hospital-ity with largesse at every opportunity and now: what was this sullenness, this resentment, these shifty dark glances, too many lies and their lies were so obvious! ("No, *habibe*, I was never in the Party!") And always always they wanted money, and more money as if you were an ATM machine! And then all they did was complain: Why were they not given this? Why had they not received that? And the checkpoints and the curfew and the electricity cuts and no jobs and where were they going to get their car registered now that the ministry annex had been looted by "those Kuwaiti gangs"? One Iraqi, who had lived two decades in Vienna, told me, "I don't recognize these people any more; it's as if I had nothing in common with them."

Nabil described his homecoming dabbing his leaky eyes with the corner of a white handkerchief.

"They killed sheep of course, they shot in the air. A nephew came up, 'Do you remember me?' and he had gray hair! I wanted to sleep on the roof but they told me it was risky—gunfire. My youngest child was nine months old when I left and I found him a qualified engineer!" He stopped himself in remembrance of the long hard Saddam night, but those days of 2003, when things seemed open and possible had vanished too.

"Saddam was bad," he said, as everyone did, exile or not, "but this regime is worse. Worse!" And he wiped his eyes again. "Khalid?" No, he could not find Khalid. Khalid had been killed sometime in the latter months of 2004. Shot on the street. Nabil wasn't more forthcoming, he said he didn't know who killed him, stories were vague, gunmen . . . Mehdi Army . . . Nabil had left Baghdad by then—no one was interested in a monarchy. Bombs, Shia groups everywhere, too many revenge assassinations, "Well, you know how it went"—and returned to London.

Chapter 16

THE CARCASS OF AN ABANDONED REFRIGERATOR

AT 7 A.M., ON 16 DECEMBER 1998, LIEUTENANT Colonel Khalid Obeid bin Walid, head of a section of Abu Ghraib prison, woke in the narrow single bed in his office. Stretched his barrel pugilistic frame, rubbed his stubble chin. Lt. Colonel Walid had the meticulous habits of an army officer, proud and polished, but as a Director in the Amn, he dressed in civilian clothes. He always wore a tie ("Always, always!" he told me, chopping his hand vertically, definite, nostalgic for his more sartorial days), he polished his brown loafers every morning, his Chevrolet was kept clean and shining. On this morning he washed his face in the basin in the adjoining bathroom and put on one of the brown suits that he favored. On his bedside table was a book by an Arab author called *The School of Spying*, about the practices and methods of the KGB. Next to it was the gold watch that had been a gift from the Governor of Mosul; he picked it up and checked the time.

He had a wedding ring on his finger and three children and a pleasant home in the Western suburbs of Baghdad, but had slept at the office that night because the Amn had been placed on maximum alert. The Americans had threatened bombing and their bombs were expected. For three days he had been accommodating Amn prisoners evacuated from different Amn offices in Baghdad. Four hundred prisoners had to be found room for in his section, which usually housed 3,500 prisoners in conditions of such extreme overcrowding that fifty or sixty men were routinely crammed into cells built for eight. Prisoners slept on the floor because there were not enough bunks, on the steps of the staircases that connected two tiers of barracks-halls if they were lucky. Lt. Colonel Walid had cleared one hall, redistributed its inhabitants and told the Baghdad Amn officers their prisoners could be put there. He did not concern himself with food or other amenities; these were a matter for his Baghdad colleagues.

IN THE RETELLING of this day, Walid displayed the usual flourishes and gestures of the Baathie: a florid, jovial expansiveness, finger splay and jabbing or slapping the table. His hand would sweep into an upturned palm and then flick like he was waving, for emphasis. Gesticulations that dismissed as they explained.

"What could I do?" "It was like this!" "This was usual then!"

He was forty-five when I met him in May 2006, fleshy, but still trim. A striped gray suit and a shirt, well dressed enough, but poor now; his shoes were scuffed. He was seeking political asylum in Britain and living in the grim northern town of Middlesbrough. After the war he had worked for the Interior Ministry and found himself on Shia and Sunni death lists. His garage was blown up and he had fled, smuggled across Turkey and through Europe in the back of lorries, thousands of dollars paid to the traffickers, landed in Liverpool and presented himself to the authorities. He had come to London to meet me and attend some other business and we talked over a whole afternoon up and down the Araby Edgware Road, in the basement of the Costa Coffee opposite the British Islamic Bank, in a restaurant over plates of stewed okra and gravy and rice, in a teahouse with brass tray tables and *shisha* pipes.

In his reduced circumstances, as a refugee, he had changed his name to Walid and shaved off his Iraqi Baathie mustache, into a strip of bristle. It was as if he could not quite bear to shave it off completely and needed a comfort reminder of the past, a tactile touchpoint. As he talked, I checked his face, jowls and dewlaps, the aging lines and expression for a sign of casual barbarity. He had a faint pox scar on one cheek, a deep trench in his nasal labial fold, a crease in one earlobe. His lips were wet and mobile, easy to laugh, quick to joke, genial, but there was a darker occluded cast behind his brown eyes and when he stopped talking he would hold my gaze for a moment before looking down. As he folded his arms against his chest, flat and defensive, I thought I could discern guilt—no, not guilt, that would have been impossible, too devastating to admit, to articulate, to allow, to even suspect. I looked carefully: hoped I could see that there were things that were difficult to think about because there might be chinks of unease in them, things which he hid from himself, an emotion folded between the images of a lost memory—but I suspected that this was my own imposition, wishful thinking. In general we had a nice friendly chat, and who among those Arabs, single men, mostly, along the Edgware Road, that day or any day, did not have scarred souls, long journeys, complicated motives and the shadows that accompany lives that have been lived between tribe-dictator father, bride fight-flight and the internal-external dichotomy, the face shown to the world and the unacknowledged private ego. In every brown face I could see an existential dislocation;

these were men who had left behind a country that was dreadful enough to abandon but which made them homesick, and found themselves in a city that was freezing cold, unbelievably expensive and faintly hostile.

"I do not like England, to be honest," Walid told me. "I do not like Middlesbrough."

In December 1998 he had enjoyed his status, his privilege and his position. A cushion, a smugness; he held himself in confidence. A servant brought his breakfast of tea, yogurt and eggs and afterward he drove to his office. It was his routine to listen to the report of the night duty officer and then take the report in hand and investigate, walking the corridors checking.

There might have been a prisoner escape overnight, for example. A group of prisoners would distract the guards by chatting to them, telling them jokes or cadging cigarettes and then the escaping prisoner would sneak past them and wait until the dead of night to creep between guard posts. Once outside the blocks he would watch the guards up in the watch towers around the perimeter and when one came down to take a piss, get some more matches or some food, he would climb up and jump over the wall. One morning, Lt. Colonel Walid had to disentangle the problem of a prisoner who had assumed the identity of a friend of his he knew was going to be set free by drugging him and presenting himself for release. After the deception had been discovered, Lt. Colonel Walid had to release the real prisoner and face the embarrassment of having let the wrong man go.

Sometimes there had been fights between the prisoners who made knives from pipes and dismantled iron bed struts and sharpened them to points by scraping them on concrete and

wrapped shoe leather into handles. These fights could be fatal;
one night six prisoners were killed, another time prisoners
took over their section so that the guards could not enter for
three days. This violence, the sodomy and murder, was mostly
contained in the section for criminals sentenced to long prison
terms. In general however, although political prisoners not sentenced to execution generally received long sentences, at least
20 years and sometimes forty, even seventy, they were educated
people: doctors, professors, army officers, and the violence in
his section was far less. Once, in his Special Section, a guard
had been taken hostage with a knife to his throat. For this
reason Lt. Colonel Walid was always escorted by a bodyguard
of prison guards armed with batons. No one, not even himself,
carried a gun inside the prison, in case a prisoner snatched it.
The main problems that Lt. Colonel Walid had to deal with
were drugs, which were endemic, brought in by family members who visited, anything, but often Valium, and scabies,
spread by the overcrowding.

Walid laughed. In the corner of the basement of Costa Coffee
a young Arab man leaned closer to a young Arab woman wearing a headscarf. Walid looked behind him.

"It was too busy!" he said and lowered his voice more seriously, "Abu Ghraib was one of the most ugly unfair prisons in
the world, there was no freedom for prisoners, no real food,
the food was simply inedible, they were dependent on their
families bringing food. The most difficult situation, for me, as
a human, was then scabies, there was no water, no sun—"

They were never allowed outside?

Walid put up his hands, "What can you do? What can you
do?" He made mock offering to God above in his might.
"Where could I put them? It was impossible to manage such a
thing."

The prisoners were locked in without any provision for fresh air or exercise. Toilets in the corner of the cells were filthy. Pipes broke and water taps dripped scant water, once sewage leaked into the water pipes and a load of prisoners went down with dysentery and three men died. The food was "air soup" made of water and tomato paste added for a brownish color and rice; meat once a year, maybe.

Walid told me he was always concerned about the prisoners and he would try to separate the worst cases where the skin rash covered the whole body. He had heard stories of a prisoner who had killed himself with the suffering of suppuration and itching.

"*Wallah!*" Walid brought his arms around in a great circle and clapped his hands together, "What can you do?"

After his morning rounds Lt. Colonel Walid went, as he often did, to play billiards.

He had set up a shed and decked it out as a leisure room, a few chairs and tables and a billiard baize, for guards and trusty prisoners. He was particularly fond of playing with Abu Seif, a prisoner who had been sentenced to twenty years for smuggling currency to Jordan. Prison befell so many Iraqis that better conditions could be always be arranged if the prisoner had protectors. Special handling for those prisoners who could pay or display *wasta*, letters from the Presidential Office or from Ministers who asked for preferential treatment for relatives or the children of friends. Prisoners with pull had access to money, food, television, luxurious double cells all to themselves, drugs; sometimes even wives were allowed to stay overnight.

At noon Lt. Colonel Walid decided to release a few prisoners from crushing punishment cells into the regular halls. At lunch he and the Amn officers, who had been evacuated from Baghdad, discussed whether the Americans would bomb or not. One of them was sure they would bomb Baghdad. Lt. Colonel Walid said he thought the Americans were threatening more than they were serious, they wanted to shake Saddam and keep him in line.

After lunch he changed into a tracksuit and played more billiards with Abu Seif and several other prisoners. Lt. Colonel Walid liked playing billiards. He always won. In the late afternoon he took a shower and changed and called his wife.

In the evening around 8 p.m. he was walking down the main road of the prison with several of the Baghdad officers. They were smoking and talking. The road ran though an open tract toward the main gate and the guard towers were quite far off. The lights were still on in the prison (lights out at 10 p.m.) and there was no black out because Abu Ghraib was not expected to be a target.

Their stride was measured, the conversation strained. The Americans would most likely bomb when it got dark and now it was dark. They felt a heightened sensitivity, tension; there was a surreal quietude waiting among the prison blocks and the officers found themselves talking softly to each other as gravel crunched under their heels. The night carried an unknown potential.

Then the bombs began. The horizon burst yellow flashes and the earth shook low tone vibrations. The center of Baghdad with its targeted ministries and security offices was thirty kilometers away, but the Radwaniya Presidential palace complex next to the airport was close to Abu Ghraib and the Americans were bombing Radwaniya. Close and thudding. Anti aircraft guns erupted from all over the city, white flecking streaks and red tracer arcs.

"From everywhere they were firing. Ha! Everyone wanted to show their bravery!" The flak made a crisscrossing matrix in the sky, but the bombers flew high unseen and could not be hit.

The small group of Amn officers stood on the road, stopped their paltry conversation and listened. Presently, unexpectedly, two new landcruisers drove up to the main gate. From where he was standing, Lt. Colonel Walid could see an officer get out of the lead car and begin an argument with the guard to open the gate. The guard was uncertain and looked over for him to come and give him authority to let the landcruisers in. It was a time of maximum alert, the Americans had just commenced bombing the capital and it was extremely unusual for cars to drive up unannounced at eight o'clock at night.

As he walked toward the confrontation Lt. Colonel Walid saw that the officer who was remonstrating was of the same rank, a Lt. Colonel in the army. Without introducing himself the Lt. Colonel asked for Colonel Hassan, the commander of Abu Ghraib.

Lt. Colonel Walid told him that Colonel Hassan had been summoned to Baghdad earlier and was on his way back.

"What do you want?" he asked the officer. The officer seemed troubled, weighted with a heavy duty, as if he had been ordered to do something he did not want to do. His speech was simultaneously rapid and hesitant. Lt. Colonel Walid noticed his hand was shaking.

Another officer got out of the second landcruiser. As he opened the door, the light inside the car went on automatically and Lt. Colonel Walid could see, sitting on the back seat, a man, blindfolded and handcuffed, leaning forward slightly with his head bowed. He thought he glimpsed a military uniform, but could not be sure. The second officer walked briskly toward him and Lt. Colonel Walid could tell, by the well-cut quality cloth of his smooth olive green uniform, the elaborate and non-regulation woven leather belt, the expensive Browning pistol in a hand tooled leather holster and the deliberate absence of rank insignia on his shoulders, that he was an officer in the Presidential Bodyguard.

The Lt. Colonel stepped aside. The officer of the Presidential Bodyguard listened to Lt. Colonel Walid's remonstrance that Colonel Hassan was not yet back from Baghdad and that in his absence he could not authorize—

"If Colonel Hassan is not here, we cannot wait," insisted the officer of the Presidential Bodyguard. "We have someone we must execute by the order of Mr. President (God protect him)."

Lt. Colonel Walid asked him if he had a written order or a signed sentence from a judge. The manner of their arrival was highly irregular and outside the usual process. It bothered him, it made him nervous, he could not take responsibility for it. There should be notification and documentation.

"Where is the judge who will attend and witness the execution?" he asked the officer of the Presidential Bodyguard. The officer of the Presidential Bodyguard made a gesture that indicated that this was not the kind of case which needed a judge.

"I have to verify this," Lt. Colonel Walid told him. "This is an extraordinary situation. I should make sure."

"Look, brother, Lt. Colonel," explained the Presidential Bodyguard determinedly, "we have the order of Mr. President (may God protect him), to execute this order for execution—"

Just at this moment Colonel Hassan's car (a single car, which was unusual because he usually traveled in a convoy of two cars) drew up at the gates and the Colonel got out.

"What's going on?" he asked, "is something wrong?"

The officer of the Presidential Bodyguard took Colonel

Hassan to one side. Lt. Colonel Walid could see his boss listening and then nodding curtly in concurrence. Colonel Hassan got back into his car and signaled for the others to follow him. The four cars, Lt. Colonel Walid's bringing up the rear, drove, not to the execution block in the prison, but to a disused corner of the prison grounds. Lt. Colonel Walid had never visited the area; he knew about it only dimly and now, in the dark, his impression was garbage, waste, mud, stands of high reeds. There was no track and the cars bumped over the uneven ground toward a clearing. When they stopped and he got out, he could smell the rotting scrap food, stench of fetid salt-rimed swamp dump. His shoes caught on the thin rustling edges of scudding windblown scraps of plastic bags and he shook his feet with disgust.

It occurred to Lt. Colonel Walid that Colonel Hassan knew this place and that he knew what he was doing there. In the distance the bombing continued and mingled with the adrenaline of the urgency of the situation in front of him. The officer of the Presidential Bodyguard and Colonel Hassan got out of their cars and Colonel Hassan called out to the other guards, "Bring him!" The words came out as easily as he would have called for an extra chair to be fetched. Then he leaned back inside his car and took out a Kalashnikov with a folding metal stock.

The handcuffed figure who was, Lt. Colonel Walid could now see, wearing a neat, clean well pressed uniform with the badges of rank removed, was brought out and held upright, arms pinioned on either side by two guards. A black and white *kaffiyeh* was wrapped around his head as a blindfold. He was a tall man with the erect grace and proud bearing of a leader. He stood straight up with dignity and said in a clear strong voice,

"By God, I am sorry: I have done nothing wrong, I did nothing for this to happen to me. Why? But we come from God and we return to God."

It was a strong clear voice and as he retold these final words Walid dropped his eyes for a moment of impression, a mark of respect.

At the time, however, his thoughts were an agitated veering blur. They spiraled and collapsed in on each other and watching this scene, taking in the rush, the smell of the filthy earth beneath, the brutality of speed and dispatch, he felt his own execution hurtling toward him.

Lt. Colonel Walid was typical Amn officer. Imagine him a regime everyman. Competent enough, immured: he was not a monster although he saw monstrous things and then ignored them. "What could he do?"

His curriculum vitae could have been written by template.

1960	Born in the Province of Salahuddin. Father, poor farmer. Sunni.
1983	Graduated Police Academy, excelled at personal combat, boxing, tae kwon do. Selected to apply for the Amn.
1983–1986	Trained bodyguards for VIPs and consulted on Iraqi Airlines security.
1986	Trained the bodyguards for the Iraqi soccer team in the World Cup in Mexico. (Ali Hassan al-Majid, then head of the Amn, had personally recommended him to Uday, who was in charge of the Iraqi Olympic Committee and the national soccer team.)

"I have heard about you," Uday told him
when he was summoned for an interview.

Not long before the Iraqi team had won a
qualifying match against Qatar in Calcutta and
afterward the opposition had torn up the Iraqi
flag in defeat. Uday was determined that this
insult should not be repeated. He told Walid,

"If this happens again cut the man who
tears the Iraqi flag into pieces and if you cannot
manage this, cut off his hand. If anyone touches
the Iraqi flag they should not leave the stadium
with his hand.")

1987–1990	Attained the rank of Major. Appointed to Mosul, responsible for overseeing the security of visiting VIPs.
1990–1997	Director of al Amn at a town on the Syrian border.
1997–2000	Lt. Colonel, in charge of a section of Abu Ghraib prison.
2000–2003	Director of Amn in Kut.
2004–2005	Appointed senior officer by Interior Ministry and put in charge of 5,000 anti terrorist forces in Baghdad.

When the war against Iran ended in 1988, Walid, like many
in the security services and the army, felt betrayed. What had
they been fighting for? What had eight years of blood been
worth if Iran was to be given its border at the midway point
of the Shatt al Arab, exactly where it had all begun in 1980?
When Saddam invaded Kuwait and the consequences were di-
sastrous many questioned, in the melee of the *intifada* that followed, *openly*, the efficacy of the President. Lt. Colonel Walid

was among them. He began to want to kill Saddam and restore his country. He knew about the injustices, the thousands of prisoners, good officers executed for desertion and the corruption of the regime, its criminality, he had seen Colonel Hassan beat prisoners to death with electric cattle prods—these things were extreme and not right; but these things he was used to. His main concern was that of the country, reduced and outlawed, brought to its knees and subjected by a President who gripped power by its neck and choked it.

Walid said that in 1992 he joined a secret opposition movement, a network of officers led by a General, within the army and security services. It was very difficult to organize such a group in the circumstances of informant terror—indeed plenty of fake opposition movements were set up as traps to lure the less than loyal—and it was dangerous to meet and impossible to talk in offices, on the telephone or in each other's homes or in earshot of more than three members at a time. Some funds were apparently procured from Arab countries, some plans, perhaps even a coup, were mooted. Ultimately this group— and it was probably not the only one—dared not or could not risk action.

As Lt. Colonel Walid watched the tall officer stand up straight and defend his last living dignity before his God he felt he was watching himself. He was stabbed with the premonition of his own death. His mind raced and flickered paranoia. He imagined that the bound officer was connected with his opposition group, that he had already been betrayed. Perhaps Colonel Hassan, who he usually enjoyed warm relations with, was watching him closely to see how he reacted through this elaborate terminal charade.

On the waste ground, the killing ground, Colonel Hassan and the Presidential Bodyguard officer began arguing.

"I am the one who will execute him," said the officer of the Presidential Bodyguard.

"No. I will shoot him, it is my job and position to do this."

The nervous army Lt. Colonel wanted nothing to do with it, stepped back and told Colonel Hassan, "Do what you want."

Lt. Colonel Walid got into his car and drove away. He could not bear to witness the killing. He did not want to see himself shot on some patch of waste shit.

"You were frightened?" I asked him gently.

"No. I was not frightened," he insisted; I never heard an Iraqi admit to fear.

When he was half way back to the main paved road he heard the three bursts of automatic gunfire, thirty bullets maybe, and then a gap and then a single ringing shot.

His mind was in turmoil. He imagined in a rush what would happen to his family if he was shot. He thought: Who was that officer? Could it have been my General? Could my mind be so disoriented with torment that I did not recognize his voice? Could I not gauge anything beyond the blindfold? Who was this man, high rank and proud, who had stood up straight and been shot, summarily by that thug criminal bastard Colonel Hassan?

If it had been his General he should find out immediately and face his fate. In his hyper concentration, this information became a desperate focus of needing to know. His own words came back to him like a taunt. Some months before he had told his General: "We will all be shot for sure. Let's revenge our-selves before we are arrested. It is better to be killed fighting them, than to wait to be executed by them like sheep."

He slowed his car and parked it on the side of the road and

decided to walk back toward the clearing. He hoped to encounter Colonel Hassan and find out what he could. He felt himself in a stumbling dreamnightmare. He began to retrace his steps, "I don't know why but I will tell you why. I couldn't wait for Hassan to come back before asking him who this person was."

Colonel Hassan saw him and got out of his car and the two walked back to their quarters together. Colonel Hassan shook his hand and asked him why he had left like that. His manner was perfectly normal, warm and collegial.

Lt. Colonel Walid told him that he had sensed that the Presidential Bodyguard were hiding something.

"They did not tell me who he was so I had the impression they did not want me to know, so I thought it would be better if I just left."

Then in his overwhelming desperation, he attacked him with the question burning his thoughts: "Do you know who it was?"

"You didn't recognize him?" Colonel Hassan was amused.

"No, I didn't know, I thought maybe it was a Minister."

"No." said Colonel Hassan, "It was Kamel Sachet."

Lt. Colonel Walid's panic had taken hold and even with this exonerating information, he could not let go of it. Perhaps Colonel Hassan was lying in order to lull him into a false sense of security. He asked him where they had put the body and Hassan told him they had stuffed it in the carcass of an abandoned refrigerator that had been lying on the dump.

"If you leave it there, the dogs will eat it," Lt. Colonel Walid advised him, making his horror sound like a logistical concern. "It will be a problem. Why not put him in the morgue."

Colonel Hassan thought about this for a moment and then agreed that he would go back himself with a few guards and take the body to the morgue.

They said good night and parted. Walid could not settle. The bombing had stopped, Kamel Sachet's body lay close by cooling into death. The hour had become late and silent and the stars came out brightly against the partial blackout. Walid walked alone for an hour around the prison grounds and then he got into his car and drove home. He waved at the Abu Ghraib checkpoint where they knew him and a second, farther checkpoint set up during the alert. He was driving a government car and he was not stopped. There were no other cars on the deserted roads. The bombing could start up again at any time. The area that he was driving through was a likely target. He couldn't feel the fear through his fear that he couldn't feel, or later, even admit to.

When he reached his home he found everyone still awake, listening for more bombs. He greeted his wife and she saw the wildness in his face and asked him what was wrong, but he said only, "It's the bombs: didn't you see the bombs?"

"You didn't tell her?"

He shook his head from side to side to side, rocking his thoughts.

"No, never, never. No one."

He sat in his garden in the middle of the murdering night and drank three glasses of arak and declaimed Mr. President, may God shit on his grave.

"Baghdad is on fire and he doesn't care," he said out loud. His receding adrenaline left a residue of anger. Still he could not bring himself to articulate what he was really thinking. He blamed his anger on the bombs, but it was not the bombs that night that had touched him.

"He only wants to keep his power! He doesn't care about people when they are killed! Only his position!"

In the morning, back at the prison which he should never

have left during an alert, Colonel Hassan invited everyone to breakfast to show his hospitality to the evacuated officers.

Afterward Lt. Colonel Walid and Colonel Hassan went over to the Long Sentence section of the prison. They talked about Kamel Sachet. Walid said, no he had never met him, although of course he knew him by reputation. He was lying, because during the night he remembered, once, maybe ten or twelve years before, he had met Kamel Sachet at a friend's office, a man who had an import-export business, just once, he had shaken his hand.

"Do you want to see him?"

They went to view the corpse, retrieved, shelved and refrigerated in the prison morgue. It had been wrapped in a black shroud as an insult to signify a deserter, a traitor. Colonel Hassan unwound the black folds to reveal Kamel Sachet's face striped half red blood. There was a crusted entry wound at the top of the skull indicating that the final coup de grâce had been shot from above, vertically downward.

Colonel Hassan pointed this out and said, "That was my bullet!"

WALID'S OWN POSTSCRIPT to the story was neat enough; a certain justice. Colonel Hassan was assassinated in Baghdad three months after the events of the night of Desert Fox. Two men sprayed his car with automatic fire and then managed to make their escape. It was said that they had been prisoners at Abu Ghraib and had been sent to kill him by opposition parties in Iran. Somehow this made Walid smile.

After eight hours of listening to Walid's story, I went home and poured a drink, drank it and poured another. Walid was not his real name. Our mutual friend and interlocutor, an

Iraqi former Sunni officer I had known in Baghdad, called him F——, but he told me not to write it down. "Everyone in Middlesbrough knows me as Walid. In the book," he told me, "call me Khalid Ben Walid," he said smiling. The original Khalid Ben Walid had led the Muslims to victory against a Byzantine army at Yarmouk in 697. "I like this name."

Chapter 17

COLLECTION

FEBRUARY 1999. AT NINE O'CLOCK ONE MORNING the phone rang. Um Omar answered it in the kitchen, and shouted for Ali to come and take the call. Ali was not expecting a call and he held the receiver to his ear with some trepidation.

Scratching through the static, metal rasp voice asked,

"Are you the son of the traitor Kamel Sachet?"

Ali turned his back on his mother and replied monosyllabically.

"Yes."

"Do you know where Abu Ghraib prison is?"

"Yes."

"Go there to receive his body."

Ali hung up and stood still, shocked, feet planted, motionless. His mother looked over at him. She had heard only the flat half of the conversation but saw something in her son's face.

Before she could ask, Ali said, "My friend is stuck at a checkpoint. I am going to help him out."

Ali dared not tell his mother or his sisters for fear that their alarm and wailing would provoke the watching agents; his younger brothers could not be trusted with the confidence. He hurriedly changed from his *dishdasha* to a pair of trousers and a shirt. He took a jacket, the weather was wet. He put some money in his pocket and worried that it would not be enough. His elder brother Omar was staying at their aunt's house and Ali got in the car and drove there first. Omar was not in. His cousins didn't know where he was and he could not tell them it was urgent. Ali sat in the car and thought for a moment: who he could go to? He decided to go to his father's driver's house. Ali Mishjil had worked for his father for twenty years, since before Ali was born—it was he who had told Kamel Sachet to call his son Ali instead of Nasser—and when Ali explained to him the phone call, the faithful servant began to shake with emotion. Ali had someone to help, but they needed a relative, an older man, to accompany him to Abu Ghraib. Ali was only eighteen, perhaps they would not release his father's body to him. So they drove back to the aunt's house to check if Omar had returned.

At every intersection, Ali Mishjil beat the steering wheel with his hands and repeated, "Abu Omar is gone, Abu Omar is gone."

Omar had not returned and could not be found. They next drove to an uncle's house, to Khalid, one of Kamel Sachet's younger brothers. He was also out. Another uncle, Hamid, was away. They went to another uncle, Mohammed. Not at home.

Ali felt burdened with unluck—it was God's will, and not for the first time: When Grandmother Bibi died he had been the first to receive the news; when his mother's sister died he was the first to receive this news. Why had God chosen him again, to suffer the loneliness of death and the misery of having to share it, to tell it, give it to other people to suffer with?

They turned off the highway into a bland, walled residential district.

"Abu Omar is gone!" Ali Mishjil was distraught. After these

weeks of waiting, the shadows behind the eyes that could not meet their inquiries, untold but knowing anyway, Ali realized he was dry eyed. His father had been missing for more than 50 days. He had left for work in the morning of 16 December, weighed down by the imminence of the American attack, but looking forward to the opening of his third mosque in the afternoon. He never came home. At first his secretary said that he had a meeting with the President, then the meeting was stretched to some unspecified mission. A few days passed, when there was still no news and those friends he and his brother Omar knew to call stopped answering their phones, his father's secretary had come to the house with a small package, that he said, fumbling with the words, unable to look any of them directly in the eye, Abu Omar had asked him to deliver to his eldest son. It was his father's pistol and his gold watch.

The cul-de-sac logistics driving to and fro, this fraught mission, absorbed Ali's anger. An hour, two hours passed this way. Finally they went to the house of his father's sister and found her husband there. Abu Shakur was not a brother of his father, but he was all that could be found and would have to suffice. Abu Shakur was kindly and a little bit old, he carried a venerability, but he was not a close relative. Somehow this made Ali ashamed; the three of them seemed to be an unworthy cortege.

At the main gate of Abu Ghraib the guards would not let them through and told them to turn off the engine and wait. After an interim they were told a car would be sent to collect them. Abu Shakur told Ali to wait in the car, he would go and do the paperwork.

"Stay here, if you come with me, in the state you are in, you will curse the government and they'll arrest you—"

Abu Shakur was shown into the office of Colonel Hassan.

Colonel Hassan greeted him with an expression of regret. He opened his palms ("What could I do?"), then pressed his fingertips together in mock supplication.

Abu Shakur sat stiffly and cut through this false sympathy with a direct ambiguity.

"If Kamel disobeyed an order," he stated clearly, in full reference and memory of his brother-in-law's unimpeachable reputation for loyal obedience, "this was his destiny."

Colonel Hassan looked down at his dirty fingernails and replied, perhaps in an effort of mild justification, "It was for the interests of the country. I hope our God will help you to be patient."

A form was presented to be signed.

Colonel Hassan asked politely where they intended to bury the body of Kamel Sachet. Abu Shakur told him, in Kuthar, near Hilla, where the family had some land.

Colonel Hassan warned him, "Take the body there and only there and no other place. If you take the body through Baghdad or stop the car in any other place we will take it back from you and bury it ourselves."

Abu Shakur signed his name.

"A funeral is not permitted," continued Colonel Hassan, in case he had not made himself perfectly understood. "A gathering of any kind is not permitted."

Ali was in a state of slow shock and could feel nothing but an emptiness, an awful emptiness swirling with dull rage. Abu Shakur explained that they were not allowed a funeral, Ali nodded. Then they went into the town of Abu Ghraib and hired a taxi with a roof rack for the coffin. It was probably not the first time the taxi driver had been hired for such an errand. His parking place was in the middle of a low row of vegetable sellers next to a restaurant that served rice and kebab to the families of the prisoners who came to visit. Opposite, up a track screened by dusty eucalyptus trees was the place where they buried the executed prisoners whose families did not know they were executed. The bodies were buried in trenches marked with the prisoners' metal wrist tags stamped with a number. No one ever told the relatives that asked, sometimes, in the restaurant: "What happens when the food and clothing parcels are returned unopened? Is the prisoner transferred? Where?" To Abu Shakur, the driver offered no pleasantries where none were to be had and agreed the fare without much haggling.

The coffin was narrow and made of cheap reused thin wooden boards; gray, plain and without markings. Ali Mishjil pried off the creaking lid and looked inside. The general's jacket had been laid over his face; he was still wearing his uniform, although it looked dirty and scuffed. For confirmation, Ali Mishjil pulled back the jacket. Ali stood a little way off and waited, hope running into grit. He wanted it not to be true and some terrible mistake, he wanted to hear any thin thread of lie—but Ali Mishjil cried out, screwing fists into his eye sockets, wailing incoherently at God and Ali knew it was him.

It was difficult and awkward, watched by the guards who offered no assistance, to lift the coffin onto the roof of the taxi. Ali and Ali Mishjil, strong with the imperative of the task, hoisted the coffin up. The taxi driver pretended to lift but didn't put much strength into his effort. As they heaved it up and rested it on the rim of the roof for a moment, Ali saw at eye level through a gap in the planking, a sliver of his father's naked foot. He recognized the long delicate scar along the ankle, an old familiar shrapnel wound from an attack outside Basra. As the last filament of hope fell soundlessly, he summoned strength from his pain and anger and pushed the dead weight of his father across the roof rack of the scratched up taxi.

They set off followed by an Oldsmobile and a landcruiser, each carrying four Amn officers. A little way out of the gate, the coffin grated dangerously on the roof and they were forced to crawl slowly to the roadside souk in Abu Ghraib where they bought some more rope and tied it down properly. They resumed their journey and took the highway west, stopping in Mahmoudiya, near their destination, to buy perfume with which to anoint the body and lengths of white fabric in which to shroud it for burial.

By this time, delayed and circuitous, it was afternoon prayer time. They went to the mosque at the graveyard and asked for gravediggers and for those who washed the bodies for burial. Abu Shakur attended to these details, Ali stood on the sandy verge and remembered his father walking with him through these very graves. He had told him he wanted to be buried next to his grandfather. Ali crouched in grief, winded by the sound of his father's voice in his memory, and touched his fingertips to the dust.

He remembered his father teaching him how to shoot. He was nine and his father was commanding a unit in Diala. One of his officers showed him all the different kinds of weapons, put them into his small hands to feel, the barrels, the safety catch, the heft and responsibility, and stood over him while he practiced disassembling a Kalashnikov. In the afternoons sometimes he would be given fifteen bullets to fire at rows of cans. Ali would always ask for more bullets, try to wheedle them out of the bodyguards, sometimes even steal them from his father's office. He liked to shoot geckos but he was not allowed to; all around was the detritus of battle, old and unexploded ordnance, a stray bullet could hit something and blow it to kingdom come. An orderly hovered to one side and picked up the spent cartridge casings. His father stood behind him, correcting his grip.

"Relax a little," he would tell him, "hold steady," "aim carefully," "no, not like that, place your feet further apart."

A few men had come to pray but they passed Ali without greeting him and washed their hands at the outside basin, wiping carefully between each finger, sharing a vanishing slip of pink soap, without turning their heads to look behind them.

Ali had wanted to go the Military Academy and train to be an officer. He wanted to be like his father, like those officers his father commanded, respect, loyalty—an expensive pistol on his hip, a Mercedes to drive, or a Toyota Crown, something that carried and conferred status. His father had refused. He told Ali that the army had once been a good place, but not now. Ali had tried to argue, he did not understand, he saw his father with all his medals and decorations, the many people who revered him, visited, petitioned, the many he helped, the daughter of one of his officers killed in battle he had paid to train as a pharmacist, the mosques he had built, the way the ordinary people in Amara had looked to him for protection, like a guardian lord.

His father brushed off his son's admiration and his ambitions, he told him, bitterly, "Saddam always keeps the people he needs close to him; when they are no longer needed, he ignores them."

As they waited for prayer to conclude, Ali felt his temper tremble and the inadequacy of this funeral.

Abu Shakur had gone to find the Sachet family plot but he could not locate it. He came back and asked the mosque attendants to find a map of the cemetery.

"Who is this you are burying?" they asked.

"This is Kamel Sachet we have here."

Then the mosque attendants began to cry and lament, they knew Kamel Sachet, they knew a good man had been killed, they bemoaned Saddam and asked how could such a hero have been executed?

Five cars full of local Amn officers drove up. They parked and the officers positioned themselves on the road and around the mosque. They had been told to keep an eye on the burial of an executed man; they had no idea who was being buried. Adnan Janabi, hearing the news through Janabis in the intelligence network, drove up to pay his respects, no matter the consequences.

The Sachet family plot was found and the gravediggers started to dig in the dusk. The corpse washers laid the body out on a slab over a drain and brought buckets of hot water. Ali came into the mosque to see what was happening but Abu Shakur touched his elbow and led him away, "It's better that you don't see this." Ali demurred, he was afraid to look at his father's dead face and imprint this as his last memory of him. Through the door to the washing room, which was slightly ajar, he could see the sleeve arm of his father's uniform, brown with blood, stiff and unnaturally rigid, bent across his chest, and the dried blood between his father's fingers—a corpse washer came over and drew Abu Shakur to one side. There was a problem, he explained. The body was in a bad state; it had been dead for some time. He paused uncertainly, respectfully. They could not undress him, skin and flesh would peel away stuck to his uniform. The man held out his hands apologetically. For Kamel Sachet, such a man who had built three mosques and kept his prayers, for such a man to be buried unwashed!—He was very sorry about all of it. Presently the imam came over and soothed things.

"No, no, don't concern yourself, God knows these problems: for a martyr, in these situations—it is not necessary to wash a martyr. Do not worry. If there is any responsibility that needs to be taken, I will be responsible."

So the corpse washers carefully folded the General's arms across his chest in death repose and wrapped the body in a shroud. Ali came in when they had finished and put his hand on his father's white cotton hand.

Final prayers were said. Ali wiped his hands over his face and hung them at his sides, through the reassuring sibilance of prayer, the familiar, the repeated, the cyclical, the continuous, the everlasting certainty. He felt, however, no solace in the promise of paradise.

The chief of the local Amn came over and made inquiries.

"Who is the body?" he asked. He had been told nothing, only that there was a burial that needed to be watched and that no gathering was to be permitted. When he heard the name of Kamel Sachet, the Amn officer inhaled and looked at the ground, coughed at the sudden lump in his throat. As the word spread some of the other Amn officers began crying openly. Ali heard their grief and he let his outrage fly loose at last. He railed, shouting at the sky, at the President, at the men who followed his orders.

The chief of the local Amn took him aside gently, put a sympathetic arm around his shoulders and said, in a kind whisper, "Look, this talk is of no use to you. Be brave as your father was. Go home and take care of your family. This talk will be of no benefit to you."

Chapter 18

GENERALS IN GENERAL

I SPENT THE SUMMER OF 2007 LOOKING FOR GENERALS and sergeants and anyone who might have known Kamel Sachet. I wanted to hear new stories and overlap and confirm the ones I already knew. Two million or more Iraqis had fled Iraq, mostly to Jordan and Syria, and I spent weeks in Damascus and Amman, sitting in cafés or hotel lobbies or on a thin pallet in a refugee hovel drinking, accordingly, glasses of tea or orange juice, or cans of warm Pepsi.

"And how is your family?" I would ask and then horror stories came out. Everyone, without exception, had a horror story. Kill kidnap kill kidnap kill kidnap. In various permutations: brother, self, wife, five-year-old son; ransomed, shot, missing. They had stopped blaming the Americans; somehow the horror had gone beyond anger or fault. One woman I remember, a modest, educated, English-speaking, handsome woman in a long black abaya. She was Shia married to a Sunni—inter-sect marriage was common in Baghdad—and her husband had been killed in a bombing. During her mourning, her brother-in-law had come to her and threatened to tell the insurgents she was a Shia spy unless she gave her fifteen year old daughter to his son for marriage and took her fourteen year old son out of school to work in his garage. Frightened, she had fled with her children to Damascus, her son was out of school, there was no one to send more money when the little she had ran out. She told me this all quite matter-of-factly, emotion betrayed only by a deep engraved vertical stress line in the middle of her forehead. One story of many, and many worse. My translator had been kidnapped and kept a picture of her dead son hung around her neck. A Scandinavian psychologist who was married to a UN official at the UNHCR told me she didn't know how to begin to counsel the hundreds of women who had been raped—*"hundreds of women raped?"* I repeated. She nodded. "Sometimes gang raped. One raped more than eight times in front of her husband! I don't know how to treat these women"—rape for Iraqis was indelible shame—"and they can't talk to their families. . ." Among the women I met there was no theatrical wailing and threshing; the public display of grief that I had known from the early stages of civil war and car bombs in Baghdad had been replaced by a sullen endurance.

In Damascus the displaced Iraqis lived with a little money scraped, dwindling, not much, in small rented apartments in Seyda Zeinab, near the Shia Shrine to the Prophet's hostage granddaughter, where many Iraqis had settled during the Saddam years, or in the Palestinian areas (another, previous wave of refugees) or in farther, outer suburbs. The apartments were concrete, tiled floor, rolled up mats for bedding, a couple of plastic chairs for visitors, a harsh strip light overhead, a television tuned alternately to MTV and Al Jazeera, a small statuette of the Virgin in the Christian households, a picture of the green mantled Hussein in the Shia, a poster of the ranks of faithful kneeling in prayer rings around the Kaaba in Mecca in the Sunni. Almost everyone complained the rent was high and they couldn't find a job and the Syrians kept changing their visa criteria and they couldn't get the new G series Iraqi passports that were only being distributed in Baghdad and money was running out and their children were disrupted from school. They telephoned family members back in Baghdad and Mosul: Was it any better? Was it safe to come home? And heard only news of new bombs and dead relatives.

It was a very dispiriting time. The former officers I found in Damascus were tired and worried. They carried their lives in plastic carrier bags, photocopies of ID cards, military records, birth certificates for their children, house deeds, license details for a car they had sold two years before, letters from the UNHCR, Red Crescent affidavits, registration forms for emigration from the Canadian Embassy. Some of them had been officers in the new Iraqi Army, allied to the Americans, manning checkpoints and operations against insurgents and militias. They had fled firebombing and assassination attempts and hoped (hopelessly, because the Americans were taking very few refugees and even those who had worked directly for them as translators were stranded) to be resettled in the United States and proffered photographs of themselves in uniform standing next to "American Colonel Bob" or "Major Hudson very good man and my good friend" along with certificates of their service and typed letters of recommendation from American commanders.

They sighed and looked over their shoulders to see if there were any listening agents sitting nearby. Often we would see a lone man reading or pretending to read the newspaper and we would have to pay the check and walk down the street to find a park bench or another, more anonymous café. Iraqis were very afraid. The old Baathies were afraid of the Syrian Mukhabarat, a familiar security blanket, which occasionally deported former high rank officers back to Iraq, like throwing morsels as appeasements at the Americans. But more terribly, Iraqis were

afraid of each other. The internecine violence was a centri-
fuge that pulled apart colleagues, neighbors, cousins, scattering
families and friends among parties, factions, militias, nefarious
business arrangements. Whenever I asked someone for help in
asking a friend of theirs to talk to me, they always said, politely,
that they would call them first to ask their permission to give
me their phone number and often people refused to talk to a
Western reporter; who knew who might get to hear of the ren-
dezvous or what consequences it might have.

Iraqis were wary of the tensions and threads of war feud that
overspilled borders. One former officer in the new Iraqi army
told me that three Shia militia thugs had broken his door down
at three in the morning and interrogated his pregnant wife as
to his whereabouts. Damascus was full of militia bandits and
insurgent foot soldiers on R & R for the summer, disgorged
with the refugee families from dusty buses into the choking
rubbish-ridden lanes around the Shrine of Seyda Zeinab. They
adjusted to sleeping without gunfire interruption, went under
false names and monikers, calculated the risks and the prices
of the people smugglers who promised to get them as far as
Greece or Bulgaria and gathered in the hole in the wall cafés,
around charcoal braziers grilling kebab, and in airless basement
Internet cafés. Sometimes, watching old Iraqi sitcoms from the
eighties in the corner of a tea house, catching a refrain of an old
Baghdad love song wafting from some open window, they remembered they were all Iraqis again. When the Iraqi national
soccer team beat the Saudis (!) in the Asian Cup final, crowds
went out into the streets cheering and gunning their motor-
bikes in lieu of Kalashnikovs until the Syrian police came to
quell and beat and remind them where they were.

In Amman the atmosphere was calmer. There were fewer
Iraqis in Jordan and they tended to be more middle class Sunnis.

The officers in Amman I met were more senior and had fared better. General Hamdani and his friends had good apartments, with gold chenille sofas and gilt edged ashtrays, money from somewhere. They passed the time writing accounts of the Saddam years under grand delusions of big American publishing advances. They called them memoirs but there was nothing personal in them, they wrote like academics without facts, great tracts of self serving hindsight, epigrammatic assumption, polemical swathes of history downloaded from the top of their heads. Some made apologies for Saddam, some blamed his "evil councilors," the Tikriti thug-cousins he surrounded himself with, some praised his intelligence and wondered how it could have twisted itself into such catastrophe, others heaped scorn on Saddam and his peasant roots and told me that they had known all along, even from the early days, that his power was built on the foundations of murder.

There were varying shades of hypocrisy and after a while the faces and the excuses and the old war stories blurred into each other, the former general became a type. I joked with my translator that I could pick one out of a crowded café: a man in his fifties or vigorous sixties, straight military back, close cropped gray hair, a mustache (usually trimmed thinner and smaller than its prime), tribal tattoo dots at the base of his thumb (sometimes one, like an old worn freckle on the end of a nose). They were always friendly and affable, often they had a sense of wry humor. A pair of thick black scimitar eyebrows above a pair of orange aviator shades, a rolled up sleeve to show me the skin graft scars to cover the damage from a heavy machine gun bullet caught in Fao in '86, a chunky brushed steel watch ringed with pavé diamonds (whose gift? I wondered), a strand of turquoise prayer beads rubbed between restless fingertips, the framed photograph of Saddam pinning a medal on his chest proudly explained, "The Sash of Rafidain, 1991. After the Mother of all Battles." I always told them that I could use pseudonyms if they were more comfortable, that I had no desire to cause them trouble. At first they would look at me skeptically, but then I dropped names of battles and commanders: Mohamara, Sachet, Khazraji, Fish Lake, and they would warm up and unfold their edited memories. One colonel I remember, white hair and white mustache, was initially hesitant to give me his name, but later told me with a flourish, "use my name, use all of it! We have a saying. Why should a drowning man be afraid of a drop of rain?"

The officers told me war stories from the eighties and tended to defend the use of chemical weapons and ignore the terror of the Anfal, conceding only that "mistakes were made" and that in war and counter insurgency bad things happen. Their dates were a year or two off kilter, their accounts were full of ellipses, their versions palimpsests, subject to the vagaries of oral history. They were dumbfounded and aghast at the current situation and blamed both the crass American heavy handedness and the delicate machinations of the Iranian *Pasdaran* and, according to the tropes of Iraqi hospitality, never let me pay for coffee no matter how reduced their circumstances. Together we shook our heads at the mistakes and the violence and even at the indignity of Saddam's execution, the last awful noosed moment when the Shia balaclavas taunted him with Moqtada's name, and made an effort at grim black humor, "Who knew then, four years ago, that we would be missing him so soon!" I liked them, I joked with them, I sympathized with them. But not one ever looked at me straight in the eye and admitted responsibility for the crimes of the government which they had served.

At times my long running narrative quest for *how-why*

seemed moot against the twisted fragments of news that came out of Baghdad those summer months: triangular battles between Al-Qaeda factions, Sunni tribal insurgents and Americans, Shia-on-Shia fighting in Amara, militia gang turf war in Basra. "Civil war" was almost a polite euphemism. Twenty four years of Saddam had been followed by an even nastier era, the bottom pulled out of purgatory, fallen into some deeper hole. Where did this vile carnage come from? *How-why?* I recalled my Baghdad interviews during the summer after the invasion (four years ago, four years already!) and all the different kinds of brain damage I had seen that Dr. Hassan had gamely tried to diagnose as paranoia, depression and anxiety. I had absorbed all their stories and now, as Sheikh Adnan sometimes jokingly admonished me, "I knew too much." In Damascus that summer I dreamed of Saddam. In my dream I was at a huge fancy reception in one of his palaces, all his henchmen and both his sons were there, gilt trays of crystal glasses of whiskey were passed by thin, obsequious, nervous waiters. The atmosphere was an uncomfortable forced jollity and I was trapped—I was a "guest" and dared not refuse such pointed hospitality—but when Saddam himself nodded a greeting in my direction from his dais, I felt strangely smug and gratified. In the morning I laughed at my empathetic Saddam anxiety dream but I noticed, toward the end of a month of dense, difficult, dolorous interviews, that every time I went to the toilet, I closed the door behind me and found that my first thought was not, clean? toilet paper? but: could I survive in this space if this was my cell for six months? Is there enough room to lie down to sleep, for example, is there a window? Would I get used to the smell? Probably . . . there was no sink, but never mind, I thought, I could wash in the cistern.

THE GENERALS, IN general, recalled Kamel Sachet with ha-
giographies, affection and reverence:

> "He cared very much about the ordinary people, he was
> always defending the rights of the ordinary people, he was
> ready to stand against even higher ranks . . . He did not get
> angry, his wishes were simple, realistic . . . he never had the
> ambition for money . . . he was quiet, he did not say much
> . . . he was faithful, truthful . . . during battles he slept on a
> simple folding mattress . . . he never had a guard outside his
> house although this was something normal for leaders . . .
> he himself served his guests with his own hands . . . he was
> frank; this is something natural for you in the West, but for
> us—I advised him often to calm down, to not speak about
> such things . . . may God bless him . . . amazingly coura-
> geous . . . close to Saddam Hussein . . . He was so honest in
> his work, so clean . . . He had a high standard, he was exact
> and correct in his job . . . He never hurried a decision . . .
> He concentrated on being correct in his religious duty . . .
> He prayed five times a day and if military duty of a meeting
> prevented a prayer he went as soon as he was able to . . . He
> ate with his soldiers, he hated to be in a bunker . . . . Kamel
> Sachet was my good friend . . . a very qualified officer . . .
> he was very quiet . . . very brave . . . very deliberate . . .
> he never paid attention to the Iranian forces, he would say,
> don't worry, this is easy . . . He was a simple man, he was
> like Rommel—but Hitler was cleverer to make Rommel
> commit suicide! . . .

About the reasons for his execution there were various theories, second hand rumors, one of the most prevalent, put about
by Khalid, his unreliable defected brother, was that Qusay
himself had shot him out of pique.

Kamel Sachet was arrested on December 16 1998, against the gathering imminence of an American and British air attack. In preparation for this and to counter the ongoing no-fly zone Allied provocations, Saddam had reorganized his general staff, notably putting Ali Hassan al-Majid in command of the southern theater. He asked Kamel Sachet to assist him, according to some, to be effectively his deputy. Kamel Sachet may or may not have been formally ordered to serve under Ali Hassan al-Majid, whom he despised; but in either case he never went south to actively take up such a command position. In some versions he refused in a meeting with Saddam and Qusay and several top commanders in the Presidential office on the morning of December 16th. In others his reluctance had already been noted for several weeks. But there does seem to be a general consensus that Kamel Sachet attended a high level meeting chaired by Saddam that morning, that there was a disagreement, that Kamel Sachet excused himself in order to pray, and that he was arrested very shortly after returning to his office by special security agents who were under the command of Qusay.

I heard various flowery versions: that Kamel Sachet refused point blank to serve under the murderous Ali Hassan al-Majid and that Qusay called him aside to remonstrate, Kamel Sachet remained proud and defiant, lost his temper and insisted that he would never take orders from an *"aji"* (a village word for a runty sheep or a small naughty boy with a recalcitrant and petulant cast) and, furious, Qusay had shot him on the spot. That Kamel Sachet had been taken to the Istikhbarat headquarters where Saddam had personally interrogated him and that Kamel Sachet had shown no fear for his life and insisted on his innocence and that Saddam had slapped him across his face in raw anger. One poignant anecdote came from Saddam's personal physician, Ala Bashir, who also designed vast non-representational monuments in Baghdad that he afterward claimed were deliberately subversive. Ala Bashir told Jon Lee Anderson of the *New Yorker*, who met him many times and wrote about him, who told me that after Kamel Sachet was shot, he attended Saddam for some minor ailment and found him distracted and morose and that his skin was a strange purplish color, "as if suffused with blood."

Kamel Sachet was not the only officer, although he was the most prominent, to be executed around this time. Dates have been confused by the Desert Fox attack, and by the varying number of weeks it took to acknowledge arrest and release the bodies to their families, and it is difficult to superimpose a conspiracy onto these deaths. Janabis heard different stories from other Janabis, the networks inside the security forces crossed accounts. By March 1999, after Ali had buried his father without a funeral, but before Saddam offered his family blood money in some effort to rehabilitate the execution of such a famous General into an unfortunate mistake, his death was being picked up by foreign intelligence monitoring websites and assigned various and vague significance.

People said he was killed because he was a Wahhabi, because he had connection to the Saudis, because he had shouted back at Saddam, because he was too proud, because Ali Hassan al-Majid hated him, because he had picked a fight with Qusay, because he was involved in a conspiracy, because the gang of Tikritis around Saddam felt threatened by his moral authority and good standing in the army and convinced Saddam that his use of Kamel Sachet's gifts of cash and cars and land to build mosques was a direct rebuttal of his respect and gratitude due to his President.

Ali, his son, once told me that Kamel Sachet's brothers had

tried to encourage him to stand against Saddam, but that he had refused to betray his President. Dr. Hassan told me that Kamel Sachet had visited him in his office, several days before his arrest, ostensibly to recheck the amount of money he had borrowed in several installments from Dr. Hassan for the building of his third mosque. (Dr. Hassan always teased him that he did not like anyone else to contribute to his mosques. Once when Dr. Hassan had brought a prayer carpet, as a gift, Kamel Sachet had barely been able to bring himself to thank his friend and said, "Yes, well, we will put this in the women's section.") Dr. Hassan wondered at this odd visit, but Kamel Sachet waved away his concerns. In retrospect, Dr. Hassan thought, perhaps this was an accounting he undertook because he had some premonition of his arrest. Dr. Hassan said he had been very withdrawn in his final months; but others who knew him told me they noticed no outward difference in his behavior. Nejar told me, extraordinarily, that he had arranged for Kamel Sachet and his whole family to be smuggled safely to Kurdistan but that at the last minute, on the morning of the proposed flight, Kamel Sachet changed his mind and said, no, he would remain with his fate in Iraq.

The general consensus however, and one I heard repeated from many sources, although his family always claimed they had no idea why he had been arrested, was that he had received a letter from Nizar Khazraji, his old commander in the Special Forces and the former Chief of Staff of the Army who had defected in the mid nineties and was then living in Denmark. Others had received letters from Khazraji around the same time (Nabil was not the only exile engaged in a letter writing campaign) and the Mukhabarat was aware that Kamel Sachet had also been sent one. It was not the reception of the letter that caught him, it was the fact that he did not report it. This was the final proof, a single sheet, the only serious charge that his enemies could count against him.

Nizar Khazraji had been Chief of Staff of the army during the time of Anfal. Throughout his time in Denmark, where he lived with his family, quietly plotting, for several years, human rights groups and Kurdish groups tried to have him arrested for crimes against humanity. At the end of 2002, as the Americans gathered their "Coalition of the Willing," and began to cast around for exiles to make phone calls to old colleagues inside Iraq convincing them not to fight, human rights groups scored a coup and an arrest warrant was issued for Khazraji. Between Washington and Copenhagen and the vagaries of international law and the realpolitik of diplomacy, Khazraji was charged but remained at home at large. Nabil Janabi says he remembers that Khazraji called him in London to ask him to help negotiate asylum in Jordan. But before Nabil could finalize such an arrangement, just days before the invasion in March 2003, Khazraji simply disappeared. There was a suspicion that he had been spirited away by the CIA; he was in fact reported to have been spotted in the south of Iraq during the invasion, perhaps negotiating with commanders behind the lines. There was even a report that he had been killed in Najaf, until the Danish police tapped a phone call he made to his son. After that he vanished completely. When I asked different generals what had happened to Nizar Khazraji they rolled their eyes and said the word was that he had been given Saudi protection and was keeping his head down in Saudi Arabia somewhere.

I often asked people who knew him whether they thought Kamel Sachet had been seriously involved in a conspiracy against Saddam or if he had remained, despite all his anger, agonies and misgivings, loyal.

In the plush surroundings of the Hyatt in Amman, a senior

Janabi, a former colonel in the Mukhabarat, considered this question.

"This is the thing. Did he have a real plan against Saddam or was it just in his mind or was it a maneuver he had not thought about? Nobody knew this except him."

The Colonel, when pressed for an opinion, thought on balance yes, Kamel Sachet was actively plotting against Saddam. Plenty of others I talked to said no, it was not in his nature to play politics, and that he would never have set himself up as a figurehead for the nefarious ambitions of others. But the Mukhabarat Colonel in Amman took another sip of tea and stretched his thoughts back to that time of stuck-stagnation and imposed a little of his own frustration on Kamel Sachet's state of mind.

"He must have had something up his sleeve," he guessed, "with all his activities in the military, social and religious fields . . . he had a strong belief in himself; he was a strong person who made decisions. We all knew the status quo couldn't last, perhaps he was contemplating something for the future. Many of us would talk about it. What comes after Saddam? Uday or Qusay?"

The tragedy of Kamel Sachet was tripartite:

It was an ordinary everyday tragedy, the same as any other of the unnumbered millions, a man killed.

It was the tragedy of self-sacrifice: Kamel Sachet would not compromise his religion or his own values and he was killed because he was brave and would not run away but would rather accept his own death in order to spare his family further wrath.

It was a tragedy of hubris: of pride, overconfidence, self-certainty.

Kamel Sachet's end was a very Iraqi tragedy, but Iraq was

not a Shakespeare play, plotted as one man, his destiny and a final curtain. It was only an episode in a long running serial. His sons inherited his death as a scar, but they inherited his pride and his reputation also. A year after his father was killed, Ali was arrested at the border, trying to get into Jordan on a fake passport, looking for work, for a way out. He was beaten, shoved into crammed prisons, sentenced to twenty years in Abu Ghraib (released in the general amnesty of November 2002, just missing his elder brother's wedding the day before), but he always managed to find one among his guards who had known his father and in remembrance smuggled him antibiotics when he was sick, or transferred him to a better cell.

Beget begat. Generation to generation. Pain and injustice, tyranny and sufferance was as much the Sachet sons' fate as every other Iraqi son. War and impoverishment and repression had led to moral disintegration and religious fanaticism, two sides of the same coin.

It was easy enough, even facile, to just shake your head at the whole blasted mess. Whenever anyone asked me where I thought Iraq was headed I always said, "God only knows!" The plot had already lurched in several different stupefying directions and prediction is a fool-pundit.

I did however, glimpse a small chink in the pessimism. For years Iraq had been getting worse, but that didn't mean it would continue to. For years Islamicism had screamed at an ever higher radical pitch, but that didn't mean it would continue to. If Iraq had taught me anything it was the complexity of reactions to events and ideals and isms contained within each human mind. Iraqis carried the scars and memories of good and bad and mad and sad and bits of Baathism, globs of pride and an inferiority complex; they carried Koranic *surahs* in their heads along with the precepts of grandfathers, memories of war slogans and the chorus of a Britney Spears song. Fractious, miasmic and changeable: Communist to Baathist. Jingo to war weary. Religious to skeptic. Fanatic to cynic. History doesn't necessarily progress, and people don't follow straight-line lives either.

IN JORDAN THAT summer I re-discovered Dr. Laith, the psychiatrist friend of Dr. Hassan's who had reported on army morale during Kuwait and who had got out of Iraq in the mid nineties after being arrested. Dr. Laith had gone back to Iraq in 2003 and become adviser to the Minister of Defense. I had heard reports that he had been severely wounded during an assassination attempt in 2005, and so I was very happy to find him safe in Amman, healthy and smiling.

"No! Not wounded!" He laughed at my concern. He had not been wounded in the attack, although two of his body-guards had. Afterward he was sent to Paris as Defense Attaché in the Iraqi embassy for a few months before returning to Iraq for a year, "it was unbearable, violence, chaos" and leaving again. Now he and his wife, Bushra, had apartments in Amman and Damascus and split their time between the two. Bushra, Dr. Laith explained tenderly, felt more comfortable in Damascus, but for him it was too familiar: "all those posters of the dictator!" It was in Damascus in exile that Bushra had first worn *hijab*, it had felt somehow more comfortable for her, socially, morally, when she was living alone there. But now, as she came out of the kitchen with a tray of tea glasses, I saw that she was out of *hijab* again. He hair was highlighted and glossily blow-dried, she wore a pair of trousers and a sleeveless camisole and lipstick penciled carefully outside her natural lip line.

"Bushra! What happened?" I asked her.

She smiled and shrugged. She said that she had finally given in to the nagging of her husband and her daughter, Louisa, "the feminist." Wearing the *hijab* in Europe, she said, was the opposite of comfortable, and here in Amman, well, in the nicer parts of the city, it was perfectly normal for a woman to be bareheaded.

I asked for their news and how was their family?

Louisa lived in Holland, "Oh, she is completely European now!" said her father, half proud, half lamenting. Another son was in Germany, working hard, and well, but their youngest! Dr. Laith looked unhappy. His youngest was supposed to be studying in Germany but he had taken up radical Islam, "It's like we have completely lost him," said his father.

Shifting feelings, priorities, values, country, context: this was one family as microcosm. Somehow, the combination of Dr. Laith's rueful wisdom, Bushra's in-and-out of *hijab* and the juxtaposed irony of their feminist daughter and Islamicized son both living in Europe, made me realize that just as nothing is to be assumed, nothing is set in stone.

Epilogue

T HE LAST TIME I SAW THE SACHET FAMILY WAS IN
January 2005 when I went back to Baghdad for the
first elections. I flew to Baghdad from Amman, braced myself
against the sickening g-force of the spiral descent (to avoid insurgent missiles) as the earth spun around the windows and
the ground came rushing up like a crash, filed through immigration (Iraqi officials asked "D o D?" Department of Defense, instead of for my passport), collected bags with the other
somber travelers: a *Washington Post* reporter, two MPs, miserable to be home, and several beefy contractors wearing khaki
trousers and gun holsters strapped to their thighs; rode the bus
to the car park collection point, met with the driver who had
brought an abaya for me to wear as disguise, sat in the back of
the car looking out at a city that had become, in the previous
six months, too dangerous for me to be in. There was plenty of
traffic on the highway, tinny smashed-up orange-and-white-
quartered taxis, second hand Hondas, pick-up trucks piled
with bedding and small children. The palm trees and bougain-
villea bushes in the median strip had all been torn up to deny
cover for insurgent attacks, American tanks squatted like great
toads amid the wasteland trash, high chain link cages had been
erected on the highway bridges to stop people throwing rocks
and IEDs at American patrols passing underneath. At one point

the traffic slowed to a jam behind an American army convoy, keeping their distance, as mandated—"KEEP BACK FIFTY FEET" read the sign on the Humvee, "or we will be shot at" added the driver—like crawling supplicants.

I had been away six months. When we drove across the Tigris into Jadriyeh, the upscale peninsula opposite the Green-Zone where the Hamra hotel was located, I looked around to see what differences I could notice. The ice cream parlor was still open, but the alcohol shop was closed, the Australians were still garrisoning the upper floors of a building site on the main road, but the bridge to Dora (once a mixed neighborhood, Sunni, Shia, Christian, violent, random, lots of gunfire, and one of the new no-go areas) was almost empty of traffic. I saw that the big traffic circle by the bridge was now guarded by the black clad Badr brigade, the militia of the Supreme Council for Islamic Revolution in Iraq, one of the main Shia parties who had their headquarters nearby. The Babylon Hotel, where I used to go swimming, the vegetable stall man under a striped umbrella where I used to buy spinach, the entrance to the cul-de-sac where I used to live, the cordoned road past the old police station that had been refurbished into some kind of Interior Ministry bunker (later revealed as a torture prison), the heavily fortified American checkpoint that had got blown up the previous spring and since been hit again—I watched all these familiar landmarks go by outside the moving window, now overgrown with war detritus: concrete barriers, metal tank jacks, rolls of concertina razor wire, sandbags, plywood signposts crudely daubed with red paint arrows. The unseen fear hung low like the gray winter sky; the kidnap risk was so high I could not get out of the car to walk down the street.

The first morning I was woken up with a car bomb, four or five blocks away; boom, 8 a.m. alarm call. The second morning I was woken up with a car bomb two blocks away, aimed at the Australians. It blew the windows out of the hotel on one side and killed a boy who sold cigarettes on the corner. We all went out onto the main road to kick over the ashy debris and watch the firemen hose down the soot skeleton of the car. The bomb had scorched some of the raw concrete pillars, but the Australians on the floors above reported no casualties. We stood around watching the desultory scene, as a few photographers went closer in to capture the last tongues of flame against the wreckage, and remarked to each other how nice it was to get out of the hotel and walk around a bit, and what a funny irony it was that the deranged atmosphere of car bomb aftermath could provide respite from the usual unease—

I RANG ALI Sachet when I first arrived. Saidiya was, like much of Baghdad, no-go for foreigners, under de facto insurgent control, IED alleys, the odd American patrol that ventured there was invariably shot at. Ali said they were happy to hear from me, that he would come and pick me up from the hotel the following afternoon.

He and his younger brother Mustafa came to collect me. I remembered Mustafa from the previous summer as a skinny, lanky, diffident youth in awe of his older brothers. Now he looked like a bodybuilder, tall, rippling muscles, strong.

"He has been working weights!" Ali told me laughing, cuffing his brother on the ear, "like a good bodyguard!" Mustafa grinned abashed and put his foot down like a kid in a video game, speeding, veering through the traffic as if he owned the road. Ali told him to calm down as we turned off the highway into Saidiya.

There were plenty of people out on the street, shopping and

going about their business. Did I imagine insurgent spotters on the corners? Men sitting in cafés with a mobile phone at their elbow, teenagers hanging around the intersections?

"This area is ours now!" Ali told me, boisterous and boasting, "the Americans don't come here anymore! They know we will kill them!"

"What about the police?" I asked. I had seen, in my first few days, the nascent police units on the street in Jadriyeh and I even pretended to myself that this made me feel safer somehow.

"The police?" Ali snorted. Mustafa giggled. We drove past the unfinished mosque, there was a pile of ragged razor wire balled up on the corner next to a heap of rubble. "That was the police station! Ha! Blew it up yesterday! They don't dare to come here now!"

We parked outside the house, inside everyone was waiting to say hello, except Omar, who was characteristically absent and busy. They all seemed pleased to see me and jolly. Um Omar gave me a hug and Shadwan poured me some tea and they said they were not surprised I had not come back earlier, yes, they had seen the footage of kidnapped journalists over the summer. Yes, *hamdilullah*, they were all well, everyone was well. Ali had a son now and they had called him Kamel! They had redecorated the reception room, pale yellow and blue—what did I think? Did I like it?

"When the lights come on it is very nice," said Um Omar, smiling, "but the electricity is very bad."

"It is cold in here now and we don't have kerosene for a heater," said Ali. Shadwan added they had no water for seven days. They used water from a well they dug in the garden during the war to wash the dishes with, for other water they go to different districts and fill up at taps or out of water tankers.

Mohammed, the eldest toddling grandchild, was brought into the room by his mother. Shadwan said she was teaching at a teachers' training college for women now; it was not far and it was a safer neighborhood than her last school, which was all Shia.

"And the bombs and the violence? And all the kidnapping? Are you worried about Shadwan when she goes to work? Or the little ones when they play in the street?" I asked.

Um Omar laughed, no no! Not at all, in their neighborhood they felt very safe; everyone knew them here and the Americans did not dare to come and the municipality office had been blown up so they didn't have to worry about police interference.

"They come sometimes—the Americans arrested a friend of Abu Omar's who lives in the neighborhood and they took all his sons; some of the sons they released. Yes, it's true, a general's son was kidnapped a few streets away, but we don't worry." Everyone knew the *mujahideen* and they took care of things. They felt safer with them.

They brought me tea and gave me holy zamzam water from Mecca (apparently Ali and Omar had gone to visit the Holy Places recently). They did not have any questions for me, they were not interested in my explanations of American policy and intentions like they had been a year and a half before when I had first met them; instead they had plenty of their own answers and opinions. *Jihad*, they maintained, was important for its own sake because it was a holy undertaking in front of God. The result of *jihad*, they said, its successes or failures or consequences were not so important. "The Resistance is winning now. At least it is stopping the Americans from running everything and imposing all their plans."

"In Samarra the Resistance held the streets for three

months!" Ali told me with pride. "They even had traffic police! They occupied the police stations and kept order. They regulated prices in the vegetable market and distributed rations of kerosene. And now Salman Pak southeast of Baghdad is almost under control of the *mujahideen* and some people who suffered kidnapping there went to the *mujahideen* for help and the *mujahideen* executed four kidnappers and now it is one of the safest areas in Iraq!"

The Sachets were an anomaly; they were the only people I talked to in Baghdad that winter who were not pale and tense and shocked by the general situation and talking worriedly about leaving Iraq and how they could find money, jobs, passports, visas. Schools were intermittently closed, people were afraid to send their kids to them, the University faculties were intimidated by Shia parties, refugees from Fallujah and Ramadi were camping in empty houses, electricity, water, sewage, hospitals were all terrible and groaning—it was a litany of collapse and the criminal banditry, often mixed up with the insurgency, car jacking, robbery, kidnapping was epidemic. The going rate for a kidnapped boy, the most common victims, was about $5,000; but the kidnappers, often neighbors, former colleagues, even extended cousins, knew their targeted families well and researched their means. If they thought the father had money stashed somewhere, or a rich brother overseas, the price could be $50,000 or more. But the Sachets did not seem perturbed. On the contrary, there was a strange ebullient confidence about them: they were fighting back and they thought they were winning.

"Will you vote next week?" I asked them.

"No. No!" they all shook their heads with emphatic distaste. The Association of Muslim Clerics had decreed that Sunnis should not vote and most of the Sunni population were boycotting what they saw as an American engineered Shia takeover.

"It is written in the Constitution that you cannot have an election under occupation," explained Ali.

"We don't want to give the election legitimacy," put in Shadwan. "Our vote would be like adding a brick in the wall of that government."

So I drank my tea and admired their new décor and gave them the presents I had brought them from England and said my goodbyes. They told me to come back and visit soon! And Mustafa drove me breakneck back to the hotel, grinning maniacally all the way.

A COUPLE OF years passed. I moved between London and Beirut, Damascus and Paris. The war in Iraq convulsed into different contortions. It was a Sunni insurgency against the Americans and then it was a civil war between Sunni and Shia for control of Baghdad and then the Americans realized they had spent too much time pandering and arming the Shia death squads attached to the Interior Ministry and it became a kind of American-Iranian proxy war and then the Sunni insurgents got fed up with their alliance with Al-Qaeda in Mesopotamia and joined with the Americans to push them out of their neighborhoods and then the Americans put in a new commander, David Petraeus, who upped the number of combat troops, "the surge," and managed to mitigate some of the worst excesses of the violence in Anbar Province and Baghdad for a while and then the south turned out to be an internecine patchwork of rival Shia battles and Kirkuk rumbled violently in opposition to Kurdish ambition and the Turks periodically bombed the PKK over the border and there were massacres of sects in remote areas that no one could figure out.

Or some approximation of the above. Reports narrowed. Western journalists could not move without being embedded and Iraqi journalists were being killed by the dozen. The fact of the violence, myriad and terrible, continued.

DURING THE SUMMER of 2007, when I was talking to Iraqis in Damascus and Amman I always asked for news of the Sachet family. There were various rumors. I had come to assume that Omar and Ali and Ahmed and probably Mustafa too had been involved in the Resistance. They were their father's sons after all, religious, righteous, prideful and brave. An occupation would not stand. I remembered that Ali had once told me, for example, how he had brought food and water to Syrian Fedayeen (Syrians who had volunteered to fight an urban guerrilla war against the Americans) who were holed up in a Saidiya mosque as the Americans rolled their tanks along the highway during the invasion of 2003. The rumors and snippets of news confirmed my thoughts. Saidiya had become one of the worst front line battle grounds between Sunni and Shia in Baghdad. The area was virtually uninhabitable and I heard several times that the Sachets had left Saidiya, possibly because their house had been burnt; certainly Kamel Sachet's Sadiq mosque, which had been a rallying place for the Resistance, was hit several times by Shia militias, bombed out and abandoned. From different directions, some cousins in Damascus, an old bodyguard of Kamel Sachet's who came from Baghdad to Sulaimaniyeh to see me, ex-Mukhabarat Janabis, I heard that two of the Sachet brothers—no one knew which ones exactly—had been arrested by the Americans and then, variously, released after several months, or not, depending on the version. I heard that one of the younger daughters (who had married a member of the Iraqi archery team, I recalled) had gone to live in Dubai, that the rest of the family was still in Baghdad, but living in a different neighborhood, that they had moved to Damascus.

The insurgency was a kaleidoscope of gangs: the 1920 Revolution Brigade, Islamic Conquest, Jihad Base Organization in Mesopotamia, Iraqi Hamas, Islamic State in Iraq, Knights of the Land of Two Rivers, Anbar Saviors, Mohammed's Army, Salahuddin Bridges, Heroes of Iraq. Some had fought under an Al-Qaeda umbrella, some fought turf wars with Al-Qaeda groups, some turned against Al-Qaeda and began to work with the Americans to re-establish control in their own areas. The situation was fluid, mutable, clandestine. News filtered through of a big summer battle between Al-Qaeda elements and disenchanted local insurgents and Americans in the tribal areas of the Albu Hassoun. Whispers in the wind. Every time I got close to finding a Sachet relative—Kamel Sachet had several brothers at least two of whom were living in Damascus—the door slammed shut. People were wary and frightened. Interlocutors hung up the phone and hurled insults at my translators and friends who made overtures on my behalf. Wherever they were, the Sachet family did not want to be found.

During the following winter, the new American policy of arming local Sunni groups to defend their neighborhoods against Al-Qaeda groups spread from Anbar province, through the Western suburbs of Baghdad and down into the Janabi tribal lands south of Baghdad. But news remained sketchy: there were no phone connections with that region, rival checkpoints sprang up overnight as militias battled, enveloped and withdrew, travel was virtually impossible, a tribal leader that I had hoped to contact via an interlocutor in Baghdad who was

going to and from the area regularly was besieged in his compound and in the middle of cutting ties with a local Al-Qaeda
group and going over to an alliance with the Americans. Some
of my Iraqi contacts in Damascus and Amman told me bits of
this story, others didn't want to tell me anything in case I was
a spy. Of the Sachet women, of Um Omar and Shadwan and
Amani, there was virtually no news at all; it was not seemly for
men to ask after the female members of a family.

After the summer battles, a brave and determined Iraqi journalist friend of mine went down to Jurfa Sakr, the main town
of the Albu Hassoun tribe, several times to check out the new
developments and he asked after the Sachet brothers among insurgent commanders and tribal leaders that he talked to. According to one, a senior commander in the Islamic Army, one
of the local former insurgent militias, Omar Sachet had joined
the insurgency in 2004 and graduated to commander level the
following year, running pitched ugly battles against the Shia on
Saidiya's border with Dora. The commander was contemptuous and angry.

"Their father was a hero, but they desecrated his name."

A local Sheikh was more specific.

"If I see Omar Sachet I will shoot him on the spot."

For a while it seemed that Omar and his brothers were
on the run, but then came reports that Omar and another
brother—which one was unknown—had been detained by the
Iraqi government. Of Ali, news trickled through even later,
third or fourth hand through the tribal grapevine: he was dead,
apparently, maybe, killed fighting in Salahuddin.

I thought back to the Sachet family I had known in the
months after the invasion, now torn by events, out of contact,
lost, dead, imprisoned. I remembered Omar's tall gravity; his
father's height, his father's taciturn quietness. He had always

avoided sitting down and talking to me one-on-one; he was busy, he was out, he sent his greetings. Now I understood why. I thought of Ali who I teased because he got fatter and fatter every time I saw him. I remembered how funny and abashed he had been, showing me the room he had decorated for his new bride and pointing out, blushing, the pink tulle draped over the lamps and the satin pink bed spread and the vases of cloth roses, shyly, asking my opinion, "Will she like it, do you think?" I thought of their father, whose picture I kept as I wrote—as I write—to watch over my efforts and of Shadwan of whom there was no news at all. And I thought of Ali's baby son, named Kamel after his grandfather, and the legacy of war and anger and revenge and pride that he would inherit.

I mused these final paragraphs into an unfinished conclusion. So many unintended consequences. How/why had the sons of Saddam's Iraq come to break their country, deracinate family and murder neighbors? Who knew when it might be possible to go back to Baghdad and drive through the scarred and scabbed and re-wounded neighborhoods, look up the Sachets, and other friends, those that had managed to survive and ask, again: What happened here?

Cast of Characters

THE SACHET FAMILY

Of the sub tribe of the Albu Hassoun of the greater Janabi Tribe.

General Kamel Sachet Aziz al Janabi   Abu Omar

Um Omar   Shamh, his wife

Shadwan   Kamel Sachet's eldest daughter, and his favorite

Omar   his son

Ali   his son

Sheima   his daughter

Amani   his daughter

Ahmed   his son

Zeinab   his daughter

Mustafa   his son

Zaid   his son

Abdullah   Kamel Sachet's elder brother

Khalid   Kamel Sachet's younger brother

Abu Shakr   Kamel Sachet's brother-in-law

Abdul Qadir   Kamel Sachet's nephew and driver

Ali Misjil   sometime servant and driver of Kamel Sachet

OFFICERS IN THE IRAQI ARMY

General Raad Hamdani   Commander of the 2nd Republican Guard Corps until 2003. Cooperated with the Americans after the invasion. Now lives in Jordan.

General Latif Commander of the battle of Seif Said 1981. Died of natural causes sometime in the nineties.

Adnan Khairallah Saddam's cousin and brother-in-law. Khairallah was the popular Defense Minister throughout the Iran-Iraq war. He died in a helicopter crash in 1989. There were always rumors that Saddam had Khairallah killed; earlier that year there had been a family dispute, when Saddam imprisoned his eldest son Uday for killing his favorite bodyguard and Uday's mother and close relative of Khairallah's tried to intervene. It was not the first time a prominent military figure had been killed in a helicopter crash. Khairallah's was the only Baathie statue to remain untouched in Baghdad after the destruction and looting of 2003.

Nizar Khazraji Chief of Staff of the army 1985–88, defected to Jordan in 1996. Khazraji spent much of the '90s conspiring with other exile groups, from exile in Denmark. Human rights groups demanded his arrest for crimes against humanity for his involvement in the Anfal campaigns against the Kurds, but he fled prosecution before the war in 2003 and was last spotted in southern Iraq just after Baghdad fell. He has since disappeared and is rumored to be living in Saudi Arabia.

Barakh Haj Hunta Special Forces General, friend of Kamel Sachet's and famous for throwing Kurds out of helicopters during the Anfal operations. He was involved in an officers' plot against Saddam just after the uprisings of 1991.

Major Nejar Special Forces officer and Kamel Sachet's sometime adjutant. In 2003 he fought with Ali Hassan al-Majid in the south against the British.

BAATHIES

Sabawi Ibrahim Hassan Saddam's half brother and head of Mukhabarat during the 1991 Gulf War, head of the Amn from 1991 to 1996, later a Presidential adviser to Saddam. When the Americans invaded he sought refuge in Syria from where he organized insurgent operations inside Iraq until the Syrians handed him over to the Americans in 2005. He was put on trial in Baghdad for crimes against civilians during the 1991 uprising and sentenced to death in 2007.

Sultan Hashem The popular and well respected commander of the First Army Corps on the northern front in 1988. Sultan Hashem later served as Defense Minister at the time of the American-led invasion of 2003. After the fall of Baghdad he went into hiding in Mosul; General Petraeus offered him a dignified surrender and there were intimations of a brief detention, but the new Iraqi government put him on trial on Anfal charges and he was sentenced to death, along with Ali Hassan al-Majid, in 2007. His execution has been delayed as the Sunni faction in the Iraqi government argues that he was just a career soldier discharging his duty and President Talabani has stepped in, refusing to sign his death warrant, saying that Sultan Hashem had good connections with the Kurds while he was serving in the north.

Ali Hassan al-Majid Held many key posts in Saddam's regime: head of the Mukhabarat, Defense Minister, Acting Governor of Kuwait. But it was his role as Saddam's ruthless instrument of the Anfal campaign against the Kurds in 1987–88 that defined his career. He oversaw the forced deportations of Kurdish villages and was given the nickname Chemical Ali in reference to his enthusiastic gas attacks against civilians. In 2003 he was Commander of the South and was captured by American forces soon after the fall of

Baghdad. In 2007 he was convicted on Anfal charges in the same trial as Sultan Hashem and also sentenced to death. At the time of writing he is still pending execution.

Aziz Salih Numan Governor of Basra, Najaf and Kerbala during the eighties, Governor of Kuwait during 1990–91 occupation, Baath Party Chief of Maysan province early nineties. In 2003 Numan was Regional Baath Party Commander for West Baghdad. He was captured by American forces near Baghdad in May 2003 and remains in detention awaiting unspecified charges.

Hussein Kamel Saddam's son-in-law and cousin. Rose through the ranks of the Mukhabarat to head Iraq's Military Industrial Complex until 1995 when he defected, along with his brother and both their wives (Saddam's daughters), to Jordan. For several months he gave information to Jordanian intelligence and to UNSCOM and the International Atomic Energy Agency, about Saddam's weapons programs and capabilities. Unbelievably he and his brother were persuaded to return to Iraq in mid 1996. Apparently they trusted that their family status would offer some immunity; instead Saddam forced his daughters to divorce them, and then ordered the house where they were staying surrounded. Hussein Kamel and his brother, Saddam Kamel, were killed after a twelve hour shoot out.

Saddam Kamel Hussein Kamel's brother, also married to one of Saddam's daughters. Head of the Republican Guard in the mid eighties, afterward consigned to "Presidential Adviser." He died along with his brother after their defection to Jordan. His wife and children, together with Saddam's other daughter and her children, now live quietly in Amman.

Arshad Yassin An Air Force Lt. General, Saddam's cousin, brother-in-law, sometime chief of his bodyguards and personal helicopter pilot. Yassin was notoriously involved in the looting of archaeological treasures from Baghdad's National Museum in the nineties and selling them abroad. He was captured by American forces disguised as a poor farmer in November 2003 and remains in American custody in Iraq.

Sheikh Khalid Al Janabi Adnan Janabi's elder brother, close friend of Saddam's and Mayor of Baghdad. Died in Rome in 1996, Adnan suspects, poisoned on Saddam's orders.

Uday Hussein Saddam's eldest son, head of Iraqi Olympic Committee, Commander of Saddam Fedayeen, main oil smuggler during the sanctions years and heir apparent. Uday was notorious for his drinking and playboy ways and for his psychotic sadism. He tortured his friends and raped whatever pretty girl was unlucky enough to walk into his view. In his two more famous bouts of murderous excess he killed his father's personal servant at a party in 1988 (in front of Suzanne Mubarak, wife of the Egyptian President, who was a guest), and shot his uncle Watban (wounding him only) at a family party in 1995. He survived an assassination attempt in 1996, but the eight bullets he took left him with seizures and a limp. After the American invasion he and his brother went on the run until they were betrayed to the Americans in July 2003 for a combined $30 million reward. Both were killed in the house where they were hiding in Mosul after a four hour battle with American troops.

Qusay Hussein Saddam's second son, quieter and more responsible than Uday, sometimes tipped as Saddam's successor over his brother. He oversaw the intelligence and security services, the Republican Guard and the Special Republican Guard. In the final shoot out with the Americans, Qusay's fourteen-year-old son, Mustafa, was the last to die inside the house.

POST INVASION

Ayad Allawi   Secular Shia and former Baath Party member, later Prime Minister of the interim Iraqi administration under the American occupation. In the mid seventies Allawi left Iraq to pursue medical studies in London and began to break with the Party. In 1978 he and his wife survived a vicious ax attack at their home, widely believed to be an assassination attempt by Saddam in retaliation for plotting against him. In the eighties and nineties he remained politically active among exile groups, eventually founding the Iraqi National Accord and maintaining myriad links to foreign intelligence services. In 2004 he became the Prime Minister of Iraq in a temporary government responsible for drawing up a constitution before national elections. Allawi's party polled only 14 percent in the election in January 2005, much to the disappointment of his American backers, his secular model of liberal democracy losing to a coalition of Shia parties. His party continues to be represented in the Iraqi parliament, although his MPs withdrew their participation during a boycott in 2007 and Allawi now spends much of his time in London with his family and traveling throughout the Middle East, maintaining his networks and garnering support for the future.

Ahmed Chalabi   Hailing from a prominent Shia family, Chalabi left Iraq in 1956 and has spent much of his life in the United States and Britain. In the seventies he headed Petra Bank in Jordan, but was forced to flee over fraud charges, which have never been reconciled. In the mid nineties Chalabi founded the INC, Iraqi National Congress, an opposition group, funded by the Americans, among others (he always had close ties with the Iranians) and based himself in Kurdish controlled northern Iraq from where he tried to overthrow Saddam. In the run up to the American invasion, he was the Pentagon's favorite to run the country, but reports of his fraud and unpopularity with Iraqis curtailed American support. In particular Chalabi was accused of supplying some of the faulty intelligence used by the British and American governments as part of their arguments for the urgency of a war. In post-Saddam Iraq Chalabi has proved himself a wily chameleon, allying himself to the Shia parties in power and positioning himself as acting Oil Minister and head of various political committees, ever the operator.

Jalal Talabani   Leader of the PUK (Patriotic Union of Kurds Party) and currently President of Iraq. Talabani fought Saddam from the Kurdish mountains for almost all his life. After the uprisings of 1991 Kurdistan became a de facto autonomous enclave, divided between Talabani's PUK and his rival Masoud Barzani's KDP (Kurdish Democratic Party). Despite a civil war in 1996 between the two, Talabani was instrumental in establishing a reasonably functional administration in Kurdistan during the nineties. After the war he became President of Iraq, a largely ceremonial position, to which his grandfatherly elder statesman air is well suited.

Moqtada Sadr   Head of the Sadr political block in the post war Iraqi parliament and one of the largest militias, the Mehdi Army. Often referred to as the "firebrand cleric" by Western media, Moqtada's sudden rise as the champion of millions of the poor urban Shia underclass surprised many Iraqis as much as the Americans. He has consistently opposed the American occupation, alternately fighting an insurgency, clashing with rival Shia parties and their militias and then offering periodic ceasefires. He remains a key player, one of the few in the current political firmament who remained in Iraq throughout the Saddam years.

SCIRI Supreme Council for the Islamic Republic of Iraq, now renamed, more tactfully, the Supreme Iraqi Islamic Council. During the Saddam years it was based in Tehran and funded by the Iranians. It is one of the main Shia parties of the post Saddam Iraq and maintains its own militia, the

Badr Brigade Now renamed the Badr Organization. SCIRI and Moqtada's party and militia have continued to battle for control over southern Shia cities, in particular Basra.

Dawa Party The Dawa Party was founded in the sixties by a group of prominent Shia leaders, some from the Shia religious establishment, as a political party that would promote religious laws, use Islam as a framework for governance and combat the secular promises of the Communists and Baathists. By the early seventies it had attracted a strong following among young disenfranchised Shia from the South and was militantly opposed to the new Baathie regime. There followed the inevitable brutal crackdown. The Dawa Party was naturally attracted to the success of Khomeini's Shia revolution in Iran, although there were fundamental ideological differences between them. When the Iran-Iraq war broke out fragments of the Dawa Party fled to the safety of Iran, split into SCIRI, ideologically and financially much closer to the Iranians, and continued to organize attacks on the Baathie high command inside Iraq. In fact it was Dawa assassins who tried to kill Saddam Hussein in 1982 in the town of Djeil. This assassination attempt was punished with a mass execution of local men and it was these murders which provided the case against Saddam for which he was ultimately hanged in December 2006.

Dawa returned to Iraq from impoverished exile after Saddam's fall and became part of the Shia ruling coalition, along with SCIRI and Moqtada's party, based on their bloc victory in the 2005 election.

Nouri Al Maliki   Leader of the Dawa Party, was chosen as Prime Minister as a compromise after weeks of stalemate between the other Shia candidates.

SECURITY SERVICES OF SADDAM'S IRAQ

The Iraqi people were subject to a vast and overlapping network of state security agencies. In general terms it's easy enough to think of the Mukhabarat as the CIA and the Amn as the FBI; but in Iraq this comparison is a bit disingenuous. Both agencies pummeled the private lives of Iraqi citizens in the cause of state security.

Mukhabarat   Mukhabarat simply means "intelligence" in Arabic, but it's a word which virtually all Arabs, no matter which king/dictator/Emir/President they find themselves subject to, have learned to utter in a whisper. In Iraq the Mukhabarat attracted the cream of the Sunni state bureaucratic elite; its senior officers were often erudite and more flexible and cunning in the discharge of their duties than the more thuggish Amn.

Amn   Amn means "security" in Arabic. The Amn, with its various branches, operated in the space between the police and the Mukhabarat. The Amn were responsible for the mid-level, everyday business of state control: piles of gray files containing handwritten reports on teachers and doctors, Imams and café proprietors. Matters of petty but terrifying concern were recorded: a brother who lived in Frankfurt, failure to regularly attend Baath Party meetings, a critical comment overheard in a restaurant, a nephew who was a military deserter, an application for an exit visa, a new car in the time of sanctions that might indicate a black market income, an overly religious cousin. . .

Istikhbarat   Military Intelligence.

Fedayeen   Translated as "those who sacrifice." Throughout the Middle East the word Fedayeen has come to refer to volunteer militias who are devoted to their cause and will fight until martyrdom in its service.

In Iraq Saddam created the Saddam Fedayeen, "Saddam's men of sacrifice," as an elite military cadre of around 30,000 men. Saddam's Fedayeen swore loyalty to Saddam rather than to Iraq and are widely reported to have been used as a death squad, in particular exterminating prostitutes as part of a crackdown on vice in the nineties.

Peshmerga   Kurdish fighters. *Peshmerga* in Kurdish means literally "those who face death." The Kurdish *peshmerga* fought a series of effective (although not necessarily victorious) guerrilla campaigns against Saddam's government much as they fought for independence from virtually every government in Baghdad over the past century. In the post-Saddam Iraq the *peshmerga* remain a military force.

OTHER IRAQI COMPLICATIONS OF A RELIGIOUS NATURE

There are two main sects of Islam.

Sunni and **Shia**   The split has its origins in seventh century battles over the succession to the Caliphate; today Sunni and Shia are separated by differences of religious culture, traditions and observance. The Shia, for example, revere early Shia martyrs and Imams, the most famous being Hussein, almost as saints, while Sunnis find this idolatrous.

Throughout the world the Sunni are the majority of Muslims. But the Shia heartland is in the south of Iraq around the shrine towns of Kerbala and Najaf. Estimates differ, but perhaps 60 percent of the Iraqi population is Shia, concentrated in the poorer south, while the Sunnis are in the center and the north of the country, and historically formed the trading and political elites in Baghdad and Mosul. During the Ottoman period, the British mandate, several dictators and twenty four years of Saddam, Iraq was governed mostly by Sunnis. Herein lies part of the resentment which has given rise to the sectarian violence of the post Saddam era. It should be borne in mind, however, that the preceding paragraph is a vast over simplification; that Shia and Sunni Iraqis all come essentially from the same tribal and Bedu traditions that migrated out of the Arabian peninsula during the Muslim conquests, that many tribes contain both Sunni and Shia and that intermarriage, particularly among the middle classes, is common.

Wahhabism   A Sunni strain of Islam based on the fundamental teachings of the eighteenth century Islamic scholar Mohammed ibn Wahhab. Wahhabism is a strict form of fundamentalism which emphasizes the literal application of the Koran and the Hadith, the book of the Prophet Mohammed's sayings and teachings. For example, Wahhabis often grow a long beard but keep their mustache trimmed carefully above their top lip and wear their *dishdashas* short, at mid calf level, according to the example of the Prophet Mohammed. Wahhabism is espoused by the Saudi royal family and is the predominant strain of Islam in Saudi Arabia.

Salafi   The terms Salafi and Wahhabi are often used interchangeably. Salafis also take the example of the rule of the Prophet Mohammed and the early Caliphates as the template for observance and decry any innovation or modern interpretations of Islam. Modern politics, for example, are a distraction from the true path of Sharia (or Koranic) law.

Imam   A religious leader or preacher, most likely Sunni.

Mullah   A Shia religious leader or preacher.

Sheikh   Confusingly the world Sheikh can refer either to a religious leader or to a tribal leader.

Acknowledgments

WHEN PEOPLE LEARN THAT I HAVE SPENT A lot of time in Iraq and the Middle East they often cock their heads to one side and say, "Really, but for a woman, a blonde one . . . isn't it, well, a bit—" The simple answer is no. In Iraq no one ever harassed me or threatened me personally or showed me any disrespect. On the contrary, in difficult and violent circumstances; in the circumstances of an occupation for which (by virtue of my half American–half Brit nationality) both my governments were responsible, I never received anything but the most gracious hospitality. Iraqis helped me, fed me, talked to me, took me into their homes and, most important, patiently explained their lives and their experiences.

For finding and translating these experiences I am indebted to several Iraqis in several countries, who must, in these dangerous times, remain on a first name basis only:

Othello (first day on the job, I said: "Let's go to Abu Ghraib!" Can't believe you stuck with me for six months), Salih (very patient with the absurdity of me holding a pink umbrella against the Baghdad August sun), Mona (incomparable, indomitable, simply the best), Mahmoud (truly above and beyond . . .), Maher (short, but very effective), Ahlam (I hope, I hope, you got out of Seyda Zeinab and to America) and Sirwan (the great picnic organizer).

The support of friends and colleagues and comrades-in-car-bombs is sometimes the greatest solace for the loneliness of the long distance correspondent: For all those conversations, bottles of wine and evenings; floors to sleep on, advice and difficult roads traveled together: Jon Lee Anderson, Michael Goldfarb, Omar Abdul Qadr, Molly Bingham and Steve Connors, Abdul Rahman Al Jobouri, Dan Murphy, Jill Carroll, Rory McCarthy and Juliette von Seibold, Sean Langan, Ghaith Abdul-Ahad, George Packer, Matt McAllester, Patrick Bishop, Patrick Cockburn, Adrien Jaulmes, Charlie Glass, Damien Quinn, Lina Sinjab, Khalid Oweis, Malika Browne, Ramsay Al Rikabi, Deb Amos, Kate Brooks, Maen Abdul Salam and Aliya Mawani, Oliver August, Hassan Fattah, Janine Di Giovanni, Viyan Sherif and Katherine Zoepf.

I would also like to thank the International Crisis Group who write the best reports on Iraq and whose towers of experience and knowledge were invaluable to me: Joost Hiltermann and Peter Harling were especially kind and helpful to me.

Finally thank you to my Beirut family: Lina Saidi, Nadim Mallat, Jeroen Kramer, Ferry Biedermann, Emilie Seuer and especially especially Imma home from home and to those in Paris who kept me going through long winter paragraphs, in particular Mounir Fatmi and Blaire Dessent and Robert Hudson. And to my dad, who always picks me up from the airport, tells me not to worry too much about having a proper job and who bought me a new laptop when mine got fried by Lebanese electrical surges.